Praise for Rear Admiral Michael Giorgione's
Inside
CAMP DAVID

The Private World of the Presidential Retreat

"A captivating stroll through the storied Maryland mountain retreat seen through the eyes of the Sailors, Marines, gardeners, cooks, handymen, and their families who all cater to the presidents. Rear Admiral Michael Giorgione, a charming raconteur, takes us behind the scenes and shows why, from Kennedy to Obama, presidents found Camp David (aka Naval Support Facility Thurmont) the ideal place for both white-knuckle international diplomacy and desperately needed decompression: a walk in these woods can restore presidential sanity."
—Chris Whipple, author of *The Gatekeepers: How the White House Chiefs of Staff Define Every Presidency*

"Toasts a great perk of the presidency, one that almost none of us will ever see...Full of firsthand glimpses into a secret world and fresh insights that may delight even the most politically cynical among us."   —Adeel Hassan, *New York Times*

"In this intimate and informative book, Giorgione blends the presidential with the personal and casts a loving eye on a seldom seen but consequential place...With grace, candor, and humor, he makes what, in academic hands, could have been dry as dust breathe with life."   —Jay Strafford, *Richmond Times-Dispatch*

Inside
CAMP DAVID

The Private World of the Presidential Retreat

REAR ADMIRAL MICHAEL GIORGIONE, CEC, USN (RET.)

BACK BAY BOOKS
LITTLE, BROWN AND COMPANY
New York Boston London

Back Bay Books / Little, Brown and Company
Hachette Book Group
1290 Avenue of the Americas, New York, NY 10104
littlebrown.com

Originally published in hardcover by Little, Brown and Company,
October 2017
First Back Bay trade paperback edition, May 2020

Back Bay Books is an imprint of Little, Brown and Company, a division
of Hachette Book Group, Inc. The Back Bay Books name and logo are
trademarks of Hachette Book Group, Inc.

The publisher is not responsible for websites (or their content) that are
not owned by the publisher.

The Hachette Speakers Bureau provides a wide range of authors for
speaking events. To find out more, go to hachettespeakersbureau.com
or call (866) 376-6591.

ISBN 978-0-316-50961-9 (hardcover) / 978-0-316-50959-6 (paperback) /
978-0-316-43991-6 (large print)
LCCN 2017936280

10 9 8 7 6 5 4 3 2 1

LSC-C

Printed in the United States of America

For Michele
Thank you for making Cedar our home.

CONTENTS

Inside

CAMP
DAVID

Introduction

INTO THE WOODS

There's just something about this place.
—Marine stationed at Camp David

O
N AN EARLY-WINTER day, the mountain is quiet during my
long, winding drive to the top—eighteen hundred feet up
from the town of Thurmont, Maryland. I go past the now-silent
campgrounds, buried in the last fallen leaves of autumn. Past the
deep woods, with their streams and brush and spectacular bluffs.
Along the way, the barren oak, tulip poplar, and red maple trees
stand like a dense army of frozen sentries, thousands of them lin-
ing the road on both sides.

I have made this drive in all seasons. On a late-spring day, the
woods are abloom, the fragrance of honeysuckle, mountain laurel,
and wildflowers hanging in the air. The summer heat gives way to
a cooling effect the higher you climb—the temperature at the top
of the mountain is ten to fifteen degrees below that of the towns at
its base. Late fall brings an icy rain that coats the ground in a
treacherous sheen. By December, the woods are quiet, as if hiber-
nating. Snow, when it comes, encases every branch in a sparkling

glow. Each season brings its own special wonder to the Catoctin Mountains, home of Camp David, the presidential retreat.

Camp David is actually a Navy installation, though hardly a typical one. Its official name is Naval Support Facility Thurmont. It is commanded by a U.S. Navy Civil Engineer Corps officer of the commander rank—as I was when I served there—and is staffed, maintained, operated, and guarded by an extraordinary team of Sailors, Marines, and other military personnel under the White House Military Office (WHMO, pronounced "whammo"). We're the force on the ground, so to speak, and the story of Camp David is very much our story too.

It is easy while I'm on that drive to the top to feel the history alive in these mountains, because this is a very American kind of place. George Washington probably visited the area, which was clear-cut for charcoal to produce cannonballs at the Catoctin Furnace during the Revolutionary War—the mountain's first national service.

Camp David is purposely hard to find unless you know where to look for it. One writer described it as "a place that doesn't exist," an apt portrayal. The turnoff, which I know so well but which would easily escape the eye of a casual traveler, is a crack in the almost seamless landscape, marked with a small sign that reads CAMP #3, an anonymous designation tracing back to an old WPA site from the 1930s. There is no grand entrance, no stately front gate or barrier on the main road. Even David Eisenhower, for whom the camp is named, had a hard time locating it one day on a drive through the mountains with his wife, Julie Nixon Eisenhower. And both of them had been to the camp many times. Its very anonymity is its best defense against intruders, as there is nothing discernible—no visible security, nothing at all, just the woods and a high fence that's mostly hidden unless you get up close. It can feel, on a dark winter afternoon, as if the nearest human being is a thousand miles away. But if, by accident or intention, you turn in and proceed a few yards down the path, everything changes. The silent landscape springs to life in the form of some of the most capable and observant military forces known to man. Here, the trees really do have eyes.

It can give the place an eerie atmosphere.

Chuck Howe, the commanding officer (CO) at the end of the Kennedy administration, recalled that First Lady Jackie Kennedy once asked his six-year-old daughter, Polly, "Do you like it up here?"

Polly replied enthusiastically, "Yes, I love it!"

Jackie leaned in and said, "But it's so *spooky.*"

Howe's wife, Jo-An, listening to the conversation, laughed. "Oh, Mrs. Kennedy," she said, "you don't know how hard they work to keep it spooky for you so that you won't see them and you'll feel free to be anyplace here."

The point was well taken by Jackie, and she would come to appreciate the remote feeling of Camp David as a welcome respite from the constant attention she and the children received in the outside world.

One could be forgiven for thinking the camp has ghosts. At night, the silence and unnatural stillness can creep up on you. After FDR's death, the Filipino stewards who had served him were afraid to enter his cabin alone after dark. They reported seeing the glow of a cigarette on the screened porch where they had often watched FDR smoking at night. I could relate. Going to the woodshed after dark and in a misty fog to get firewood could be its own spooky experience, and the patter of mice scurrying around and beneath the stacked, rotting logs added to the sense of unease.

Every commanding officer has had a similar feeling. "It's a

mystical place," Commander Mike O'Connor, who served during George W. Bush's presidency, said of his first impression of the camp. "You hear about it, but experiencing it is different. It's mystical. It gives you goose bumps."

Camp David is functionally invisible, as it's designed to be. In the beginning, during FDR's time, as World War II raged on, the administration went to great lengths to deny the camp (then called Shangri-La) even existed. The best efforts of the press were thwarted again and again as the White House put them off the scent, and it wasn't fully unveiled until after the war. Such secrecy is understandable in a time of war, but there was another reason for it too: a president needs a small corner of the universe where he can truly be alone with his thoughts and relaxed in his demeanor. Before Reagan took office, Pat Nixon confided to Nancy, "Without Camp David, you'll go stir crazy." And most presidents since have agreed.

Today, absolute privacy is the gift Camp David continues to bestow on presidents. Press access is limited and invitation only, and those invitations are usually given only when there is an international summit. At the White House there is such a constant clamor, so many demands, that there is literally little chance to think. At Camp David, the clamor subsides, if not the weight of obligation. A White House photographer is on hand only when requested to capture personal moments in the manner of a family scrapbook. Even these photos are guarded. Unlike at the White House, where every moment is observed and recorded, at the camp, it is possible to close the door and draw the curtains, shutting out the nation for a precious brief time. Presidents can *breathe* here. Reagan spoke of the "sense of liberation" he felt at Camp David.

The intrigue of the place, its mystery, begins with the difficulty of accessing it. While many guests fly in with the president on Marine One or on separate military helicopters, most of the Sailors and Marines who run the place take the route up the mountain by car from their housing below and are subjected to the rigorous security process every single time.

The goal is to keep the world out. Occasionally, though, even a president might feel a bit fenced in. George W. Bush sometimes took runs outside the camp—much to the displeasure of the Secret Service. Once when he reached the gate, he cried, "I'm free!"

It's definitely easier to get out than to get in. I won't talk much about the security—for security reasons!—but suffice it to say that the search is thorough. It takes some time to get in, even if you have high-level security clearance. Sometimes there can be a wait to go through the process. During one change-of-command, a CO's wife offered this tip: "When the president is at camp, the gate does not open if he's moving around. Bring a book—and don't buy ice cream!"

Once you're inside, the busyness of the security area quickly gives way to the camp feeling. Golf carts are the primary mode of transportation, most of them four-seaters (two facing forward, two facing back), with the president's cart designated Golf Cart One. When the winter chill sets in, zippered plastic canopies are added to the carts, though they do little to cut the cold and only slightly reduce the wind. Riding along the narrow, winding paths through the woods, a visitor will note that everything is pristine. Even in autumn there is not a stray leaf to be seen, a remarkable feat considering the abundance of trees. Legend has it that Nancy Reagan was bothered by the scrubbed look, which seemed unnatural.

"Where are the leaves?" she asked. That night a crew of dutiful Seabees, who make up about 60 percent of the Navy enlisted crew, went out and sprinkled leaves along the path in front of Aspen, the president's cabin.

The landscaping efforts always have two goals, sometimes at odds with each other: make it look natural—and perfect. Nature often wins. White-tailed deer, who live and breed inside the fence, are frequently spotted and given names. On the Reagans' first visit, the couple stood in Aspen and looked out the rear window to find eight deer staring back at them. "Look," Reagan said, "we have a welcoming committee."

Commander John Dettbarn, who served for nearly four years during Nixon's administration, recalled that Julie and Tricia Nixon were fond of one doe in the camp and named her Apples. Apples loved cigarettes—the crew was allowed to smoke openly throughout the grounds at the time—and she would try to steal packs from their pockets, often chasing crew members. When Tricia and Ed Cox were honeymooning at Camp David, Dettbarn received a call that Apples had gotten inside Dogwood cabin, where they were staying. It was never discovered how this happened, although there was speculation that Ed coaxed her in. Concerned for the safety of Tricia and Ed and not wanting the newly rebuilt Dogwood cabin to be damaged, they hurried to the area. Dettbarn's master chief arrived first and was able to coax Apples out of Dogwood with no harm to the couple or the cabin.

Deer can be pests, as many homeowners know; they nibble at flowers and trample gardens. The number of deer at Camp David and in the surrounding forest is the subject of some controversy, as their birth rate is high enough to compromise the sustainability of the woods—they have voracious appetites and destroy saplings and low-hanging branches. The deer are constantly in a battle with Seabees over the prized flower beds around Aspen, despite fencing that's put up when no guests are around. From time to time the National Park Service comes in to cull the herd.

Living in the woods means unusual encounters with wildlife, including snakes and raccoons. "Anything can happen in the woods," said CO Keith Autry, who was called to Aspen by an alarmed Obama family when they discovered a snake in the house. In the fall, my wife, Michele, traditionally decorated our front and side doors with hay, cornstalks, and an assortment of pumpkins and gourds. One night a determined raccoon pounded away at the display and attacked the side door's glass pane, seeing his reflection and thinking he was in a duel with another midnight scavenger. Once again, our friends at the National Park Service came aboard to help; they trapped the raccoon without harming him and relocated him to another part of the Catoctin forest, well outside the fence line. Chuck Howe remembered capturing a rattlesnake and putting it in a glass jar to show his kids, only later realizing the danger. "If I'd dropped the jar, I would have pissed off a rattlesnake."

The camp interior consists of over twenty cabins, among other facilities. There is a gym, a chapel, a health clinic, a fire department, maintenance buildings, and a hangar to hold Marine One when the president is on-site. There are also offices, a mess hall, barracks for unmarried enlisted men and women, and a recreation facility.

On first impression, the place has the rustic aura of a campground, familiar to most Americans; the rough-hewn oak cabins are all painted a moss green. The color was Franklin Roosevelt's choice. He told the crew he wanted green. "What color green?" they asked. "I don't know—just take white and add green to it." In most respects, the camp is the polar opposite of the White

House with its stately grandeur—a place apart and deliberately distinct. There's a reason Camp David is not listed on the historic registry: to keep bureaucrats from meddling.

A tour of the camp along the winding paths, just wide enough for a medium-size vehicle or golf cart, begins at Aspen, the president's cabin. First named the Bear's Den by FDR, it was later renamed Aspen in homage to Mamie Eisenhower's Colorado home.

The lush acreage, appealing to most, disturbed Harry Truman, a product of the flat midwestern plains. When he first entered Aspen, he complained, "I look out the window and there's nothing but trees." The forest pressed up against the president's cabin and made Truman feel hemmed in. He instructed Lieutenant Commander William M. Rigdon, his assistant naval aide, to have the area cleared, and a work party from the presidential yacht, the USS *Williamsburg*, set about cutting down trees and clearing out the heavy underbrush.

Rigdon wrote that once the forest was cut back "it looked more like a suburban spot than a place hidden in the forest." Not quite. But the cutback had the desired effect, and today a president can stand at the back of Aspen and take in the stunning vista of the manicured lawn of Eisenhower's three-tee golf green and the magnificent heated swimming pool added by Nixon. An old stone barbecue pit was Eisenhower's favorite spot; he loved to cook big fat steaks on the fire. From time to time people have suggested a more modern grilling area, but it has never happened. Terraced gardens surround a patio where world leaders have relaxed with presidents over meals and drinks.

I remember seeing Aspen for the first time. I entered it through the side door; I rarely used the front door that is captured in almost every photo you see of the president's mountain lodge.

The side door leads to a mudroom, and through that is the kitchen, then the main living and entertaining area. Bedrooms are on the opposite side of the cabin.

Like much of Camp David, Aspen has a sense of history suspended in the air and embedded in the paneled walls. The conversations, the arguments, the intense discussions, the welcomes, and the dismissals are all part of how presidents have used Aspen diplomatically. Beyond the history, I felt the cabin was incredibly simple and basic, very much your grandparents' longtime home — dated but comfortable furniture, aged-stone fireplaces, bookshelves filled with leather binders containing press clippings and articles of historic events. There's a functional pantry and kitchen with simple plates, cups, glasses, and utensils; certainly no china or crystal for this extraordinary residence.

And yet to me, this simplicity, this country comfort, made Aspen even more revered and special — it was almost like looking at an original Founder's document. I often felt that you wouldn't want to modernize the cabin too much. Plumbing, electricity, heating, air-conditioning, all those things behind the walls, yes. They need constant upgrading and more efficient operation, but the walls, the ceilings, the doors, and the palpable sense of history in the air — leave those alone!

And presidents mostly have, with some improvements. The Nixons added the swimming pool and made one other change — they asked CO Dettbarn to replace the king-size bed and headboard that had been there since Kennedy's time. The headboard was a large overstuffed item with the presidential seal in the middle. The Nixons thought it was too formal. When they scrapped the furnishings, Dettbarn removed the seal, and Pat Nixon told him to keep it. It now resides in his living-room curio cabinet. Talk about a keepsake!

Other presidents and First Ladies have left their personal stamps on Aspen. In her memoir, Nancy Reagan, who was often criticized for lavish expenditures, wrote, "For me, one of the best parts about Camp David was that there wasn't a whisper of controversy about the renovations I made there. Because the entire place is off-limits to the press, nobody ever knew what I did." She took some pleasure in that, although her improvements to Aspen were relatively minor—new slipcovers, landscaping, and the like—and did not change the character of the place.

George W. Bush wrote in his memoir of the cozy atmosphere, which appealed to his family. "Its interior is simple but comfortable. The wooden structure has three bedrooms, a perfect size for our family; a sunlit living room where I watched football with my brother Marvin and friends; and a stone fireplace beside which Laura and I liked to read at night."

In front of Aspen is a small pond that FDR had constructed because he had a terrible fear of fire and wanted water nearby. During his time, the pond was stocked with trout, but later it was filled with koi. In the icy winter of 2015, the pond froze and so did the koi. Since then the water has been temperature-controlled to prevent a similar catastrophe. A small bench, hewn from a tree log, provides a spot for contemplation. My young daughter Briana liked to sit there, commune with the fish, and make up stories about living in the woods.

During Reagan's administration the pond was also stocked with goldfish. One day Commander Bill Waters received a panicked call from the president. "Commander, you've got to do something! The poor devils are dying!" Thinking the camp was under attack, Waters sprang to his feet and raced over to Aspen, where he found Reagan staring morosely into the fishpond. Two goldfish were floating on top, clearly dead. Waters promised to get to the bottom of it, and having no idea what goldfish die of, he ordered autopsies of the fish. He learned that some fish had trouble acclimating to the high elevation, and he passed on his report to the concerned president.

Beyond Aspen are Birch and Dogwood, cabins located, diplomatically, equidistant from the president's residence. During the 1978 negotiations, Israeli prime minister Menachem Begin stayed in Birch while Egyptian president Anwar Sadat stayed in Dogwood. Other leaders who have bunked there include Leonid Brezhnev and Russian prime minister Dmitry Medvedev. During Clinton's 2000 Middle East peace summit, PLO chairman Yasser Arafat occupied Dogwood, and Israeli prime minister Ehud Barak occupied Birch, both for over two weeks.

The interiors of both cabins are cozy but modern, each with two bedrooms, stone fireplaces, a kitchenette, and closets with the signature Camp David jackets and bathrobes, which at times disappeared into guest suitcases and have had to be retrieved.

Further along the scenic camp road is historic Holly cabin, which was originally named Laurel until the new Laurel was built. The revised Holly was created by connecting two smaller cabins— the goal is always to repurpose wood—but the original porch, where FDR and Churchill sat to plan D-day, remains. The interior features a large meeting room with a stone fireplace where the Camp David Accords took place. Carter chose this more intimate setting rather than the larger Laurel conference room, thinking it would encourage conversation. He also added a pool table and a movie projector, and the delegations watched fifty-eight movies during the thirteen-day summit. An office, used by the president for secure communications, is lined with bookshelves.

Down from Holly is the new Laurel cabin, built in 1972, which in many respects is the centerpiece of camp life and diplomacy.

It has three conference rooms, a full kitchen, a dining room, a small presidential office, and a large family room with cozy chairs and tables. Hillary Clinton made further improvements, opening up the main room with windows that take advantage of the beautiful view. There is a piano and a beautiful antique sideboard from the 1800s added by Laura Bush. Laurel is ideal for larger gatherings, such as the big Christmas dinners both Bush families held every year of their terms. Ronald Reagan used the largest conference room to give a hundred and fifty Saturday addresses to the nation.

Somewhat separated from the guest cabins, Cedar, the CO family's home at Camp David, is a comfortable, charming cabin with three bedrooms, a glass-enclosed sunporch, and a spacious family living area—at least, it's spacious by Navy standards. As CO Jim Broaddus told his young sons, "We have a modest house with a great yard!" When I was CO, the quaint cabin was dated, cramped, and in need of some upgrades, and I asked the Navy to invest in its redesign and make some improvements over the next few years. Though I kicked the project off, I didn't have to live with the inconvenience, noise, and intrusion of construction, so I give credit to the two COs after me who endured this. Today, upgraded bathrooms, a new great room, and a separate garage are used and enjoyed by the CO's family.

Across the road from Cedar is Rosebud, which housed the Secret Service and the Soviet security team during Nikita Khrushchev's visit in 1959. Today the interior is modernized and has the only ADA-accessible accommodations at the camp.

Other, smaller cabins include Witch Hazel, the closest one to the president's, if not the fanciest. The Kennedys used it as a nursery for Caroline and John. Walnut, Hawthorn, Sycamore, and

Linden were original cabins that were rebuilt in 1956, with indoor plumbing installed. All are used as guest quarters today.

Backtrack along the path toward the gate and you come to Hickory Lodge, the recreation center and undoubtedly one of everyone's favorite locations. Here is the bowling alley, built by Eisenhower, and a movie theater with Barcalounger-style seats that are so plush one can imagine many movie watchers falling asleep. There is a full game room with a pool table, a library, a gift shop for purchasing souvenirs, and the Shangri-La bar and grill. A favorite delicacy at the bar when I was there was the Shangri-La Bar Frito Pie. The recipe: a bag of Fritos, a can of Hormel chili, and a sprinkling of cheese, all of it microwaved for one minute. Everyone loved that Frito pie, especially the Secret Service agents coming off of a night shift.

Right next door to Hickory is the cabin Poplar, the staff offices for the CO, executive officer (XO), command master chief (CMC), and administrative staff. Because it is close to the gate, a small lot outside allows select visitors to drive in and park there. One of my favorite artifacts in Poplar is a very large black-and-white photograph taken at the end of Eisenhower's presidency; it shows Eisenhower with his familiar amused smile, Mamie, and the entire crew. Above and behind the historic setting on the Aspen flagstone patio are two Secret Service agents looking on, casually smoking.

My homey office in Poplar was where I would welcome and say farewell to every Sailor and Marine who reported to Camp David for duty. During my time, from 1999 to 2001, our entire staff was military, unlike the White House staff of long-serving civilian ushers, butlers, valets, housekeepers, florists, chefs, grounds-keepers, and maintenance workers. All of us arrived at Camp David after an intensive screening process, yet we knew that at some point we would receive orders to our next stations, a routine that almost every military member experiences throughout his or her career. It is the military way of life, how we do our very important business for the nation, and as unique as Camp David is as an assignment, we all know that one day we will have to move on and get back to what we really do for a living. This is part of the bittersweet experience of serving at the presidential retreat, knowing that this very special time will end—and for most, that will mean never entering the camp again and having only memories and great stories to hold on to.

Among the most striking buildings at the camp is Evergreen Chapel, an octagonal structure of wood and stained glass with seating for up to one hundred and fifty people. Reagan selected the site and broke ground for it, and the chapel was completed in 1991 and dedicated by George H. W. Bush. Before the camp had its own chapel, presidents either traveled down the mountain for services or had clergy come to the camp. Breathtaking stained-glass windows frame each side of the interior, designed and created by 1936 Olympic biathlon gold medalist and renowned artist Rudolph Sandon. On the left is the Tree of Knowledge, on the right the Tree of Life, with depictions that appeal to all faiths. "When the president attends, he sits between the religious Tree of Life and the secular Tree of Knowledge," noted the current Navy chaplain, reflecting the tension that is very dear to Americans.

There's a tangible weight to the atmosphere at Camp David—the sights and sounds and smells, yes, but also the invisible gravitas of the place, its inimitable heft. The history that happened here—the *type* of history that happened here—could only have happened *here*, away from the barbed swelter of DC, away from the scrutiny of the press, away from the party lines and partisanship. Within Camp David is a whole hidden side of the presidency that Americans don't know well but are definitely curious about.

The amplification of the work ethic, a puritanical standard, scorns vacation and relaxation—considers it slacking, even. Presidents inevitably get unfairly criticized for their time off, but Camp David is no more a resort than the White House is a cushy mansion. There is a special chemistry to the place that has been important for every president who has come here. Among the trees, a clearing of the chief executive's mind is possible that results in tangible benefits for national policy.

Laura Bush, a frequent visitor, told an interviewer that what she loved about Camp David was spending time outdoors. In her words, one gets a sense of the shut-in nature of the presidency, the claustrophobia that sets in at the White House but is released at Camp David, where "there are no tourists peering through the fence."

"To me, Camp David is more a psychological journey than a physical one," Lady Bird Johnson once said. "I leave my troubles outside the gate."

There are many moments that capture the flavor of Camp David for me, but I'll always remember one in particular. It was January 2001, right before George W. Bush's inauguration. President Clinton wanted to come up and be at Aspen a little bit and have some downtime to go through personal things and pack up before the move date. As a career military officer, I've done this countless times in my career, and I thought to myself, *Yeah, makes sense. Even the president has to pack up his stuff before he moves.* For this visit, I asked Lieutenant Commander John Coronado, our executive officer, to handle the arrival at the landing zone; I would wait in Aspen to greet the president with the Aspen steward. It was a nice opportunity for the XO. Normally, the command master chief (Kevin Timmons and then George Havash during my two years) and I would be at the landing zone, and Coronado would be at Aspen. That's how a typical visit would start, especially if the president arrived on Marine One.

It was a brilliantly sunny day at first, but there was snow in the forecast, and soon it started to fall. Throughout the morning, the snow came down heavier and heavier, and it became obvious that the trip by air would be scrubbed. It was doubtful that the president would take the time to travel by motorcade.

Waiting in Aspen, the fire glowing, I looked out the picture window to a robust snow falling peacefully onto the lawn with the eastern view of the land beyond. Feeling the sense of something big about to happen and standing in the president's cabin with everything ready to go, this was probably one of the most dreamlike experiences I ever had at Camp David. I was used to the scene by then, but the beauty and wonder were still capable of catching me off guard.

And then the moment ended. Snow was too heavy and not going to let up, and, as anticipated, a motorcade was not an option; the visit was canceled. So the fire was put out, the lights turned off, the kitchen cleared, and we went back to our normal duties. For me, that experience was a snapshot of the sometimes jarring paradoxes of Camp David.

THE IDEA OF writing the story of Camp David had been brewing in my mind for years before I finally sat down to work on this book. I feel so privileged to have been there, and I appreciate how rare the opportunity was. The experience changed me in ways I am still defining, and I wanted others to be able to peer over the gate. Much has been written about the presidents occupying the White House residence—what they say and do there and how they behave. But I think, from my own observation and the accounts of others who have served there, that the presidents are different at Camp David—more reflective, playful, and energized by the hills and forests that surround them. There, they are briefly removed from their pedestals, the strictures of protocol loosened just enough to reveal their humanity. My intention in writing about Camp David is to illuminate the central character of the presidency and of America that emerges here.

It is not just the presidential families who are on display; it is also the high-level military crew that serves them. Everyone agrees there is no job like it in the military. The daily encounters with the utterly mundane mixed with moments of awe is something all who serve here find. And for the commanding officers, all of this is heightened by the fact that Camp David becomes our home too. We bring our spouses and children to live in the woods, the crew becomes extended family, and all of us are different as a result. Over the years, the most common question people ask me is: "What was it like?" It's hard to describe it in a simple way, so in this book I will take you through the experience of living there. Along with the many former commanders and crew who contributed their memories and reflections, I will be your eyes and ears on the ground.

Soon after I began writing this book, a significant event increased my desire to tell the story. In September 2016, the current Camp David CO hosted a reunion for sixteen former camp commanders, five former command master chiefs, and their families. Over a hundred and twenty-five people visited the camp, all of us walking the paths and remembering together.

Throughout the day, I experienced the history that each of

us brought to the gathering, and I felt pride, honor, and gratitude that I'd had the extraordinary opportunity to lead in such a unique environment. While each of us had different experiences, depending on the presidents we served and the events that surrounded them, we still had a common bond as members of this exclusive club.

The grown children of many of the COs especially enjoyed seeing Cedar, their former home, as each family lived in Cedar at different times in its history of upgrades and expansions. Someone coined the term *Cedar kids* as a moniker for yet another exclusive club. It was a moving, exhilarating experience to be back at the place that had, in one way or another, dramatically affected all of our lives.

In some respects, you'll find that the commanders and their families, along with members of the crew, are the main characters in this book. Commanders, alone among the crew, have a home and regular family life at the camp, and their memories offer an inside look at this secretive setting. The average term for a commander is two to three years, so there have been many of them. I was able to speak with all of the commanders who are still living, and their recollections provide a previously untapped view of Camp David.

Some, like me, served two presidents. The oldest is Chuck Howe, who was there for the end of Kennedy's presidency and Johnson's first year and a half. You'll also meet John Dettbarn, CO during almost four years of Nixon's presidency. Jim Rispoli, Jim Broaddus, Bill Waters, and Mike Berry served under Reagan, with Berry also serving two and a half years under Bush 41. Joe Camp served for six months under Bush 41 and at the beginning of Clinton's administration. Rich Cellon and Bert Ramsay served under Clinton. I served under Clinton and Bush 43. Mike O'Connor,

Bob McLean, John Heckmann, and Bob Reuning served under Bush 43, and Reuning also served for the first six months of Obama's presidency. Keith Autry, Wendy Halsey, Russ Rang, and Jeff Deviney served under Obama. Deviney is still CO at the beginning of the Trump administration.

Most of them were present at the reunion. Sitting together with the other commanders, I sensed from them the same thing I was feeling—that Camp David never leaves you.

Let me take you there.

Chapter One

THE GOOD SHIP SHANGRI-LA

This is my Shangri-La.
— Franklin Delano Roosevelt on first viewing the
site of the future presidential retreat

HOW THIS MAGICAL place came to be is a seventy-five-year-old story. Even though the camp has undergone embellishments and renovations in its history, the character and meaning have remained remarkably unchanged. Walking the paths today, one can imagine its first residents strolling those same paths, fishing in a nearby stream, smoking and chatting on the patios, or pitching horseshoes in a clearing. For three-quarters of a century, presidents have been traveling to this retreat on top of a mountain, first by car — a two-and-a-half-hour drive from Washington — then, since Eisenhower, more often by helicopter, a thirty-minute hop from the South Lawn of the White House. Thirteen presidents, from FDR through Obama, have used the retreat. As of this writing, a fourteenth, Donald Trump, has taken office.

The origin of the Catoctin Mountains site was the backdrop of World War II, but the need for a retreat close to Washington predated Roosevelt. In 1929, shortly after taking office and before the stock market crashed, Herbert Hoover bought 164 acres in the Blue Ridge Mountains of Virginia in what later became Shenandoah National Park, a hundred miles from Washington. Called Rapidan, it was a beautiful site, with two streams merging from the Rapidan River and surrounded by oak, elm, and beech trees. Hoover spent his own money to develop the area with stone structures, rock gardens, and waterfalls. He often retreated there to pursue his flyfishing hobby.

The main house was called the Brown House, a play on the White House. Thirteen small brown cabins were connected by paths, with main buildings named for their function — Town Hall, the general meeting place; Mess Hall, the kitchen; and Duty Station, base for the Secret Service.

The Hoovers entertained many luminaries at Rapidan, including Thomas Edison, Henry Luce, Charles and Anne Morrow Lindbergh, and the Edsel Fords. Some of the technologies needed for a presidential getaway, such as electricity and telephone service, were installed during the first year.

An article in the *New York Times* that appeared months before the financial collapse recounted a gathering that included Charles Lindbergh, who was "acclaimed as the horseshoe champion of the group of friends whom Mr. and Mrs. Hoover entertained in the country over the weekend.... President Hoover himself did not play, but stood on the sidelines and encouraged all concerned without exhibiting any partiality. Some of the players attributed their ill luck to the fatigue that overcame them as a result of the hard work they were required to do in collecting boulders and other material for the dam which the President is building near the camp."

Meanwhile, the press was taking swipes at this "frivolous"

expenditure, even though press secretary George Akerson insisted that "every nail and stick of wood" was paid for by the wealthy Hoover, not the nation. Once the Great Depression was upon the country, Rapidan took on a different significance. There, Hoover was able to conduct critical meetings away from the stress and the ever-prying eyes of Washington.

But the idyllic retreat was not enough to soothe Hoover's soul. Secret Service agent Colonel Edmund Starling wrote of the toll the economic crisis took on Hoover, observing that even during fishing, "President Hoover grew nervous. His hands would tremble as he worked with his tackle."

Hoover could not see his way out, and in 1932 voters swept him from office and in a landslide elected Franklin D. Roosevelt, a man who changed not only the course of the nation but the way the president relaxed. Although the Hoovers deeded Rapidan to the National Park Service for use by future presidents, Roosevelt didn't care for the spot, whose muggy atmosphere aggravated his medical conditions. Roosevelt enjoyed time away from Washington most often at his Hyde Park home—he visited there two hundred times during his presidency. But for a nearby retreat, Roosevelt preferred being on the water. Before the war, Roosevelt's retreat was the presidential yacht, the USS *Potomac*. It was put in mothballs during the Hoover administration, but Roosevelt had taken it out, and he loved that yacht. It was manned by a Navy crew, including Filipino stewards, and nicknamed "the Floating White House."

The war changed everything. With security officials contemplating the horrifying possibility that the presidential yacht could be sunk by German U-boats or attacked from the air, it was decided that it was just too risky to use the yacht. So in March 1942, officials from the National Park Service were tasked with looking for a location that could serve as a presidential retreat. There were three criteria in addition to the paramount one of security: (1) it had to be close to Washington; (2) it had to be at a high elevation to assure coolness during the summer, due to Roosevelt's allergies and asthma; and (3) it had to be cost-effective.

Three potential sites were suggested. The first was Comer's Deadening in Shenandoah National Park, one hundred miles from Washington. The other two were existing recreational areas in the Catoctin Mountains in Maryland, about sixty miles from Washington, part of the Catoctin Recreational Demonstration Area Project begun in 1935 by the Works Progress Administration (WPA). The goal of the WPA project was simple: to create parks from blighted agricultural land using mostly salvaged wood and other natural materials. It is possible to surmise that Camp David would not have existed in its present form and location were it not for the Great Depression and Roosevelt's decision to launch the WPA. Camp #3 and Camp #4 in the Catoctin Mountains were part of this project; they were about half a mile from each other, with Camp #3 at the higher elevation, eighteen hundred feet (thus its designation as Hi-Catoctin). Camp #3 also had the advantage of being a completed project, with cabins already erected.

On April 22, 1942, a presidential motorcade made the two-and-a-half-hour drive from Washington, winding up the mountain road to survey the site. When he first laid eyes on Camp #3, Roosevelt was delighted. "This is my Shangri-La," he announced, referring to the fictional Himalayan paradise in the 1933 novel *Lost Horizon*.

Writing about that first visit, Conrad L. Wirth, who was in charge of recreation and land planning, recalled FDR's enthusiasm for the view from the central cabin, whose full-length front porch faced the east and south. The president eagerly said he wanted to sit on the porch. There was no wheelchair handy, so the project director hurried down to his office at the base of the mountain, procured a desk chair, and brought it back up. FDR was lifted out of his car by two Secret Service agents and settled in the chair on the porch. But as soon as the men released their hold, the chair began to roll toward the edge. The agents dived and caught it just before the president toppled over. "It was a narrow escape," recalled Wirth, "but the president was all laughter and said he realized that somebody might try to get him someday, but he never suspected his own boys." No worries—he had found his retreat.

During the construction of the camp, Roosevelt enjoyed driving up from Washington to survey the progress. He'd call up Wirth and ask him to come along. "On one of these outings," Wirth wrote, "we stopped on the way to pick up Queen Wilhelmina of the Netherlands. At Catoctin the three of us sat on a car robe spread out on the ground right in front of the lodge under construction to have lunch and look out over the beautiful rolling Maryland farmland. Altogether, I believe, it was about as nice an assignment as a person could have had."

Roosevelt took a personal interest in every detail of the camp's development, assuming full charge of calculating the costs and assigning occupants to the cabins. In his early notes he scribbled:

Fix up one cottage for Miss Hackmeister and any stenogs
Fix up one cottage for Mr. Hassett and other male staff
Fix up one cottage for Filipinos and Valet—6 bunks
Secret Service to sleep in tents.

The president's cabin was the most important. That meant remodeling and expanding the building that had caught FDR's eye during his first visit. The completed cabin included four bed-rooms, two baths, a large living/dining area, a screened-in patio, a kitchen, and a pantry. At the time there were no plans to use the camp in the winter, but fireplaces were built in. Because of Roosevelt's constant worry about not being able to escape in case of fire, an extra-wide door was cut into the wall outside his bedroom, constructed like a drawbridge opening outward to form a ramp that could accommodate his wheelchair. (The special escape door was removed during a later renovation—a pity, given its historical significance.)

The building of Shangri-La was a daunting task. The presidential retreat had to be as secure as the White House, completely locked down. Yet at the same time, it was supposed to have the relaxed, woodsy feel of a summer camp, which meant that much of the security had to be invisible to the naked eye. In this setting, it was thought, a president could momentarily shake off the burdens of the office and luxuriate in the pretense of normalcy. That purpose set the tone for what happened over the next seventy-five years.

Roosevelt christened the site the USS Shangri-La on July 5, 1942, and made his first three-day visit on July 18. The naval designation, which was made when he moved his Filipino stewards from the USS *Potomac*, stuck, and thereafter the retreat was considered a naval facility. Much of the terminology evokes the seas, to the point where one can imagine sailing away on Camp David. For example, in line with Navy vernacular, people still speak of being "on board" at the camp. Ronald Reagan once referred to it as "the good ship Camp David."

According to Wirth, naval officers from the USS *Potomac* bent over backward to help set up the camp, and that included procuring supplies for it. One of the most difficult tasks was laying miles of cable for electricity. The captain of the yacht managed to get the cable and he charged it to yacht maintenance. One day the admiral in charge of the Navy Yard called the captain into his office and asked what he was planning to do with all that cable on the yacht — sink it?

The captain said, "Well, Admiral, you know the yacht is at Shangri-La."

At first the admiral didn't understand — and then he did. "Oh hell, all right." The supply chain continued, and a good deal of the furniture from the president's yacht was also moved to Shangri-La. Other furniture came from the White House attic. "There were no luxuries at all," William Rigdon wrote, "yet I believe FDR loved that camp more than any other place he frequented, except his own home at Hyde Park."

It can't be overstated just how *rustic* the camp was in its early days. The president's cabin had indoor plumbing, but everyone else had to settle for latrines. One can imagine late-night stumbles into the woods when nature called and guards appearing in the mist with rifles at the ready. Roosevelt loved it, but it had issues.

Wirth related a near-disaster that occurred on one of Roosevelt's early visits.

That evening the president sat playing cards with some friends at a table directly beneath a chandelier made from an old farm wagon wheel fitted with wrought iron electric light fixtures. The next morning the table was found crushed under the heavy wooden part of the wheel. Apparently it had been gradually drying and shrinking and had slipped out of its suspended iron rim some time during the night, after the people who had been sitting under it had left. Roosevelt was not told of this, nor have I seen the story published heretofore. We rushed up to the camp early the next morning and saw to it that the table was repaired and light fixtures put together again. This time the wooden part of the wheel was securely bolted to the iron rim.

Incidentally, FDR's beloved yacht did not fare well after his death. Over the years it had many different private owners, including Elvis Presley. But its most disreputable incident came in 1980, when it was seized in San Francisco as a front for drug smugglers. It was left to rot in the East Bay estuary, but weeks away from being sold for scrap, it was rescued by the Port of Oakland. There is a happy ending to this story. In 1995, the *Potomac* was restored to its former glory, and it has given over a quarter of a million visitors a glimpse of the appeal it once had for FDR.

Once the camp was built, there seemed to be a small detail left unattended to. The Navy likes to name things, and one of the camp's crew gave the cabins whimsical names that survived until the Eisenhower administration. The president's cabin was the Bear's Den. The communications cabin was One Moment Please. Quarters for the Secret Service were 221B Baker Street and the Baker Street Urchins. The Secret Service communications cabin was the Eyrie. The mess hall was the Breadbasket. The Filipino stewards' cabin was Little Luzon. The bathhouse was Hickory Limb. And the front entrance gate was Tell It to the Marines.

Like today, security was the number-one priority. When the president was on-site, Marines with war dogs patrolled the perimeter; sentry booths with telephones were located at hundred-yard intervals in case of emergency. There was a constant concern that someone would try to breach the camp's defenses and harm the president. Everyone was obsessed with achieving absolute quiet at night, presumably so any interlopers would be easily heard. Rigdon wrote that one of his duties "was to spend the night before the President's arrival in his bedroom, listening for any disturbing noises that we might be able to control. Squirrels were the chief offenders."

Of course, the Secret Service was also on hand during the president's visits. But that did not prevent Roosevelt from having a security scare. He liked to take drives along the mountain roads off the site, and one day when he was out in his car accompanied by a Secret Service agent, he became curious about a private turn-off. He decided to explore and drove down the road, ending up at a caretaker's cottage. A small woman holding a shotgun rushed out and confronted him. Refusing to believe he was who he said he was, she ominously pointed the shotgun at him. Deciding it was time to depart, he backed up the car and got the hell out of there. Later, the Secret Service contacted the caretaker and told him what had happened, and he was quite embarrassed. He went to Shangri-La, apologized profusely, and presented the president with a permit to use the road whenever he wanted. It is doubtful FDR ever did so.

At Shangri-La, Roosevelt, dressed in the casual attire that would become the hallmark of residents at the presidential retreat, conducted much of the regular business of the presidency. But he also liked to relax and let the enormous weight of a nation at war ease from his shoulders. His favorite spot was the screened-in patio where he could breathe the cool mountain air and work on his stamp collection, chat, or play solitaire. In the evenings he enjoyed cocktails and dinner there. When there were guests, his private secretary Grace Tully would sometimes organize poker games. She was such a good player that Roosevelt put up a sign in the living room of Aspen: VISITORS BEWARE OF GAMBLERS (ESPE-CIALLY FEMALE) ON THIS SHIP.

Recalling a typical weekend scenario, William Hassett, one of FDR's assistants, recorded: "The President settled himself on the porch to the rear of his cottage; said we would have dinner at 7 and cocktails in ten minutes. The President was as good as his word; lost no time in shaking Martinis on the porch. After dinner the President went back to his favorite corner of the porch and asked for his stamps, always a diversion."

During the first two summers, the crew decided to grow a vegetable garden, which they called the Kaptain's Kabbage Patch. They were quite delighted with the achievement until the waste-disposal system backed up and it was discovered that the Kabbage Patch was located directly over the septic-tank drain field. That was it for homegrown vegetables.

Given the pressures of the war, Roosevelt usually came with substantial briefing books. His close adviser Harry Hopkins was often with him at Shangri-La, as was Grace Tully, and they labored over reports and cables in the living room or on the screened patio.

In his book *Gateway to the Mountains*, Thurmont historian George Wireman wrote,

To give you an idea of the important part that Shangri-La must have played during World War II, a government official once stated that this secluded little mountain retreat not only had the data on the fighting fronts, and the potential fighting fronts, but it was actively in touch with them all. It was nothing for the citizens of Thurmont to sec General George Marshall, Admiral Ernest King and General "Hap" Arnold come tearing up that twisting mountain road at 12 or 1 o'clock at night with their aides and secretaries. Then there would be a conference with the President lasting for about an hour or more and off they would go again. Just what historic decisions in the conduct of World War II were made at Shangri-La have thus far not been disclosed. However, as one official recently stated, "they were momentous."

Winston Churchill had become a close friend and ally of FDR, and he visited Shangri-La twice during the war. They sat talking and contemplating strategy over highballs and cigars or went fishing together at Hunting Creek, near Shangri-La. Few fish were caught, but that was almost beside the point. There they would talk for hours, seated on rudimentary canvas chairs, clouds of cigar smoke rising above them. "The cigars created enough of a screen to protect both of them from mosquitoes," wrote naval aide William Rigdon.

Churchill enjoyed these times with Roosevelt. According to the historian Doris Kearns Goodwin, Churchill once told Eleanor, "You know, one works better when one has a chance to enjoy a little leisure now and then. The old proverb all work and no play makes Jack a dull boy holds good for all of us."

On one of these visits, they drove down to the town of Thurmont at the base of the mountain. When the townspeople spotted them, they poured out onto the road and cheered as Churchill raised his hand and gave the victory sign. Stopping at the Cozy Restaurant, a favorite local establishment, Churchill announced that he wanted to see what a jukebox looked like; Churchill eased his bulky frame out of his seat and strode inside. He handed the stunned owner some coins for the jukebox and bought a beer. The people of Thurmont still talk about it.

In a true sense, the two men were allies and soul mates, even if they were sometimes combatants on the field of ideas and strategy. Their closeness is reflected in the fond sign-off of a letter FDR wrote to Churchill: "It's fun to be in the same decade with you."

Roosevelt did not live to see the Allied victory. As the nation and the world grieved his passing on April 12, 1945, his beloved Shangri-La was left empty and silent. The place was deserted through the spring and summer, except for the skeleton crew of twenty assigned to maintenance. President Truman did not visit for the first time until September. Truman only grudgingly used the camp—Bess found it dull—and he made just ten visits during his presidency, although, as noted, he did manage to clear the abundant foliage from behind the presidential cabin. (Mrs. Truman might have rethought her impression of the dullness of the camp had Rigdon called her attention to the copperhead snake that appeared between the terrace flagstones a few feet from where she was having lunch one day.) While Truman was there, his main pleasure seemed to be walking the extensive trails, but Bess began using the camp a bit for informal luncheons. Rigdon recalled one uncomfortable incident: Mrs. Truman had invited seven ladies to lunch, and she informed him that they did not want steward service; they'd be fine on their own. In other words, he should stay away. But during the luncheon, Rigdon received an urgent phone call from the White House that required Mrs. Truman's attention. Fearfully imagining what he might encounter, he went to get the First Lady. "I made my approach to the pool site as noisily as I could, but nevertheless arrived unnoticed, to confront eight mature ladies sitting in a line on the pool's edge, fully clothed except for their shoes and stockings, dangling their feet in the water and apparently having a grand time."

Ironically, Truman's preferred getaway was the USS *Williamsburg*, which became his presidential yacht. The war having been won, it was now deemed safe for the president to be on the water. Since the *Williamsburg* and Shangri-La were both Navy "vessels," it wasn't unusual for crews to go between the two; it was the crew from the *Williamsburg* that was tasked with cleaning up the brush behind Aspen.

In spite of Truman's lack of enthusiasm about the camp, he took the decisive action of maintaining it as a federal property, writing to Maryland governor Herbert R. O'Connor: "I have decided because of the historical events and international interest now associated with the Catoctin Recreational Area that this property should be retained by the Federal Government and made a part of the National Park Service of the Department of Interior." And so it has been ever since.

Truman made one other important contribution: the addition of steam heat in the presidential lodge and a few of the cabins, which allowed Shangri-La to be used year-round.

More than one president initially intended to shut the place down as a cost-cutting measure, but in every instance the camp seduced the chief executive or someone on his staff. Eisenhower thought it was an unnecessary expense at first, and he changed his mind about abandoning the camp only at the behest of attorney general Herbert Brownell. Following a Justice Department inspection trip to review the site, Brownell was so taken with it that he wrote Eisenhower a "Petition for Executive Clemency" for the camp. Defending his "client," Brownell wrote, "Petitioner states that she was convicted without a hearing in the White House . . . and was sentenced to embarrassment, ignominy, and possible transfer or obliteration."

Eisenhower was persuaded. He did object to the name, however, declaring that Shangri-La was "just a little fancy for a Kansas farm boy." He renamed it Camp David in honor of his grandson, who would make many visits there, both while his grandfather was in office and after he married President Nixon's daughter Julie.

The name change was somewhat spontaneous. Rigdon remembered receiving word about it the day before Eisenhower was planning a visit. The crew sprang into action, and when Eisenhower arrived, there was a new sign at the entrance reading CAMP DAVID. "I am glad they did not touch the paint to find whether it was dry," Rigdon wrote.

Eisenhower made forty-five visits to Camp David during his two terms; he used it during his recovery from a heart attack in 1955. At that time he held the first cabinet meeting there. Eisenhower's most famous stay was the two days he hosted Nikita Khrushchev in 1959, which led to a brief rapprochement with the Soviets—thanks to what Khrushchev called "the spirit of Camp David."

Eisenhower also introduced the helicopter landing area, shortening the trip from two and a half hours by car to thirty minutes by air and making it much easier for presidents to get to Camp David.

"I don't plan to use Camp David very often," Kennedy said when he was elected. And he didn't, making only nineteen visits. Notably, JFK's first visit to the camp was in the company of Eisenhower. Demoralized after the Bay of Pigs fiasco, Kennedy called on Eisenhower for advice, helicoptering him in from his nearby home at Gettysburg. Eisenhower was then in the odd position of showing Kennedy around the camp while giving him a stern critique of where he'd gone wrong.

After that, Kennedy visited only infrequently during his first two years. Jackie favored a four-hundred-acre horse farm they rented in Middleburg, Virginia, called Glen Ora. But in 1963, the owner wanted the farm back, so they began coming to Camp David more often. They installed stables so Jackie and Caroline could ride, and they all enjoyed the site, interacting with the crew in a warm and relaxed way. Kennedy was particularly interested in the rich history of the area, including Gettysburg. By the time of the assassination, he'd grown to appreciate the camp and likely would have used it more had he lived. Jackie loved the freedom of being in the mountains, sometimes taking the kids on outings to Fantasyland Park in nearby Gettysburg or bringing them shopping in Thurmont.

Incidentally, there was some discussion when Kennedy took office about whether he would rename the camp, as Eisenhower had done, either returning it to the original Shangri-La or using a personal designation—Camp Caroline, perhaps. But Kennedy refused, even when urged to do so by some particularly partisan Democrats in Congress. Camp David it remained.

Hard-driving and sociable by nature, Lyndon Johnson didn't initially see the advantage of the getaway. But that changed soon enough. A few weeks into his presidency, he was sitting at a White House banquet, feeling bored and restless. Suddenly he leaned over to Lady Bird and whispered, "Would you like to go to Camp David?" Yes, she would! Two hours later, they were flying north. "We woke up to snow and serenity and a fire burning in the fireplace," Lady Bird recalled. It was just what they needed.

During his presidency, LBJ made only thirty visits, but the chance to get away from it all appealed to him more as Vietnam War demonstrators increased in number and volume around his house in Washington. He used the camp mostly as a meeting place for advisers, although Lady Bird's home movies show family and friends romping in the pool and cooking barbecue.

Richard Nixon dramatically changed the look of Camp David, instituting what was by then a much-needed modernization of the property and the cabins. He built the new Laurel Lodge, restored Dogwood and Birch, and, of course, built the private swimming pool in back of Aspen. Nixon made a hundred and sixty visits. He was usually accompanied by his close advisers, including H. R. Haldeman, John Ehrlichman, and Henry Kissinger. He liked to swim, bowl, and watch movies, and he frequently used the camp for governing purposes, holding cabinet meetings there and hosting world leaders, most notably Leonid Brezhnev. But as the storm clouds of Vietnam and Watergate hung heavier over his administration, he often came to the camp alone and walked the trails deep in thought.

Within a month of taking office under very difficult circumstances, Gerald Ford brought his family to Camp David for the first time. Gerald and Betty Ford enjoyed Camp David, especially the great outdoors and the way it offered them a chance to relax with their children. But Ford didn't use it that much and hosted only one foreign dignitary there, President Suharto of Indonesia. They made twenty-nine visits during Ford's two and a half years in office.

One change occurred on Ford's watch. During Nixon's administration, the press had set up a trailer, dubbed Poison Ivy Lodge by the camp crew, outside the gate. The UPI correspondent Helen Thomas complained to Ford that the name was insulting, so he arranged to have the press trailer renamed Honeysuckle. Sounds lovely, until one considers that honeysuckle is a leeching vine, a pest in spite of its floral scent. Eventually the press moved down the mountain to the Cozy Inn, and the trailer was gone forever.

Ford was uncharacteristically open with the press, though, allowing Harry Reasoner of ABC News to do an interview at Camp David; he even gave him a presidential camp jacket to wear.

Carter came into office with a dogged determination to cut government waste, and Camp David was initially in his sights. However, not only did he back down about closing the camp, he used it as the site of the historic 1978 negotiations between Egypt and Israel, which cemented Camp David's reputation as a place to foster peace. He made ninety-nine visits, going there forty-seven of his forty-eight months in office. His final visits weren't happy, though; he was miserable about the result of the election that ended his presidency, and in addition, he took a spill off a sled and broke his collarbone at the camp two weeks before leaving office. In the years since, he remained uncomfortable with what he considered the wastefulness of Camp David. When he was a guest of the Clintons while I was in command, his first comment to me, delivered in a distasteful tone, was "I see you've kept building this place up."

It was the Reagans who broke the trend of occasional use. They set a record that remains to this day — 189 visits for a total of 571 days. For the Reagans it was very much a private retreat; they mostly came alone and rarely invited others — not even their children — to join them. It was clear the Reagans craved time together without pesky aides or even relatives to distract them from their intimacies. Their visits were pretty predictable — riding horses by day and watching movies by night. But Reagan also used his time at the camp for study and reflection, and he wrote many speeches there.

One consistent feature of Reagan weekends was the live Saturday address to the nation from Laurel. According to CO Jim Broaddus, Reagan would have a draft delivered to him by his speechwriters early Saturday, and he would spend the morning going over it and marking it up. At Laurel, a staffer from the communications office would sit next to him, following along while he spoke — "So she could rescue him if he sneezed or something." Broaddus remembered one occasion when the speech had been *very* heavily marked up by Reagan. "Just before the speech, we were asked to make a copy, but as luck would have it, when the secretary printed it, the printer ate the speech," Broaddus said. It was in there somewhere, but they couldn't pry it out. Broaddus finally got a copy to the president with only three minutes to spare. "I rushed in," he said, "and the president was sitting there as cool as a cucumber. He wasn't worried at all." It revealed a key aspect of Reagan's character. "From the crew's perspective," Broaddus said, "they were motivated by him as a person — not out of fear."

Reagan was at his ranch in California when he made his famous gaffe while kidding around before a taping of the Saturday address — "We begin bombing in five minutes" — but afterward at Camp David, a giant electronic ON AIR/OFF AIR panel was added to prevent future accidents.

World leaders were not frequent guests of the Reagans, with one exception. In 1984, Reagan invited his dear friend and ally Prime Minister Margaret Thatcher to the camp. There they debated the advisability of the Strategic Defense Initiative program (known colloquially as Star Wars), but they also had time for more local adventures, riding a golf cart along the paths so he could show her the sights, including the porch at Holly where Winston Churchill and FDR planned D-day.

George and Barbara Bush were already familiar with Camp David when Bush assumed the presidency, having visited several times during Reagan's administration. They loved the camp and visited 124 times — about three weekends a month, except when

they were in Kennebunkport. They took advantage of everything Camp David had to offer, or they tried to, swimming laps,
tossing horseshoes, golfing, shooting skeet, playing tennis, and jogging, usually accompanied by their dogs. Their large family gathered around on frequent occasions, and they built a playground for
their grandchildren, which was later rebuilt for the Obama girls.

Bush 41 was instrumental in making sweeping improvements
to the camp's infrastructure. Due to political considerations and
budgetary constraints, presidents were reluctant to approve large
expenditures for the presidential retreat, and few upgrades had been
made since the Nixon administration. By the beginning of Bush 41's
term, this neglect was becoming critical. Cabins, including Laurel
Lodge, had leaking roofs; the electrical-distribution systems were
inadequate and unreliable; there were environmental problems,
such as open sewage in the lawn below Aspen; and the housing and
troop-support facilities were outdated. A main-line power outage in
August 1988 revealed that the emergency power system could carry
only a small portion of the camp's electrical load. At his first meeting with President Bush in January 1989, CO Mike Berry recom-
mended a multiyear repair-and-improvement program. Berry told
the president that many of these projects "only an engineer would
find interesting or get excited about and they may be somewhat
disruptive to guest operations." President Bush said that he'd support such a program to update this important national asset. A year
later the Bush administration approved the first ever Camp David
facilities master plan. This plan, most of which has now been imple-
mented, improved the power-distribution system, the emergency
power systems, the sewage-collection-and-treatment systems, and
perimeter security, and it authorized a reroofing program, two new
guest cabins, and a fire-crash building for the hangar.

During their eight years, the Clintons visited only sixty times, definitely a slower pace for the crew, who had enjoyed the frequent visits of the Reagans and Bushes. When they did come, they were often accompanied by friends, and that included big Hollywood celebrities. One night Matt Damon, Ben Affleck, Robin Williams, and Gwyneth Paltrow were on hand to watch the movie *Good Will Hunting* with the Clintons, and the next day Damon and Affleck joined the president at Laurel cabin to watch football. The Clintons liked to relax with Chelsea and their friends and perhaps felt the healing aura of the camp. One tradition that they did keep was going to the camp for Thanksgiving with extended family and friends. In 1998 Clinton spent the holiday playing golf while articles of impeachment were being drawn up in Washington— reminiscent of the way many presidents gravitate toward the camp during times of personal crisis.

Clinton appreciated the significance of the camp as a place where one might attempt to heal international tensions. In his last year in office he held a Middle East peace summit, bringing Palestinian leader Yasser Arafat and Israeli prime minister Ehud Barak together in an effort to resolve their conflicts.

Like his father, George W. Bush made great use of the camp and felt right at home, given how many times he'd visited when George H. W. Bush was president. He made 150 visits over 464 days and hosted twenty heads of state there. Bush soon learned that Camp David had value in times of crisis; he brought his cabinet, advisers, and security agency chiefs there after 9/11 to do the hard work of crafting a response to the attack. In the process they also grieved and worshipped together, gaining strength from the spiritual energy of the camp.

Bush enjoyed bringing foreign leaders to Camp David, among them British prime minister Tony Blair, who visited three times;

surely those visits strengthened their friendship, which had grown since 9/11. He also hosted Russian president Vladimir Putin.

At the start of the Obama administration, rumors flew at the camp that the new president wasn't likely to be a regular guest — in the words of Michelle Obama, "He's an urban guy." There was also speculation that, much like the Clintons' with Chelsea, the Obamas' weekend schedules were affected by their daughters' activities in Washington, DC. In eight years, Obama made only thirty-nine visits. When he was at camp, the president's favorite spot, not surprisingly, was the basketball court, called Leatherwood Court, which had been refurbished especially for him at the very end of George W. Bush's administration; it's no doubt the only one in existence that features a large presidential seal in midcourt.

Michelle Obama and the girls tended to visit more often, the First Lady taking the advice of her predecessors to make use of the camp. She loved hosting groups of female friends or hanging out with Sasha and Malia.

In a bitterly partisan era, there was some talk of hosting bipartisan meetings at Camp David, but they never materialized. Obama did invite Senate majority leader Mitch McConnell to join him at the camp after the 2014 midterm elections; however, McConnell declined — giving as his excuse a scheduling conflict.

At the G8 Summit in 2012, Obama earned the distinction of bringing together more heads of state than any other president ever had. It had originally been scheduled for Chicago, but Obama changed the venue, saying, "G8 tends to be a more informal setting in which we talk about a wide range of issues in a pretty intimate way." It was an extension of Camp David's role as a place where the world's leaders could talk about the most important issues on the planet as they walked in the woods.

The long and the short of presidential use of Camp David is that each president has added his own signature to the camp, regardless of the frequency of the visits. In this way, the history of Camp David does not stay in the past but is fully present today. When you're there, you can almost see Roosevelt smoking on the porch with Churchill. You can imagine George H. W. Bush in the wallyball court slamming the balls across the net. You can picture Eisenhower at his rustic grill with the steaks sizzling, Caroline Kennedy riding her pony Macaroni, and the Clintons talking as they walked down a tree-lined path. Blink and you can hear Reagan's warm voice coming over the radio as he gave his Saturday address to the nation. Like an archaeological imprint, it's all still there in the dirt, in the air.

Chapter Two

REPORTING FOR DUTY

We're moving to Camp David. It's where the president
goes on the weekends.
—CO Michael Giorgione to his daughters

MY FIRST DAY on the job at Camp David proved one of the truisms of working for the president: there are no absolutes. That said, as the Clintons demonstrated, some presidents are more unpredictable than others. Weeks earlier, my family had been uprooted from my last post in what many of us cheekily call sunny Mayberry—Coronado, California. My wife, Michele, and our daughters, Briana and Ryanne, were getting used to moving, but this was the biggest change of all. How to explain to a seven- and four-year-old that you're moving to a cabin in the woods?

I'd first visited Camp David in 1992 when I was serving at the Bureau of Naval Personnel at the Pentagon as the rating assignment officer for the U.S. Navy Seabees. I was asked to go and talk to the troops at the camp. I remember coming away from that visit thinking, *What a pain to work there!* Everyone was so formal and polite, and everything had to be perfect, right down to the last blade of grass. Now, seven years later, I was preparing to take over as the commanding officer.

Reflecting on this, I saw that there were several times in my career when something I thought I didn't want ended up being the best assignment or opportunity for me. Fortunately, I forgot all about my first impression of the camp!

Getting the position was a long journey. Just to reach the first interview, I had endured an intensive yearlong vetting process. My life had been scrutinized to the minutest degree. Not just my professional background and intellectual aptitude, but my financial history, my health history, my military performance, my personality and "fit." One week when I was traveling, Michele noticed a car parked down the road from our house for a few days, and it followed her during her busy daily routine. My family, friends, neighbors, classmates, co-workers, former co-workers, former neighbors, former friends, and anyone else the adjudicating authority deemed relevant had all been interviewed to make sure I could be trusted with the highest level of security permission. Meanwhile, my family was happily situated in idyllic Coronado, where I was serving as the public works officer at the naval base. We were really enjoying our life. As a Navy family, we knew we wouldn't live there forever, but we weren't exactly angling for a move. My wife and I had both grown up in Pittsburgh and we were quite familiar with those winters. The idea of returning east to live on top of a mountain seemed like a challenge, even as the opportunity beckoned.

We were used to moving around and living in obscure places. We'd lived overseas twice before we had children, and we knew the drill: questionable housing, secondhand furniture, all the stuff military families face every day. Camp David would be a unique and special assignment—and yet.

I was called for an interview and a visit to Camp David in November 1998, and on the same trip I spent a day in the East Wing of the White House with the White House Military Office. There were three of us under consideration, but in meetings with the WHMO staff and as I sat and talked with the White House director, I sensed that I was going to get the job. I got the phone call two weeks later telling me that the assignment had finally come through, and I had to tell Michele we were moving back east the following summer. It was a little bit hard. If you can imagine it, there was a sense of excitement, but also some upset. I won't deny there were tears shed.

One of Michele's biggest concerns was work-life balance, which, fortunately, had always been very good for us. Coincidentally, our life in Coronado was the perfect example of Mrs. Clinton's concept that it takes a village to raise kids; we actually called Coronado proper "the Village." That's what we had in that posting in California, where everyone—colleagues, friends, neighbors, teachers, and coaches—was invested in our family. The isolation of the Catoctin Mountains would be a challenge. But the opportunity and adventure were too great to pass up.

When I spoke to other Camp David commanders, I found that this combination of excitement and strong reservations was often shared by others, most of whom had had young children— even infants. The idea of moving your family to the woods at the top of a mountain can take your breath away. "I was a reluctant draft choice," Bob McLean, who served during Bush 43's presidency, told me. His reluctance wasn't about going to Camp David; it was that he wanted to be an operational Seabee during a time of conflict. In addition, Bob and his wife, Lisa, had a one-month-old son and an eighteen-month-old daughter. But Lisa was pushing for him to say yes, and they actually found the experience easier with babies than it would have been with older children. They didn't have to worry about school buses, and their family doctor was occasionally the White House physician when he or she was on board. In spite of any initial reservations, all the families who were admitted to the exclusive Camp David club were glad and grateful they'd had the opportunity.

But at the start, you don't know what to expect, so I approached my first day, June 25, 1999, with some butterflies. Scheduling a change-of-command ceremony that Friday had seemed like a safe bet, and my immediate predecessor, Commander Bert Ramsay, knew this well. There was no indication of any presidential visit on the horizon, and the event was booked. So when the morning dawned temperate and sunny atop the Catoctin Mountains, my biggest concern was keeping my dress whites pristine for the ceremony. My only job that day was a simple one: Take command. It was someone else's job to worry about all the planning for the event.

Surrounded by the camp's lush green grounds, the modest WPA-era cabins just beyond the trees behind the dais, I felt a strong sense of history and promise in the air. I was about to accept responsibility for the day-to-day operations of a facility that had hosted some of the most important figures in modern times. But just as I was enjoying the chance to contemplate this, we received word that there had been a slight change of plans: The Clintons were coming. That very night. In military-speak, immediate pucker factor.

I would soon learn that unpredictability was a hallmark of the Clinton rhythm. Many visits went off without a hitch, but there were enough scheduled visits that were suddenly canceled and canceled visits that were suddenly on again that the staff was always speculating: Were they coming? Weren't they?

This first visit, all I knew was that they most certainly were. And I didn't actually yet know what a presidential visit entailed.

During the ceremony, my mind was buzzing with questions about the details that would need to be arranged before the Clintons' arrival. A presidential visit is an intricately choreographed affair, and everything has to be just right. I had received an early glimpse of this preparation process and protocol when Ramsay invited me to camp to observe an actual presidential visit with Clinton before I took over, a practice done for many years between successive camp commanders. Now I was on my own, although there was a very capable and competent staff there to support and execute everything.

Normally, the preparation consists of a morning kickoff meeting, usually on the Monday before a weekend visit — *if* we know of the visit at least a week out. During my time, the Poplar conference room with the iconic Eisenhower photograph was used for this meeting, which was attended by a representative from each department of the camp plus the Marine Security Company and the White House Communications Agency. Now, owing to the expanded number of attendees, the kickoff meeting is conducted in another location.

At the meeting the CO typically shares what information he or she has about the nature and purpose of the visit, who is visiting, cabin assignments, desired activities, events, meals, and other minute details, plus the ever important arrival day and time. We then review any facility, weather, or security concerns for the days preceding the arrival and go over visit preps that have to be completed. We have scores of SOPs — standard operating procedures — for just about everything from firefighting to golfing off-camp at a local course.

Bob Reuning, the CO during part of George W. Bush's and

Obama's administrations, likened the preparation to the scene in *Apollo 13* when they're getting ready to launch: "Booster!" "Go!" "Guidance!" "Go!" "Procedures!" "Go!"

During my time, I worked principally with the First Lady's social secretary to receive information about the visit. If a head of state was involved or if there were other diplomatic or business purposes for the visit, the WHMO director and staff and sometimes the Department of State would also provide information.

The relationship with the social secretary was crucial during my time at camp and one that I continually had to develop. These loyal servants can take on the personalities and routines of their bosses, and I found that to be very true working with Capricia Marshall under Mrs. Clinton and Cathy Fenton under Mrs. Laura Bush. The Camp David COs learned quickly; speaking to them was the equivalent of speaking directly with the First Ladies themselves.

But on June 25, 1999, I didn't know any of this and hadn't talked to a social secretary that week, let alone that day. And even though I knew I could trust and rely on others, I hadn't been to the race yet on my own, and it is a much different feeling once you're in the driver's seat.

I had planned to show my family and friends around the retreat after the ceremony and the reception, but that would have to wait. I curtailed hugs and good wishes, and Michele, our daughters, my parents, my father-in-law, and other family members, as well as fellow officers and friends, were all ushered "off the hill," outside the gate of the Camp David compound. (Normally, Michele and the girls would remain, of course, but we hadn't yet moved into Cedar.) I stayed behind alone, thrown into the thick of things before I'd barely been handed the keys. I had work to do, but the best decision I made that first day was to do *nothing*. Yes, I was the commanding officer now, completely in charge and accountable for everything that happened. But that first day, I was also there to learn, and what better way than to be thrown into it and let this exceptional crew do their thing?

During the hastily assembled kickoff meeting, I mostly listened, asking a seemingly smart question now and then but really just watching the crew in action. I was conscious of the need for calm; I communicated to the crew that I trusted them, which in turn bolstered my own self-confidence. This style of leadership, which I had used throughout my career, would serve me quite well at Camp David.

It was to be a night arrival, which has its own drama because of the surrounding inky darkness pierced by the landing-zone lights and then the sudden illumination from the approaching helicopter.

Arrival is always the most dramatic time of a visit. There are so many variables — timing, weather, getting everyone arranged. The fire crew and the crash crew must be positioned in case there's an accident. The golf carts have to be standing by. Sometimes — though not on my first day — guests are invited to witness arrival, usually the families of crew members who live in Navy housing down the mountain. At those times we have to arrange for a bus to pick them up and bring them to the site at least an hour beforehand.

One interesting note: On every helicopter arrival, there is one reporter with a camera at the observation area. He or she is the press observer with a macabre duty — to be a witness in case there's a crash.

We got an alert when the Clintons took off from the South Lawn, meaning they were thirty minutes away. I was in my dress uniform and drove over in my golf cart with the command duty officer. We took our places at the head of the path, far enough that the helicopter-prop blast wouldn't knock us down or blow our uniform covers (hats) into the distant trees.

When we saw the lights in the sky we began to stiffen our backs, and as the helicopter, Marine One, was landing, we saluted. It was very ceremonial and strangely simple, yet poignant. We dropped our salutes once the helicopter landed and waited for the power to go off and the blades to stop turning. I walked down the pathway as the door popped open and Marines in dress uniform jumped out and took their posts. I walked right up to the bottom of the landing stairs to greet the president.

Out came Clinton, holding his nephew Zachary Rodham; followed by the Clintons' chocolate Lab, Buddy; Mrs. Clinton; Chelsea, nineteen; and Chelsea's friend Elizabeth. They looked perfectly relaxed and natural, despite the late hour, all dressed casually. I recognized from seeing him on TV the president's familiar lope as he came down the stairs. Chelsea, her hair a wild, curly mass, looked at me standing there saluting and asked, "Who are *you?*" I told her I had just taken charge twelve hours earlier and she laughed in a nice way, as if recognizing my anxiety.

At Camp David we are mostly set apart from the political roar outside, but I had the impression that the Clintons had survived the horrible ordeal of impeachment only eight months earlier and that they'd already figured out how to move on, their family intact, and make the most of the last year and a half in office. What I didn't know at that point was that Mrs. Clinton was already exploring making a bid for the Senate in 2000.

I shook hands and introduced myself for the first time as "the commanding officer of your presidential retreat."

They welcomed me, and then I walked them back to where the golf carts were lined up. They got in Golf Cart One, and before I knew it they were heading toward Aspen. The helicopter was pushed into the hangar, and the pilots and the crew settled in at the camp in case the president had to move quickly.

When the evening was finally over, I breathed a sigh of relief. I had survived my first day, and it wasn't at all the day I had expected.

There's a saying in the Navy that command involves the highest highs and the lowest lows, separated by nanoseconds. I was certainly reminded of this frequently while serving at Camp David. It can be humbling, but it can also go to your head if you're not careful. As a senior officer told me before I started, "Mike, make sure your hat size is the same when you come out of there." Wise counsel.

The rest of my first weekend was relatively uneventful. The Clintons relaxed together, took walks; the president might have hit a few balls behind Aspen. On Sunday they went to services at Evergreen Chapel, and President Clinton sang in the choir, as he usually did. In the chapel, the president's family sits in the front row on the right side, and the CO's family sits in the front row on the left side. Navy chaplain Brad Ableson led the Protestant service. When he gave the sermon, I wondered for the first of many times what it felt like to be preaching to the president of the United States.

Ableson was the first of two chaplains I served with at Camp David. He departed just a few months after my arrival but was a tremendous adviser and supporter as I settled into the job. He had a pleasant and gregarious personality, and he really had a connection with President Clinton; even though I wasn't the one preaching to the president from the altar a few feet away, I found his manner comforting. The next chaplain would have the same wonderful relationship with President Bush during some very trying times in our nation. (More about that later.)

Sunday afternoon, the Clintons departed, and the crew and I repeated the same process in reverse. I saluted and watched the helicopter lift off — and realized I was *exhausted*. I thought about it. I hadn't really done all that much. But I was always up, walking around, observing and learning, onstage every minute. Even though nothing of particular consequence seemed to be happening, I was perpetually on edge, even as I conveyed a relaxed demeanor. It wears on you after a weekend, enjoyable as the visit is. With time I came to see that Camp David was a place of "high risk, high yield," with the Sword of Damocles always hanging above my head. There's not a lot of room for error. All of us who serve as commanders are aware that we can be relieved at any time. Sure, everything looks calm and cool from the outside, but it's supposed to — *inside* there is often the constant unease that comes with command, the hyperalertness that something could go wrong. Much like being president, I suspect. It's part of the deal of being a leader.

As a leadership challenge, Camp David is significant. Think about it. The crew that's picked, the senior petty officers and officers, are top candidates throughout the Navy and Marine Corps. Everyone who works for you is like a gold-medal athlete, and now they're all on your team — and that's wonderful. But you take these Sailors and Marines and you tell them their jobs are to make beds, clean toilets, and plant flowers. You tell them to dress up, look nice, and salute the president. Be sociable and pleasant — but watch yourselves.

There are bound to be ego conflicts, people saying, in effect, *Wait a minute. I was the top Sailor on my ship and now I'm doing menial labor much of the time.* The Seabees, most of whom are on their very first assignments, are thinking, *This isn't why I joined the Navy!* The commander's job is to motivate the crew, to help them make sense of it, and to ensure they realize that what they're doing is important and necessary. Don't get me wrong; everyone is thrilled to get this plum assignment. But when the mundane crawl of daily life sets in — especially if the president doesn't come very often — it can be grueling, particularly for the young servicemen and servicewomen. They all get the importance of the camp when you're interviewing them and you're vetting them and they're going through security, because everyone is jazzed by it. They say, "Camp David. So cool." Then they arrive. Marines walk the patrol in February at two a.m. and it's freezing cold, shockingly quiet, and very lonely. The crew replants flowers because the deer got into them. After a while, a natural frustration sets in for many of them, and they ask themselves, *What the hell am I doing?* The leadership is ready for this; it's perfectly normal. And most of the crew come away from Camp David feeling proud to have had the unique opportunity of serving there.

On that first weekend I tried to go with the flow and make sure there were no mistakes. Most successful leaders will tell you that when you're new in command, you go in and observe for a while at first. In time you might find things that you think can be better, things you're going to tweak or make substantial changes to.

For me, the first of those changes had to do with clothing. It had been a long-standing practice — at least fifteen years — that after the president and guests arrived, the crew would change into casual civilian clothes, referred to as "Camp David casual," for most of the visit, and then change back into dress uniforms for departure honors. Typically, I would greet the president, First Family, and guests in summer whites in the spring and summer and navy blues in the fall and winter.

I noticed that the crew was following the practice very well when I arrived, but I also observed that individual definitions of what was casual and appropriate could vary. The problem was how to maintain the casual feel of this exclusive mountaintop retreat while also adding the kind of class a tourist would expect at a five-star resort.

I worked with the staff and our supply officer, Lieutenant Tim Jett, a wonderfully creative and dedicated officer, and we came up with the idea of issuing the crew three different-colored polo shirts (navy blue, maroon, forest green) with the Camp David seal on the front of each one. We would also issue gray polo shirts to the Sailors and Marines assigned to the galley to wear while they were working in the kitchen and on the serving line, and everyone would receive one navy blue sweater. Winter coats and rain gear would still be left to the discretion of the individual, and those on guard duty would continue to wear the military uniform of the day.

I was happy with this change. We looked good, and I think it added the right touch of class in a relaxed manner. The "uniform" also helped guests easily recognize who worked at the retreat. The shirt material has evolved since 1999, and only navy blue shirts are issued today, but the practice continues.

As commander, I knew that if there was one mixed signal, it all fell apart. On one visit I got word that President Clinton wanted to play golf when he arrived. When I met him at Marine One and walked him to Golf Cart One, I told him that the golf motorcade was prepared to leave whenever he was. You would have thought I'd called him a Republican from the look he gave me. At last he smiled. "There must have been a misunderstanding," he said. There was no plan to play golf. I cringed.

This might seem like a silly incident, but the tiny details keep the CO on constant edge. When I look back on my whole time there, I remember the pressure and stress. My job was to be the director of everything; I had to make sure that my family was comfortable, that the atmosphere was casual but still perfect, that the crew felt trusted and empowered. And most of all, I had to make sure that the president was happy and had a great and relaxing visit. Thus the edginess.

It wasn't just me. When Wendy Halsey assumed command in 2011, she was full of anxiety. Like all commanders, she wanted to be perfect, and she was very aware that as the first female commander, people might be watching her in a special way. Her wonderful and supportive husband, Mark, and their three kids were with her, and she was pretty tough on them in the early months. She was scared that one of them would step out of line, which would reflect badly on her. Looking back, she admitted she was perhaps overcautious, but I can understand her angst. It's something we all feel. She isn't the first CO to lecture her kids not to make a peep!

Initially, she wouldn't even allow her family to go to the landing zone to watch an arrival. The first time she did, she was concerned about her seven-year-old son, Tucker. Knowing that President Obama liked to chat with the families after he landed, she felt Tucker required advance instructions. At the time, he was going through a phase of greeting people with "Wa'sup?" She told him, "If the president speaks to you, the only words I want coming out of your mouth are 'Yes, sir,' 'No, sir,' and 'My name is Tucker.'"

Sure enough, when he arrived, Obama made a beeline for the families. Tucker had recently lost his front teeth, and the president teased him. "Do you know you don't have any teeth?" he asked playfully.

Tucker looked up at him and replied, "No, sir. My name is Tucker."

*　　*　　*

WE'RE PREPARED AT Camp David for the very worst to happen. But for the most part, the crises that occur are hardly matters of life and death. They only seem like it in the moment. When your mandate is perfection, you *do* sweat the small stuff.

Of course, some of the incidents are potentially catastrophic, like the time we almost set Aspen on fire. One winter day during a Clinton visit I was called to Aspen to talk to the military aide. The fireplace was roaring and there was a great feel and smell inside the cabin. I was standing inside the main living area when the president walked in and decided to go out to the Aspen patio through a door that was rarely used, especially in the winter months. As he was opening the door, someone came in the front door, and the rush of air stoked the fire and instantly filled the room with smoke. The president quickly shut the door, but time stood still as my eyes met his and we both wondered, *What the hell just happened?*

Quickly assessing the situation, which is something we all learn to do well at Camp David, the Aspen steward, the military aide, and I saw no random embers or damage to furnishings and no threat to any person. We apologized and calmly went into reaction mode. We asked others to leave the room, opened the Aspen patio door for airflow, brought in a fan to help dissipate the smoke, turned the fire alarm off, and notified the firefighting team to stand by. Then we left, thanking God it hadn't been worse.

Fortunately, near-catastrophe is rare, although our mandate to make the First Family happy keeps us hopping. When I spoke to Chuck Howe, it had been fifty-two years since he was CO at Camp David, but he still had vivid memories of the tussles over Lyndon Johnson's problems with water and temperature control. Many people have read about Johnson's obsession with the force of his showerheads, colorfully recounted in Kate Andersen Brower's book *The Residence*. Well, it turns out the same issue came up at Camp David. On Johnson's first visit he immediately determined that the shower in the master bathroom at Aspen was completely inadequate. The pressure was too light and there weren't enough showerheads. Johnson liked the shower water to *assault* his body from all sides. The White House crew would surely have commiserated with Howe when he got the call to fix the matter. At Camp David, the solution was a complete remodeling of the shower, and the crew even put in a booster pump so that water would hit the president's body really hard. Thankfully, Johnson was satisfied.

It wasn't so easy to solve the air-conditioning problem. In the summer of 1964, a month before a change-of-command was scheduled, Howe had his replacement, John Paul Jones, at the camp with him for a lengthy turnover-preparation stay. After one visit, President Johnson complained to the stewards that there was something wrong with the air-conditioning; he wasn't getting enough cold air. Howe and Jones went to look at it with a mechanical crew, turned the thermostat down to its lowest setting, and were satisfied that everything was working properly. But on the second visit, Johnson once again complained. Howe's crew investigated it and reported that the equipment was working beautifully.

The third weekend LBJ did not visit. The change-of-command ceremony was planned for the Monday after the fourth weekend, with several VIPs invited, and they were hoping for a peaceful weekend, but LBJ came up on Friday. On Saturday morning the stewards called to say that the president wondered why they hadn't fixed the air-conditioning. Howe and Jones racked their brains and finally recognized simultaneously that it was not an air-conditioning problem; it was an airflow problem.

Both JFK and LBJ liked to nap in a dark room. The crew had put up extra blackout drapes and put a shim under the carpet at the doorway so no light could leak in. However, the air-conditioning vent was in the bedroom and the return air duct was in the hallway. When the president shut his door, fresh air would come into the room until it became pressurized; after that, the air turned stuffy. Hallelujah; we had the answer! It could be fixed the following week.

But a few hours later, Howe received an ominous call from the president's special assistant, Marvin Watson; LBJ wanted to see Howe in Aspen — in his bedroom. When Howe went in, the president was lying in bed with documents spread all around him. He said, "Commander, look at the thermostat. What's wrong with the air-conditioning?"

Howe launched into the explanation about the dark room and the unintended consequences and told him how they planned to solve the problem. Johnson listened and then gave Howe a hard look. "Well, what am I going to do tonight?"

To which Howe replied, "Sleep with your door open, Mr. President."

He nodded. "Okay."

Howe left breathing a sigh of relief that they'd solved the problem. "If we hadn't," he said, "I think my change-of-command would have been Saturday afternoon instead of on Monday morning." He wasn't being melodramatic. The camp CO is always aware that any incident might end badly. One of the skills we all learn well during our time at Camp David is to be very adaptive and think quickly on our feet. After similar incidents, I often wrote in my journal, *I'm still here.*

Remember, Camp David is not a modern hotel; it's meant to be rustic, and in spite of improvements, the setting and facilities are old — not unlike the White House's. After George W. Bush's first visit, he told the Aspen steward that his bed didn't seem level. So we launched a full investigation. The staff surveyed the bed, used marbles on the floorboards to check for slope, examined the bedposts, shimmed one or two of them, measured the bed frame with a level, and so on. Finally, I lay down on top of the bed (wearing booties, which we *always* had on in Aspen and Laurel). I didn't notice anything untoward. We ended up seemingly doing nothing — but on Bush's next visit, he gave us a thumbs-up for fixing the bed.

George H. W. Bush had a habit of writing to-do lists on a Selectric typewriter at Laurel and giving them to the camp's CO. The notes always had a touch of humor — one reason Commander Berry has kept them to this day. For example, one read: *Mike — the toilet in the presidential bathroom is not responding to presidential commands. Could you do something to make it more obedient?*

On another occasion, a congressman from Pennsylvania sent a letter to Berry asking if he could donate some wild turkeys to Camp David. Berry wasn't overly enthusiastic about the idea, but he wrote to presidential aide Tim McBride about it, detailing the pros and cons. McBride forwarded the note to President Bush, and Berry received this response:

From the President

To: Cmdr. Mike Berry

Subj: Command Decision on the Turkeys (the feathered ones)

Let's try it. If they fly away so be it — nothing ventured nothing gained.

If they stick around they should make it on their own.

Decision: Go forward with only one caveat. If it costs money forget the birds.

George Bush

The climate and the setting on top of the mountain is one of the greatest challenges. The fog can roll in and make helicopter landing impossible. In those cases, sometimes the visits are canceled; at other times, the presidential motorcade has to make the long trip up from Washington. Once when George and Barbara Bush were forced to drive up on a rainy, windy day, Mrs. Bush, who was known for her wicked sense of humor, greeted CO Joe Camp, who was waiting in front of Aspen, with "Didn't your predecessor tell you that you're in charge of weather?"

In the winter, keeping the paths salted and free of ice could be considered a matter of national security. None of us wanted to cause a presidential broken bone because we hadn't performed our duty. But it wasn't so easy to manage. I can well remember being pelted by ice at the landing zone as the helicopter arrived during a subzero afternoon.

CO John Dettbarn recalled a frigid day when Nixon was scheduled to arrive. The crew had cleaned all the snow and ice off the asphalt for the landing. As Marine One came down, the powerful prop downwash instantly turned the sheen of water to black ice.

Dettbarn warned the senior Secret Service agent stepping off the helicopter ramp about the slippery surface and received a knowing look. He also warned Nixon, and after the president stepped on the ground and they both turned to walk to the car, Dettbarn lost his footing and started to fall. He instinctively grabbed the person next to him — the president! — and Nixon clutched his arm and kept him from falling. It was a close call. Unfortunately, on another occasion, the ice got Nixon.

The president loved swimming in the beautiful pool he had built, which was heated year-round. At the time there was no pool cover, though there is one today. That created maintenance problems on the flagstone deck, as the cloud of water vapor in winter would condense, land on the flagstones, freeze, and crack the stones.

On a cold Sunday evening, after watching a movie at Aspen, Nixon went outside for a walk in the winter dark, which was unexpected, as he almost always went to bed after the movie. Further, he was due to fly from Andrews Air Force Base to Paris the next morning to attend peace talks on Vietnam. Descending the steps to the pool from the deck, he slipped and broke a toe. Fortunately, he was still able to wear a shoe and fly to Paris as planned, but Dettbarn felt terrible. As he put it, "My steps, my ice, my ass."

In the time before Nixon built the Aspen pool, the presidents used the camp pool. Kennedy liked the pool to be at ninety degrees. One day prior to a visit, the crew checked the temperature and found it was elevated to one hundred and five degrees. The heat exchanger had malfunctioned, and it had continued to pump in hot steam. What to do? At first the crew considered dumping ice in the pool, but then they realized that there weren't enough trucks in northern Maryland to bring in that much ice. So they decided to dump half the pool's water and refill it with cold water. By the time Kennedy arrived, the temperature had been reduced to ninety.

Problem solved, right? Not exactly. After Kennedy went swimming, one of the crew received an urgent call from a steward wondering if he had anything that could remove tar from the president's face. Apparently, the heat had melted some of the asphalt sealing, and there was an undetectable skim of asphalt floating on the pool. A couple of stewards raced down to clean up the president's face, and they never told the commander. Neither did the president.

There is something about the pools that can produce special agita. At one point during my command, when George W. Bush was president, we had what can only be described as a madcap adventure with the pool. Most presidents used the private pool at Aspen, though Barbara Bush liked to swim laps in the staff pool. George W. Bush was never known to use the staff pool, however.

Heather Wishart was a young officer who served as the assistant public works officer during the week but was also the command duty officer that weekend. This meant she was basically coordinating and confirming everything for the visit and was constantly on call. When she heard the president was taking a nap, she jumped in the shower, but she was called midway through with the information that Bush wanted to swim some laps in the staff pool. *What?* she thought. *The staff pool? The president doesn't swim in the staff pool. Well, he* can, *but* . . . She jumped out of the shower, and with her hair still wet and possibly soapy, she called Chestnut, the cabin where our quarterdeck and duty bunk rooms are located, to get some Sailors to the pool to make sure it was visit-ready. But when she arrived, she found the newly installed roll-up pool cover had filled with rain from showers the night before and was stuck in the closed position due to the weight of the water.

With the president due to arrive any minute, Wishart and the crew feverishly tried to clear the water off the cover, but they didn't have much luck, their available tools being a broom and two small buckets from the horseshoe pit. Soon Bush's golf cart pulled up. The president hopped out, surveyed the situation, and began offering suggestions. At one point, he said, "What we need is a frogman to jump in and push the cover up from the bottom, to clear the water that way." The poor Marine corporal who had arrived to lifeguard got pressed into service, and he did his best to push as much of the leafy, dirty water off the cover from underneath while treading water in the deep end. Of course, some of the leafy, dirty water ended up in the pool.

After hearing the chatter over the radio, I approached in my golf cart, unseen by Wishart and the crew, and joined a Secret Service agent in his golf cart. We sat and watched the drama unfolding fifteen yards away. It occurred to me to go over and take charge of the situation, which seemed fairly out of hand, but I stopped myself. The mood seemed lighthearted, and Bush was in good spirits and laughing. I trusted Wishart and the others to handle things. I didn't always have to intervene. I'm a big believer in the idea that leadership isn't about doing it yourself all the time; it's also about letting the people in your command practice problem-solving on their own. It helps to have a situational awareness, and in this instance it was calm enough that I could watch from a distance.

Just when it seemed nothing would work, the pool cover became unstuck, and they rolled it back. Wishart wished the president a good swim, he thanked them with a chuckle, and she and the troops turned to leave. And then they saw me sitting there watching. They gasped. I motioned Wishart over and asked her to ride with me after I bade farewell to the agent. I knew he would relate the incident to his boss—another example of having situational awareness. As Wishart recalled, "The troops later told me they were sure I was about to get my you-know-what handed to me."

"Start to finish, tell me what happened," I said calmly. She did. "What would you have done differently if you could?"

She mentioned she could have checked the pool cover earlier, and maybe the pool mechanical room should have buckets, but that was about it.

"It sounds like you handled it as well as you could," I told her. "Good job."

She was floored by my response, but to me it was perfectly reasonable. She had solved the problem, the president had gotten his swim in, the pool cover was not destroyed in the process, and she'd learned a valuable lesson about leadership. Eisenhower always used to say, "You don't lead by beating people over the head." I took that to heart.

Some problems are easier to solve than others. One day, sitting in his office, CO Howe got a call from Jackie Kennedy. "The television isn't working and the president is speaking in Germany. I want to watch him."

He told her he'd be right over. He arrived and saw that, indeed, the television wasn't working. Jackie was very agitated. "What am I going to do?" she asked. "I want to watch the president."

Howe pointed to the next room. "Why don't you watch it on the set in the president's bedroom?" She brightened. "That's a good idea." And she went in the bedroom to watch. Howe stayed and fiddled with the TV, and as he was working, John John came running across the room and jumped on his back. "Yay, soldier boy!" he cried. He repeated the process several times, with much laughter.

As the Kennedys and Johnsons discovered, living conditions were not always stellar, even at the president's house. Although the Nixons undertook a major renovation project to upgrade the cabins, Aspen was still pretty downscale when Ronald Reagan became president in 1981. The bathrooms were old, with wheezing pipes and aging tile, and the rooms had a hodgepodge feeling. The furniture in the master bedroom and the First Lady's sitting room was of several different types of wood, as if everything were purchased at a garage sale. The TV in the bedroom sat on a tubular metal stand with gold paint flaking off.

Nancy Reagan was very sensitive about proposing renovations, even outside the public eye, but the military office agreed to some improvements to the bathrooms and furniture. CO Jim Rispoli, who is color-blind, vividly recalled sitting on the floor with Nancy looking at tile samples for the bathrooms. When she asked his opinion, Rispoli stared at the tiles thoughtfully, waited for her to indicate which she favored, and then agreed enthusiastically. They also perused Ethan Allen catalogs for furniture, specifically a cherrywood TV stand. When a Seabee who was something of a craftsman saw the stand in the catalog, he told Rispoli he could make an exact duplicate, which he did. The Reagans were so delighted, they had the Seabee come to Aspen so they could give him a hearty thank-you, which turned into a fifteen-minute chat.

This is our job and we're glad, even honored, to do it. And one thing all the commanders I've spoken to agree on is the positive feeling we have for the presidents we serve. At Camp David, it is rare to see rudeness or imperious behavior from the First Family. The presidents and First Ladies are on our side—mostly thoughtful, gracious, and appreciative of what we do. We in turn develop a fondness for "our" presidents—we're rooting for them, we want them to do well leading our nation and get exactly what they need from Camp David. And amid all the petty crises, there are moments of pure, unadulterated bliss, when the cares and woes of maintenance take a backseat and we're allowed inside.

CO Mike Berry was delighted when he and his senior officers received a standing invitation to watch movies with the Reagans on Friday and Saturday nights, an invitation his predecessor Jim Broaddus had told him to expect. They were instructed to be outside Aspen at seven forty-five sharp and wait for the president to invite them in. The president would usually come out right when they arrived and stand around with them, telling them stories, jokes, or a little of what was going on in the world. As everyone knows, he was a wonderful storyteller.

They'd visit this way until eight o'clock, when Mrs. Reagan

would appear at the door and announce it was movie time. Even if he was in the middle of a joke, the president would stop and say, "Well, boys, I guess I'll just have to finish that story next time." And he usually would, the next night they were together.

Everyone had an assigned seat in the Aspen living room. Berry's was against the back wall nearest to the projection-booth window. The projection booth was a small room accessible from the outside only. It was outfitted with two movie-theater-quality projectors and was operated by one of the camp crew members, usually Petty Officer First Class Shelborne. Inside the Aspen living area, behind a picture hung on the north wall, there was a window. When it was movie time, the picture was removed and the film was projected through the window. A motorized screen was located above the curtains on the opposite wall. The CO and XO sat near the projection-booth wall so they could slip out of the living room and go help the projectionist if there was ever a problem. Problems did occasionally crop up. "I can tell you one thing," said Berry, "the last thing the projectionist needed if there was a problem was me 'helping' him. Usually what I'd do is stand outside the projection booth and make sure everyone left the projectionist alone as he was dealing with the problem. Being the duty projectionist was extremely stressful, and I remember many times seeing Shelborne absolutely soaked with sweat, especially if he was having some trouble with the equipment."

The Reagans sat on the couch and the rest of the guests sat behind and to the sides of them. There was an actual protocol to the evenings. First, the president would stand up, introduce the movie, and tell a little of what he knew about it. (During Berry's time, they were on a routine of watching an old movie, usually one in which Ronald or Nancy starred, on Friday night and then a new movie, sometimes pre-release, on Saturday. On Berry's first night watching with them, the movie was *This Is the Army*, released in 1943, starring Ronald Reagan, Kate Smith, and George Murphy. The next night they watched *Who Framed Roger Rabbit*, a new movie starring Bob Hoskins and Christopher Lloyd.) Then the president would sit down, and Eddie Serrano, Reagan's chief steward, would turn off the lights, which cued the projectionist to start the movie. Roughly halfway through, Serrano would, quietly and in the dark, deliver popcorn and drinks to everyone — beginning, of course, with the president and Mrs. Reagan. (Serrano, a delightful guy who got along well with the camp crew, had been with the president for a long time and called him "the Boss." He stayed on with the Reagans when they returned to California after the presidency.)

As soon as the movie ended, Serrano would bring up the lights, and the president would ask what everyone thought about the film. It was a loaded question on oldies nights. When the movie starred Ronald or Nancy Reagan, what could you say?

After a few minutes of small talk, the evening would end. That first time Berry felt a sense of amazement as he headed out into the night. "As I was leaving, I had to remind myself that this was real," he said. "I just watched a movie with the president of the United States and I had a standing invitation to do it every night that they were here." That's about as good as it gets.

There's an addendum to this story provided by another CO who served under Reagan. Bill Waters had been in a river patrol division in Vietnam in 1969. One of his closest buddies was Joe Petro, who was then a special agent on Reagan's Secret Service detail. The two men found themselves together at Aspen for movie night. "When I was in Vietnam my mom used to send popcorn,"

Waters recalled. "Joe and I would pop it and watch movies. At Aspen, when Eddie Serrano passed out the popcorn, Joe and I looked at each other across the room and grinned. We were both thinking, *Can you believe this? In '69 we were hunkered down in the Mekong Delta eating popcorn. Now we're with the president of the United States.*"

Chapter Three

LIVING THERE

My home is like living in a zoo, only the
animals are on the outside.
—Seven-year-old Briana Giorgione

B<small>Y THE TIME</small> Mike Berry became comfortable enough to watch movies and eat popcorn with the Reagans, he already knew how easy they were to get along with. But his first meeting with them in the living room of Aspen was, as he described it, "surreal"—a word I also used many times throughout my tour. There the president and the First Lady were, dressed in informal camping clothes, as relaxed and friendly as anybody else, yet at the same time larger than life. It was not at all what he expected. He'd been on pins and needles going in, and there he stood laughing at the president's jokes.

Indeed, Berry would have to adjust his expectations constantly during his time at Camp David, which spanned the last six months of Reagan's presidency and the first two and a half years of George H. W. Bush's. Originally, when he'd been approached about the job, which he'd never considered, he'd had qualms. In a prior post at the Navy submarine base in La Maddalena, Italy, Berry had had a Seabee in the public works department who had been stationed at Camp David during the Carter administration, and he'd lost a finger in the pin-setting machine at the bowling alley. A machine had jammed while Amy Carter was bowling, and after he cleared it, his wedding ring caught on the frame and tore his ring finger off. He managed not to scream and quickly wrapped his hand; Amy Carter never knew it happened. But it seemed to Berry like a bad omen.

Berry's wife, Dee, had heard stories from the wives in Thurmont about their husbands working long hours performing tasks like, supposedly, painting grass. "You never want to get orders there," she told him. But when the appointment looked likely and they talked it over as a family, his fourteen-year-old son, Ken, said, "Dad, why don't you go for it?" It turned out the family was ready for an adventure. And that's what they got.

Living on top of a mountain behind security gates is not what you'd call the average family experience. But then, military families are not exactly average. They are extraordinary and patriotic people, inspired and motivated to serve our nation and others, and they all understand that moving a lot and living in accommodations that are not always the best are part of the deal. CO Mike O'Connor, who'd had a previous tour in Japan, where his lodgings had paper windows, thought Cedar was charming: "A beautiful fireplace with unlimited firewood, bucks on the lawn, the president of the United States walking by. Pretty cool."

Jim Broaddus and his wife, Kay, considered assignment to Camp David during Reagan's presidency "pretty darn fabulous." From the outset they vowed to make it a family experience for their two sons, Jeff and Scott, who were in the third and seventh grades. From the time he was six years old, Scott had wanted to become a Marine, and he was thrilled to be living around Marines, who were all very kind to him. (Today Scott is in the Marine Reserve.) Jeff was very athletic and made full use of the camp facilities, playing basketball in the hangar and skateboarding down the paths.

Joe Camp's two sons, Derek and Joseph Jr. (known as JJ), were seven and four when he became CO, and they also found Cedar to their liking. When they arrived, he asked the boys to make a choice: each boy could have his own room, or they could share a room and have a playroom. They chose to share a room, and Camp said they still talk about how closely they bonded as a result.

Overall, one fact stands out: the COs are camping with the presidents and are *in* but not *of* their world.

Being a Cedar kid is a lifelong distinction that most CO offspring come to treasure later. (At least two, one of whom was my daughter Briana, wrote about the experience for their college essays.) But when they're actually living it, it can be challenging. Kids love normalcy, and many of them are accustomed to being in communities where there are lots of kids to play with and there's lots of freedom to roam. At Camp David there are many restrictions and a rather complicated schooling scenario.

Each family living inside the bubble deals with schools in different ways. Some homeschool, some use the public-school system off the mountain, and others use private or charter schools. There's no right answer, only what is best for that family and their children. It's just one of the many decisions families make every time they relocate.

Michele had researched the area before we moved from Coronado — something she always did for every duty station — so we had a plan going forward. Briana would attend second grade at the local public school, and Ryanne would go to preschool and kindergarten in Thurmont. We later moved Briana to a magnet school in Frederick, Maryland, for third grade, as it was a better fit for her, but *getting* to school was the real challenge.

We drove Ryanne to preschool or carpooled with other families, but Briana had to catch a bus, a very unusual pickup. As every parent knows, being on time for the school bus can sometimes be a mad race. In our case, it was a little more complicated than that. We drove Briana to the end of the access road in our golf cart, which had to go through the security gate and checkpoints and still arrive on time. If there was snow or freezing rain, it was doubly intense. The school bus stopped at the end of the access road in the park, and all by herself, Briana would step out of the golf cart and get on the bus, appearing through the mist from this wooded place of mystery.

When we missed the bus, which happened due to any number of reasons, I sometimes had to go back to Cedar, transfer Briana from golf cart to car — usually amid tears and anger from her and, often, her mom — and shuttle her off the mountain and down to school. She'd sit in the car sulking, more than once crying plaintively, "Why do we have to live here, Daddy?"

Third grade brought another complication. There was no school bus that came to the camp that could take her directly to her new school in Frederick, so we had to drive Briana to the high school in Thurmont, where she caught a bus to Frederick. On that bus were a few of her classmates but also middle-schoolers and high-schoolers, and we worried about our third-grader riding a bus every day with kids who were more than twice her age. Another link, another complication that added to the fraught nature of our morning routine.

One day early in second grade, Briana's teacher asked the kids to write a description of their homes. Briana wrote that her home was like living in a zoo—she was fenced in, with the animals on the outside. Not knowing we lived at Camp David and finding the description a bit concerning from a little girl, her teacher asked for a parent conference. Michele went down to the school the next day.

"I think your daughter might have some psychological problems," the teacher said.

Michele was alarmed. "Why?"

The teacher handed Michele Briana's paper. Michele laughed. "I think she nailed it," she said, and then she explained where we lived.

Meanwhile, we were trying our best to make life as normal as possible for our girls. That wasn't easy because the list of things they couldn't do far surpassed those they could. They couldn't have a swing set or use the sandbox that Pop, my father and their grandfather, had made for them years earlier. They couldn't run around outside the cabin or play in the woods. They couldn't make noise when the president's family was visiting. They couldn't bother the guests; the rule was to speak only when spoken to. When they wanted to have a friend come and play, that child's family had to endure a background check, which could put a damper on a playdate.

And when it snowed, they couldn't build a snowman in our front yard—or mess up the snow in any way, for that matter. Our kids absolutely hated snow days because not only were they cut off from their friends due to impassable roads, they couldn't even frolic in the snow like normal kids. They knew that all their friends were down the mountain sledding and building snowmen. Michele kept pushing me. "Can't they just play in the snow?"

Finally, one day I gave in. It was supposed to warm up and melt the snow, and we weren't expecting a presidential visit, so it seemed safe. Michele and the girls had a glorious day sledding near Rosebud and building a snowman. But the next day it did not warm up, and then I heard the Clintons were arriving. I was mad at myself for letting down my guard, and I went out and smoothed the snow and cleaned things up as best I could, still worried. But of course the Clintons never said a word. "See, the world didn't end!" Michele said. Well, I knew they probably wouldn't care and might even think I was being overly sensitive, but from my standpoint, it was not proper to have the camp looking messed up like that.

We did discover one oasis of normalcy, though. There was a small, unused cabin close to Cedar that we were allowed to repurpose as a playhouse. The girls named it Sweetgum, and we put a sign up outside, just like the other cabins had. They had a Little Tikes kitchen and an easel for drawing, and they brought dolls and games and spent countless hours there. Briana and Ryanne loved to play school and imagined Sweetgum as their little schoolhouse. Sweetgum survived to be used by at least one other CO's daughters, but today it has a different use and the Sweetgum sign has been replaced by a marker reading C-6.

The camp has restored C-6 to its 1940s appearance—the interior is complete with a copy of *Life* magazine and a pack of Lucky Strikes. I've seen it several times, and they did a great job. At the Camp David CO and CMCs reunion visit in September 2016, we all took a tour, and when we walked to C-6, the Sailor tour guide gave some history of the cabin, yet she referred to it as Sweetgum in her remarks. Michele and I were very touched and proud—hey, we're parents too—and we shared the backstory with our kind tour guide.

The girls had brought their hot-pink Barbie jeep from California, and they loved driving it down the path to Hickory, where they would go in, get lollipops, and say, "Put it on our dad's tab."

The sight of those little girls tooling around in their car was a constant delight for the young Marines stationed there, who often found themselves in the role of big brothers.

When I was serving, the CO's family was not allowed to have pets, which was a disappointment for my daughters. One day Michele took the girls to the Thurmont fair and they each won a goldfish at one of the games. Bringing the diminutive prizes back to Cedar, however, became a challenge. One of the special traits of the U.S. Marines is that they have *absolutes*. That's how things get done, that's how things remain in order, and at Camp David, when you're in charge of security for the facility and for the president, there are *absolute* absolutes! So when Michele tried to bring the fish through the gate, the Marine guard informed her that she couldn't. "There are no pets allowed," he reminded her as she stood outside the car.

"They're just little fish," she protested. "In a plastic bag—we need to get them in some water." Each daughter was intently holding her bag, half asleep but suddenly very nervous about what was playing out.

"Sorry, ma'am, no pets," he repeated.

"It's our dinner." She offered the explanation with a straight face but gave a slight smile and subtle nod toward her concerned backseat passengers, and she was relieved when it worked.

"Yes, ma'am, you may get back in your car," the sentry said, not missing a beat. The goldfish were in!

Nature did provide a real pet for a while; Michele found a turtle with a cracked shell on the grounds and brought it to Cedar. The girls named him Slowy and nursed him back to health, keeping him in an outdoor fenced area near the same side door that our neighbor raccoon had visited the previous autumn. One day Slowy simply ambled off, disappearing into the woods. We speculated that he'd been digging a hole under the fence for quite some time, unobserved. Patience is a well-known virtue of turtles.

My successor, Mike O'Connor, managed to smuggle in two barn cats he got from a local farmer. In his defense, he noted that there was a tremendous mouse and snake problem at Cedar—copperheads! Once the cats were on the premises, that problem ended.

CO Russ Rang, who served under Obama, had a slightly different family experience than the rest of us. He and his wife, Patricia, had four children—Henry, eleven; Lila, nine; Elsa, six; and Anna, four. Russ and Patricia had always homeschooled their kids and continued the practice at Camp David. The sunroom at Cedar became their classroom. "It was like being in an aquarium watching the world go by," said Rang. Their classroom not only had books but a full view of the First Family and many foreign dignitaries passing by in their golf carts right outside the window. The kids also participated in Scouts and athletics down in Thurmont, but their fondest memories were of being in their sunroom school in the woods.

They reveled in the experience of nature. Elsa discovered a family of rabbits at Sweetgum and named the mother Cocoa, the father Peanut, and the baby Brownie. The children also befriended a bushy red fox—from a slight distance—whom they named David and who strolled by a few times a week. In late summer and early fall, they picked wineberries, roaming through the camp with their buckets, and learned how to recognize poison oak and poison ivy.

On the rare occasions when the president's children are the same ages as the CO's children, they can even become playmates. One morning Jo-An Howe was taking a shower at Cedar when she heard a knock on the front door. She hollered to the kids to go see who was there. Nobody went. There was another knock, and she hollered again, but then she realized that the kids were all out playing somewhere, so she put on a robe and went to the front door dripping wet. There stood Jackie Kennedy. Jackie said, "I was just wondering if Polly could come out and play with Caroline." Before that, Caroline had brought up friends to play with over the weekend, but now Polly became her friend. Caroline had her pony Macaroni there, and the two girls would often ride together.

The children all adored Jackie Kennedy because she treated them so kindly. She would frequently invite Howe's four kids, Julie, Hank, Polly, and Chip, to have lunch with Caroline and John John at a round table on the Aspen patio. "She talked to us," recalled Hank Howe. "She wanted to hear what we would say. There were no pretenses. I was stunned because I was thirteen and I was thinking, *The First Lady of the United States is being this generous and this genuine.* It stuck with me."

When Bob Reuning was serving as CO during the Obama administration, his daughter Hannah once played with Sasha at a party for camp crew and guests; the two girls were near the same age. "Can I stay overnight at your house?" Sasha asked.

This perfectly natural request gave Reuning pause. "You'd better talk to your dad," he responded, knowing it was probably not in the cards. The Obamas told Sasha it wasn't a good idea, and Reuning was a bit relieved because if Sasha stayed, that meant the Secret Service would be there too.

Kids see things from their own perspective. One day Ryanne asked Michele if she could go play with President Bush. Michele naturally said, "Honey, I don't think you can do that," to which Ryanne replied, "Well, he said I could come visit any time!"

Wendy Halsey's daughter, Kate, was eleven when they came to camp, and she was under strict instructions to make sure she gave the Obama girls their privacy and space to play with their friends. For example, if Kate was playing in the game room and Malia and Sasha came in, she was to leave casually but immediately. One day, this occurred, but as Kate was starting to leave, the girls kindly asked if she would like to play with them.

Hank Howe's friends all lived down the mountain in Thurmont or even farther, and he was allowed to ride his bike through town—to see one particular friend, that was a twelve-mile ride. "I remember being impressed that my parents had enough trust in me to [let me] do that by myself," he said. "They probably wouldn't have if they'd known that I rode my three-speed bicycle down the hill at about thirty-five miles an hour with no hands and not touching the brakes for two and a half miles."

Probably the hardest adjustment for the CO's family is the security. For one thing, Cedar kids are out in the world every day, and while there is a serious effort to maintain secrecy, everyone knows that kids talk. The idea can make an overly sensitive CO a little bit nervous. Wendy Halsey remembered how on the first day of school she instructed Tucker not to tell people he lived at Camp David—to just say that he lived in military housing. When the school bus pulled up on the road outside the camp, the bus driver exclaimed, "Do you live at Camp David?"

Shooting his mom an uncertain look, Tucker replied, "Maybe."

In truth, though, as CO John Heckmann observed, it's kind of hard for kids to disassociate themselves from the camp when they're being picked up by the school bus right outside its gate. Like other COs, he instructed his daughters, Hannah and Beth, not to tell anyone at school they lived at Camp David. The first day, Hannah came home and said, "We didn't say anything, Dad, but all the kids on the bus started asking us what it was like to live at Camp David."

The members of the Marine Security Company, assigned from Marine Barracks Washington, DC, commonly known as "8th & I" (for its location on the corner of Eighth and I Streets), were handpicked, the cream of the crop and extremely professional and committed to their task. That was good news for the president and the crew, and working with them was one of the true pleasures of my time there. But it didn't always work so well for the children, who could chafe at the high-security atmosphere. Going back and forth to school meant daily wanding and metal-detector checks on the way back in. "Julia knew how to assume the position," CO O'Connor said of his seven-year-old daughter. Sometimes the extreme security measures could be embarrassing when friends were involved. One day Wendy Halsey's daughter had a friend visiting and her father was waiting to pick her up, sitting in his car outside the gate, when the police showed up and started to question him. The next day at school a rumor spread that the girl's father had been *arrested* picking her up from a playdate.

During the early years of the Reagan administration, the White House kept camp access very tight — perhaps in response to the assassination attempt that occurred early in Reagan's term. CO Jim Rispoli was frustrated when he was told his eight-year-old daughter, Christina, couldn't have friends visit unless they were cleared by the White House. He didn't have authority as commander to clear them himself. This seemed unnecessarily overbearing to him. He went to the White House and argued, "These kids are not a threat." He got a concession — children ten and under didn't need White House clearance.

When kids slack off or forget the security routines, they can be in for quite a scare. Hank had been kind of deputized by the Sailors as an honorary Sailor. They gave him a uniform and let him hang out with them occasionally. But one time he was reminded he wasn't a member of the crew: Caroline and Polly were out riding, and Hank was at the stable with three-year-old John John. Several Secret Service agents were nearby. At one point John John told Hank he had to go to the bathroom. There was a big field house there with a bathroom, so Hank took John John by the hand, walked him the fifty yards or so there, and went inside with him. They were about halfway down the hall when the door burst open and two Secret Service agents came flying through with guns drawn. "I thought my life was over," said Hank. "I seem to recall one of them diving through the door and rolling on the floor in kind of a tactical mode, and one guy came up to me and in the most powerful voice I've ever heard, he shouted, 'Don't you *ever* take John John out of our sight again. *Do you understand?*' I thought I'd seen the Lord."

Mike Berry's son, Ken, had a similar fright involving security. Soon after the Berrys moved to camp, Ken was returning from a school activity. Typically, he would get a ride up from Thurmont to the access road, where a phone inside a box affixed to a tree allowed him to ring the main gate and get permission from the Marine on duty to advance. But being new to all this security protocol, on this day, he forgot to make the call. As he walked toward the gate, he was suddenly surrounded by Marines with guns drawn screaming, "Freeze! Freeze!" He was scared to death—and it never happened again.

Berry's daughter, Kristi, twelve, loved to run, and one evening after dark she decided to take a run on the camp's perimeter, as she had done many times before during the day. Berry, who was at an off-camp social event with his wife, got a call from the first sergeant. "Do you know where your daughter is?" he asked. Berry said she should be home at Cedar. "Could she be running around the perimeter?" Berry replied, "Could be." Security had picked up her small form where she wasn't supposed to be, and they brought her home. That didn't happen again either.

Wendy Halsey's thirteen-year-old son, Justin, decided to go over to the game room at Hickory one night around nine thirty — without telling his parents. It turned out the Marines were doing exercises in the woods, and Justin came face to face with a very serious Marine with a gun. Terrified, he raced back to Cedar.

I sympathize with Justin because the exact same thing happened to Michele and me. One dark evening we decided we would go to the gym — Wye Oak — for an evening workout, and we left Cedar a few minutes apart, she before me. When I arrived at Wye Oak, I was a bit shaken, in a good way, about the Marine Security Company drill I had inadvertently walked into; I had been promptly ordered, with rifles drawn and pointed, to kiss the asphalt road *immediately!* Michele had experienced the same ordeal and tried to call me at the house, but I had already departed. We didn't have cell phones then. A similar incident occurred when Michele's family was visiting one weekend and young nephew Michael asked Aunt Shelly why there were Marines with guns surrounding the house.

Knowing these drills were taking place, we made some changes. We agreed to notify the security post whenever anyone in our family left Cedar at night, and the Marines would notify us when they were running a drill after working hours.

Michele tried mightily to ease the difficulties of going through the gate, especially the kids' boredom during long waits. One day, the wait was longer than normal. As always, Michele had packed snacks and drinks as well as toys and coloring books. But as the wait dragged on and the girls became restless, she suddenly cried, "Chinese fire drill!" They flung open the doors and raced around the car. Over the intercom, a voice boomed out, "Get back in the car." Laughing hysterically, they complied. Relating the story to me, Michele defended her action. "Oh, you only live once. Let the kids have some fun for a minute." I, of course, was not amused.

Unfortunately, it wasn't just the kids in the family who had security issues. Michele's father, Coach, was quite a character, and one day he drove up for a visit. Having been to camp before, he thought he would be helpful, and he jumped out and put his hands in the air, which was a protocol break because you don't do anything unless you're instructed to do it. "Get back in the car," the Marine said. I was watching this from the other side of the gate, a little bit anxious. But the worst point came when the Marine asked him to open the hood. It was a new car, so he didn't know how. As he fumbled around, I stood there laughing a little. Fortunately, the accommodating Marine guard and my father-in-law eventually learned where the latch was located, and after that they let him in. Other relatives presented similar security challenges. My mother once drove to the camp with an expired license. And my cousin showed up carrying mace!

The CO's kids are expected to behave with a maturity beyond their years. At the same time, they observe the children visiting with the president not always doing likewise. Jackie Kennedy made sure her kids behaved themselves, but Commander Howe recalled the sheer chaos that would ensue whenever Bobby Kennedy brought his large brood to the camp. There were eight kids at the time (eventually there would be eleven), but in Howe's memory it was "like there were sixty-five kids." They took over the place, wildly climbing over the porches and railings, running through the woods, and generally roughhousing. The crew did its best to handle the situation—mostly concerned that one of the children would get hurt—and fortunately there were no terrible incidents. But Howe's four children, forced to sit and watch the fun without being allowed to join in, envied the wild abandon Bobby's kids were allowed.

George and Laura Bush's twin daughters, Barbara and Jenna, were lovely girls but notoriously free-spirited when they were young, and once, just after they celebrated their twenty-first birthdays, they'd planned to join their parents at camp but were late arriving. Bush called O'Connor. "Where are my daughters?"

"They're in Georgetown, sir, but headed to camp."

Later, when they still hadn't arrived, Bush called again. Still no sighting. The girls would not get to camp until very late. Bush was scheduled to fly out at eight a.m. and at the landing zone O'Connor teased, "Where are your daughters, sir?"

Bush started laughing. "When did they arrive?" he asked.

"The log says two a.m., sir."

"Better than the night before," he replied.

Children are unfiltered and honest reality checks on our adult pretensions, and this is certainly true of those who live at Camp David and get used to seeing the president strolling or riding by their houses. During the first month at Camp David, every time President Bush rode by Cedar, Julia O'Connor would get up from what she was doing and wave to him. Gradually, though, she got tired of it, and after a while, when she heard him go by, she'd simply raise a limp arm, her eyes fixed on the TV.

In the beginning, Wendy Halsey's kids loved going to the landing zone to see the president's helicopter land. Eventually, though, when she said, "Do you want to go to arrival?" they'd shrug indifferently and decline—"We've already seen it." It was much more exciting for them when the president's dog Bo strayed onto their lawn.

That doesn't mean there aren't moments of awe, especially

when the kids' friends are present. Julia had a friend visit once, and they were playing in the swimming pool. After a while, they went to use the bathroom, which was right next to the gym. When they walked out of the bathroom, there was George W. Bush on the treadmill right in their path. Julia's friend began to stammer something.

"What's wrong, young lady?" asked the president.

"I'm having trouble getting my words to come out," she said with wide eyes.

"That's okay," the president assured her. "It happens to me all the time."

Although COs try to stay in the background, I saw early on that this was a place where relationships mattered. I realized that my relationships with the president and the First Family, with their guests, with WHMO and other units, with the crew and families, and with my family were absolutely critical to my success. These relationships take many forms, and the CO must be able to meet everyone's needs silently and often invisibly. Still, the most memorable times for the CO families and the crew come when the president and First Family make warm overtures that, just for a moment, put all of them on a common human plane.

Lyndon Johnson was well known for terrorizing the crew, but he had a soft spot for Commander John Paul Jones's two young daughters, who might have reminded him of Lynda and Luci when they were young. He liked to take them to Aspen for ice cream. One morning Jones's wife, Winkie, was still in her nightgown when the president came walking into Cedar looking for the girls. She was flustered, but he apparently thought nothing of it. And off he and the girls went for ice cream.

Pat Nixon loved CO Dettbarn's sons, John, eleven, and Jamey, eight. One Halloween she invited the boys to dress up and trick-or-treat at the camp. They dressed up—John as a go-go girl and Jamey as Count Dracula—and knocked on the door of Aspen. Mrs. Nixon greeted them and gave them candy she took from a carved pumpkin by the door. The president even came out to share in the moment. The AP picked up the story, and the next morning the local paper had a headline: "Dracula Visits Nixons."

One day while the Reagans were at camp, the president's aide called Mike Berry and said that Jack Kemp had given Reagan a football, and Reagan had brought it with him. "Bring Ken to Aspen," the aide said. "The president would like to give him the football." So Berry brought his son to the president, who signed the ball and gave it to Ken. It was a thoughtful gesture.

The Heckmanns were thrilled when George and Laura Bush invited them to dinner at Laurel one evening, along with the chaplain's family, expressing a desire to get to know them better. It happened to be Beth Heckmann's seventh birthday, and it was also the birthday of Miss Beazley, the Bushes' dog. The Laurel culinary crew had made two cakes, one for Beth and one for Miss Beazley. They ate cheeseburgers and cake and enjoyed a wonderful time together.

The simplest gesture can mean so much. President Obama, as I've said, made it a practice to spend a few minutes with the family members who came to witness arrivals. These were mostly military families, the spouses and children of those who served at the camp and lived in military housing below. The president would thank them for their service and tell them how important the spouse's or parent's job was. The current command master chief, Joe Maioriello, observed, "That single two-minute encounter with the president pays for a year of goodwill. They'll shovel snow uphill for that. Families never forget it."

Chelsea Clinton had the same effect on many of the young

girls at camp; she would often spend time talking to them after chapel services and was always kind and thoughtful. Briana considered applying to Stanford solely because Chelsea went there.

At the Clintons' last weekend at Camp David, in 2001, after final thank-yous and farewells at the landing zone on a cold, dark January night, Chelsea, now grown up at twenty, handed me two stuffed animals—a cat and a panda bear. "I brought them to camp eight years ago," she said, "and I want Briana and Ryanne to have them." I was touched. It was a very kind gesture by a thoughtful and mature young woman. Thinking about those stuffed animals, I wondered how many happy and sad moments they'd witnessed, how many stories they were told and games they'd played, how many tears they'd absorbed, how many months they sat in quiet solitude waiting for their owner and best friend to appear.

When I walked the First Family to Marine One, I quickly placed the stuffed animals in Golf Cart One, not wanting to hold them while I saluted farewell. It being January, the golf cart had a plastic canopy, but I was in a hurry and didn't zip the flaps. As the helicopter lifted off, creating a stiff wind, the golf cart flaps blew open and the stuffed animals shot out onto the wet asphalt road. They were rescued by Master Chief Kevin Timmons, who broke ranks to grab them, and after a cleaning by Michele at home, they were good to go. The girls still consider them among their most cherished possessions.

The Clintons were very warm and gracious, the president as charismatic and engaging as so many people have said. When they visited camp, they almost always had guests and didn't interact with the crew much—it was just their way. The arrival of George W. Bush was a different experience. The first time he came to Camp David, on February 2, 2001, I met him with a salute at the landing zone. He addressed me by name and put his arm around me—a presidential hug! I was taken aback, but I came to see that the Bushes were extremely friendly people, and Bush loved mingling. When he noticed the people who had come to see his arrival, the new president walked through the light, crusty snow and grass to greet them at the flagpole. He shook each person's hand, asked the children their names, and greeted Michele as well. Our new neighbor was certainly making a good impression, and the first visit for 43 was off to a great start.

The Bushes' respect and love for Camp David and the crew were always evident. They could even be deferential to the crew, which was a little jarring. One Saturday morning during another visit, I was showering when my Alpha Mate—the pager I always had at the ready—began to vibrate. (Remember, this was 2001 technology.) I hopped out, toweled off, and read the message: *Please call Aspen.* Oh boy—always worrisome.

I called and Laura Bush answered. "Oh, hello, Mike. Do you think it would be okay if the president's brother Marvin came up today?"

Did *I* think it would be okay? Was she asking *my* permission?

"Of course, Mrs. Bush," I said. I hung up thinking, *That was something.* But it's just the way she was.

Bob Reuning noted that the Obamas were so kind, relaxed, and laid back that he felt it necessary to counsel the crew never to forget that Obama was president of the United States, fearing that "his congenial attitude might cause us to drop our guard."

ONE CAN'T TALK about living at Camp David without talking about dogs. Although my family wasn't allowed to have pets, other CO families were. And then, of course, there are the presidents' dogs—who were the real stars. The saying "If you want a friend in Washington, get a dog" strikes a note of truth for those who have labored in the highest office. The quote was long credited to Harry Truman, but there is doubt he ever said it, since he wasn't a dog lover. Feller, a cocker spaniel given to him as a gift in 1947, was promptly turned over to the White House physician and then exiled to Shangri-La until 1953. The crew would occasionally take Feller to be groomed in Thurmont in case the president wanted to see him, but Truman never asked. Most modern presidents, however, have had a beloved First Dog or Dogs, and inevitably their favorite place to be is Camp David. Reagan's Cavalier King Charles spaniel Rex loved the camp so much that he could sense in advance when the president was planning a visit. One military aide always knew when the president was headed for Camp David, he said, even before it was announced, because Rex was at the door ready to go. Before Ronald Reagan left office, as a farewell gift, the Camp David crew built Rex a doghouse shaped like the White House and lined it with a piece of carpet from Aspen.

On the last day of his presidency, Reagan invited CO Berry and his family to the Oval Office so he could say farewell. During this visit, Reagan was reminded by his aide Jim Kuhn that it was the Camp David carpenters who had made the White House–shaped doghouse for Rex. Kuhn asked Berry, "Did you cut a hole in the carpet in Aspen?" Hearing this, Reagan gave Berry a surprised look — as if they'd do that! "No, sir," Berry quickly assured Reagan. "We had some spare carpet."

I think I can speak for the dogs when I say that the White House was not a particularly friendly habitat for them. The Eisenhowers were forced to banish their Weimaraner Heidi to the Gettysburg farm after she soiled a twenty-thousand-dollar carpet in the Diplomatic Reception Room. And while the Barney Cam made Bush 43's Scottish terrier a national star, it also exposed his incorrigible nature and the havoc he wrought. Michelle Obama admitted that Bo sometimes made deposits in inconvenient places. All of these acts, one has to assume, were a form of canine protest against the terrible restrictiveness of the environment. Camp David, however, provided room to romp and take frequent walks with their favorite people. For the Obamas' Portuguese water dogs, Bo and Sunny, Camp David also provided them with some much needed downtime. The dogs were in such demand for public appearances, they had their own official White House schedules.

Being the First Dog confers special status, and that's why over the years CO families were rarely allowed to have pets. If they did have them, the restrictions were great. CO Howe recalled that some friends of the Kennedys often brought their wirehaired terrier George to the camp, and George was so happy there, the guests gifted him to the Howes. The Howe children were delighted, but then the inevitable happened. The Kennedys had a Welsh terrier, Charlie, and one day the two got into a big fight. After that, whenever the Kennedys were at camp, George was banished to Cedar, relegated to staring longingly out the window as the First Dog had the run of the place.

Nikita Khrushchev gifted Kennedy with a dog: Pushinka, the daughter of Strelka, the dog who had gone into space for the Russians. White House dog watcher Traphes Bryant noted that before she "could be given the run of the place, she had to be checked through security" so they could determine if she was a spy. (She wasn't.)

President Johnson's beagles Him and Her were his best-known dogs, thanks in part to a *Life* magazine photo that showed him picking Him up by the ear, which enraged dog lovers. But the Johnsons had several dogs over the years, including a white collie named Blanco. The dogs made frequent trips to Camp David.

After one visit in 1965, Johnson wrote in his diary that Him and Blanco had had a great time, running in the woods, chasing chipmunks, and barking at the sentries. "Where do I go to get a job as a dog?" he wrote.

Checkers was the most famous Nixon dog; he featured in a 1952 scandal. But Checkers died four years before Nixon was elected president. The Nixons were great dog lovers, and when they came to camp, they often brought King Timahoe (an Irish setter named for a hamlet in County Kildare, Ireland, where Nixon's ancestors were from) and Tricia and Julie's dogs Vicky (a French poodle) and Pasha (a Yorkshire terrier). At the time, the CO family was allowed to have pets, and the Dettbarns had a Samoyed named Frosty. Frosty, who was large and female, and Pasha, who was small and male, loved each other and would run around camp together. However, Frosty and Vicky did not get along.

During one visit, while Dettbarn was at dinner with the staff, he received an urgent call telling him to report to the medical clinic. He hurried to the sick bay and saw, to his horror, the chief corpsman holding Vicky on the table while the president's physician stitched her wounds. With a sinking heart, Dettbarn realized what had probably happened, and a call to his wife, Gloria, confirmed his worst fears. Gloria said that Frosty had escaped from Cedar and immediately ran to Aspen, where she knew Vicky would be on the porch. Vicky didn't stand a chance. Sickened, Dettbarn took hold of Vicky while the doctor finished stitching her up. Then, with the Sword of Damocles hanging over his head, Dettbarn brought her to Aspen, wondering how he would explain the injury to the Nixons. Their valet, Manolo Sanchez, met him at the door. He told Dettbarn to come back in the morning, leaving the worried CO to contemplate his fate overnight.

Dettbarn returned to Aspen the next day and apologized profusely to the Nixon family. The president and the First Lady seemed not to mind, but Tricia was very upset. Vicky had silver hair, yet the new hair that grew back over the wound was jet-black. Dettbarn had a constant reminder — not that he could ever have forgotten — about the nearly career-ending event.

The love between Pasha and Frosty would not be denied. One day the Nixons were aboard Marine One preparing to depart Camp David, and they couldn't find Pasha. Instant concern and fear swept the First Family and the crew. They searched everywhere, without success. Dettbarn called Gloria and asked her if she had seen the dogs. She looked around inside Cedar and, lo and behold, Pasha and Frosty were curled up together under the TV, sleeping.

Bush 41's English springer spaniel Millie achieved fame when Barbara Bush wrote a bestselling book about her, *Millie's Book*. Bush also used Millie in a campaign ad in 1992. "My dog Millie knows more about foreign affairs than these two bozos," Bush said, referring to Bill Clinton and Al Gore. But it was Millie's offspring Ranger who was most beloved by the president. Ranger was a perfect Camp David dog; he loved to prance on the paths and run in the woods. He was a great companion for the very active president.

Mike Berry's family was allowed to bring Sam, their female black Labrador, to the camp during the Reagan and Bush 41 presidencies. At the beginning of Bush 41's term, Barbara Bush told Berry's wife, Dee, "This is Sam's home. She doesn't need to be on a leash." Privately, Berry disagreed. "I know what the First Lady is saying, but Sam needs to be on a leash, just to be safe," he told his family. However, the Berrys thought it would be okay to take Sam on unleashed walks during the First Family's mealtimes, when they were in Aspen.

One day, when Dee judged the coast was clear because the First Family was at lunch, she took Sam out without a leash. They were almost home from their walk when the president and Mrs. Bush appeared with Millie. The two dogs went at each other ferociously. From his office window, Berry saw the entire presidential entourage stop in front of Cedar, and he knew immediately this was not good. In fact, there was a full-blown dogfight in the yard. The First Family was calling Millie, and Dee was calling Sam, but neither dog was paying any attention. Finally, Dee dived on top of Sam and held her down while the Bushes pulled Millie away.

The Berrys didn't hear more about it until the next morning after church, when Mrs. Bush said to Dee, "Isn't it a beautiful day?"

"Yes," Dee replied, "and yesterday was beautiful too."

"Oh, you would know about that, wouldn't you?" Mrs. Bush replied jokingly with a gleam in her eye. After that, there were no further unleashed walks and no further problems between Sam and Millie. A couple of months later, before Sam delivered a litter of nine puppies, the First Lady had Millie's whelping box sent up from the White House.

One afternoon she and Laura Bush came by to see the new puppies. They stood around talking puppies with Dee for a while in a neighborly fashion, and Sam was perfectly well behaved. But as Laura and Barbara Bush turned to leave, Sam spotted a man at the end of the driveway and barked at him. It was a Secret Service agent. "That's okay," said Barbara Bush. "Sam can eat him if she wants to."

For those COs who brought dogs to the camp, it was always a little nerve-racking—and not just because they might get into a tussle with the presidential dog. Russ Rang's family brought a rescue dog, Winnie, a Catahoula leopard hound, to the camp five months into the tour, and once during a visit, they needed to take her down the mountain to the vet. Rang knew that during presidential visits, the Secret Service canine patrol was at the gate, and he worried about what would happen when Winnie encountered the Secret Service's German shepherd. Fortunately, the trip through the gate was uneventful.

Bill Clinton's chocolate Lab Buddy was a loyal and good-natured dog, and one reason he loved Camp David was that it put some distance between him and Socks the cat, with whom he feuded at the White House. Or, to be accurate, Socks, who had been there first, feuded with Buddy. Camp David being Socks-free, Buddy was in his element. I can remember how happy he always looked bounding down the steps of Marine One. Occasionally he would roam unleashed. My daughter Ryanne still remembers the day Buddy came bounding onto the deck of the staff pool and licked her face with his big tongue as she was contentedly asleep on a lounge chair. She wasn't amused at the time.

Buddy often spent much of the day and the night in Chestnut with our duty section, and Michele would occasionally retrieve him from the post and bring him over to Cedar to play with the girls. One time around the holidays, Buddy was inside Cedar and Briana and Ryanne weren't paying close enough attention. They quickly realized that he had wandered into the next room and started munching on the elaborate gingerbread house the girls had made the week before. "He's eating our house!" the girls cried, and Michele rushed in to drag him away.

Buddy achieved national fame with the publication of Mrs. Clinton's book *Dear Socks, Dear Buddy: Kids' Letters to the First Pets*—although Socks got top billing. The letters were culled from the thousands that poured in from children across the nation. "Do you have a best friend?" one child asked Buddy. Mrs. Clinton replied, "While the President is our dog's No. 1 buddy, he has many friends—most of them people."

Barney, Bush 43's Scottish terrier, was lovable and beloved by Americans, but he was like a naughty child. Barney's goal in life was to escape restrictions. When the Bushes were at Camp David, the crew grew accustomed to hearing the president's loud cries echoing through the trees—"Barney! Barney!"—as Barney yet again disappeared to chase a chipmunk down a hole.

Barney was always with the president, his master, and many photos show Bush holding him as he came off of or prepared to get on Marine One. One Sunday morning, Laura Bush was walking Barney before services in Evergreen Chapel, and when they passed our home, Barney made a beeline for the kitchen door and darted inside. He scampered through the house, delighting the girls but leaving tiny muddy paw prints on the carpet, as it had rained the night before. Mrs. Bush was mortified; Briana and Ryanne were electrified.

Barney was very territorial, and he bristled if there was another dog around, but there was one exception—his "niece" Miss Beazley, a Scottish terrier puppy that the president had given the First Lady as a birthday gift in 2004. Barney and Miss Beazley were adorable together, featured on White House Christmas cards and in home movies. Barney was also okay with Spottie, a springer spaniel who was one of Millie's offspring, an extremely well-behaved dog. Vladimir Putin was surely correct when he bragged during Bush's presidency that his dogs were "tougher, stronger, meaner" than the president's.

When Bob Reuning was offered the job of Camp David commander, he thought he might have to decline. The Bushes were clear about not wanting staff to have dogs because of Barney and Miss Beazley. The Reunings had two dogs, a golden retriever named Maddie and a miniature dachshund named Daisy. They had been unable to find a temporary home for the dogs, so Reuning told Rear Admiral Mark Fox, director of WHMO, about the dilemma.

Fox called him in: "Are you confident you can keep the dogs away from the Bush dogs?"

"Yes, sir." So the Bushes agreed to let him keep the dogs and there was never a single incident. They were locked up tight when the Bushes were at camp.

Vice president Dick Cheney learned firsthand that it was unwise to introduce a competing dog at the camp. A confrontation between Barney and Cheney's yellow Labrador Dave sealed the latter's fate. It occurred at Laurel when Cheney brought Dave along to breakfast one morning. Unfortunately, Barney was already in the room, and according to Cheney, a "hot chase" ensued. Arriving in the midst of the bedlam, President Bush demanded, "What's going on here?" Cheney took hold of Dave, calmed him with a pastry from the table, and took him back to his cabin. Soon after, he was informed that Dave had been banned from Laurel—presumably on the order of the president.

The president no doubt let Barney get away with his shenanigans largely because of the vital role he played in his life. "Barney was by my side during our eight years in the White House," Bush said. "He never discussed politics and was always a faithful friend." That's pretty good company.

Chapter Four

HAPPY CAMPERS

The president is on the move.
—Camp David security alert

G EORGE W. BUSH liked to leave everyone in the dust on his mountain bike. He was a hard rider, always breaking bikes— the Marine crew followed with one or two spares. He'd bike no matter what the weather. Sometimes if there had been a light snow or conditions were icy, Marines would be out on the trails with blowtorches to clear the paths. When Bob Reuning became CO and received an invitation to ride along, he bought a suitable bike for himself, but he didn't know what he was in for. On his first ride, he hung back to help a guest who was falling behind. When that guest dropped out, Reuning said, "I had to ride like the devil to catch up."

"How're you doing, Commander?" Bush called over his shoulder.

"I'm good to go," Reuning said, panting. Never show weakness!

They ended at Aspen, and Mrs. Bush greeted them. Reuning's face was flushed, and she asked, "Bob, are you okay?" She offered him a power drink, which he still has, unopened, to this day.

For those around Bush, this kind of workout was a common experience. If you'd thought you were taking a bucolic ride along a mountain trail, you had to think again. Ray "Frenchy" L'Heureux, Bush's Marine One pilot, was excited to be invited on what the Marines called "bike ops" one morning at Camp David. As he recalled in his book *Inside Marine One: Four U.S. Presidents, One Proud Marine, and the World's Most Amazing Helicopter,* he arrived at Aspen on his cheap loaner bike and saw the rest of the team, including Bush, decked out in riding gear with sleek professional-grade bikes. "It was a bit like showing up to a Ferrari convention in a Volkswagen bus," he wrote. "I was in way over my head."

The ride left him dehydrated and battered and bloodied from frequent spills, but he would not give up. On the final hill, his pride at stake, he labored to keep up with the president. At one point Bush asked if he was sweating yet.

"Fuck, yeah, I'm sweating," he shouted—and then was horrified. He'd just dropped the F-bomb on the president! His life and career flashed before his eyes. But Bush never mentioned it. He was gleeful about outpacing his pilot.

Bush was always game for a physical challenge. CO O'Connor was invited to run with Bush and, predictably, got left behind. On Thanksgiving at the camp, Bush got up at six a.m. to join the annual Turkey Trot, jogging on the grounds with military and Secret Service personnel. "On the last hill he just took off. I couldn't keep up," O'Connor recalled. One year Bush set a record for the three-mile race—twenty minutes, sixteen seconds. "He lives in a fishbowl. Camp lets him stretch his legs," O'Connor observed. An understatement!

One weekend Vice President Cheney and his wife, Lynne,

joined the Bushes at Camp David, arriving in Marine Two and staying at Birch. Cheney brought three of his shotguns for skeet shooting, and the president joined him Saturday afternoon. Bush was frustrated he wasn't a better shooter, and he got that gleam in his eye; he was determined to improve. (The Kennedys also enjoyed skeet shooting. A poignant video from 1963 shows Caroline and John John looking on, rather bored, as the president and Jackie take turns firing. Barack Obama and Hillary Clinton also liked to shoot on the range.)

Clearly the Bush family, with its alpha-male mystique, encouraged rough-and-tumble behavior at the camp. After he was elected in 1988, George H. W. Bush visited the camp and told Commander Berry, "We love this environment. We're going to wear you guys out." And although Berry felt the Bushes were lovely, accommodating people, the president was very active and high-spirited. His favorite game at the camp was an intense sport called wallyball, which is a hybrid of volleyball and squash played on a squash court. Teams of Marines and the president's staff would hit the courts for an intense workout. Whether creaming the competition at wallyball or pitching horseshoes, Bush was always on the go. But as he neared his sixty-seventh birthday, he had a health scare. One day after running, Bush experienced a heart-rhythm irregularity, and it was decided that he would immediately go to Bethesda Naval Hospital for tests.

While everyone was preparing to leave, Barbara Bush, who was very worried that they would encounter a huge media circus at Bethesda if word got out, came up to Commander Berry and poked him in the chest. "I don't want anyone to know about our leaving until we're on the ground at Bethesda," she said with a concerned look. "I'm counting on you to make sure of that."

To assure that the information was quarantined, Berry directed the Camp David WHCA operators to clamp down on telephone calls between camp and the outside world. Moments after Marine One left, Berry got a call from the switchboard that George W. Bush was on the line asking for his dad, and the operators wanted to know what to do. Berry said, "Give me the call." Berry felt that immediate family would be an exception to Mrs. Bush's command, so he told George W. Bush that his dad was on his way to Bethesda for some tests. At the same time, Berry was thinking, *Mrs. Bush is going to be so mad at me,* and he pictured moving vans pulling up to his house. Ten minutes later, Doro, Bush's daughter, called to talk to her dad, and Berry told her as well. He worried that he might have made the wrong decision in not keeping it totally under wraps, but he knew how close the Bush family was. Everyone was happy when, after Bush had spent forty hours in the hospital, his heartbeat returned to normal and he went back to his usual workload. Berry never heard any criticism from Mrs. Bush about telling the kids, so he must have judged correctly.

Jimmy Carter had his own exertion-related health scare in 1979. While participating in a cross-country footrace near Camp David, he collapsed from heat exhaustion and had to be wrapped in wet towels and given intravenous fluids. Determined to outpace the other runners, he'd pushed himself too hard, but no damage was done, unless you count a bruised ego. The nation's newspapers published an unflattering photo of Carter in a near faint being held up by Secret Service agents.

Bush 41 didn't always stand on ceremony, occasionally causing interesting interactions within the ranks. When a president wanted to participate in an activity at the camp, the normal protocol was for him to call the commander, but Bush sometimes bypassed that procedure. One day he picked up the phone at Aspen and called the Marine officer of the day, a gunny sergeant, and said he wanted to go skeet shooting in thirty minutes. The gunny sergeant, never having received a direct call from the president and not believing that's who it really was, decided it was one of his fellow Marines playing a joke. He cussed him out and hung up.

Bush, nonplussed, next called the Navy command duty officer, a lieutenant, but he didn't say anything about his previous call to the gunny. The lieutenant then called the gunny sergeant. It immediately dawned on the gunny what he'd done, and he was horrified. He quickly got into his dress blues, and then he, along with the Marines, set up the skeet range. Ten minutes later, the president arrived in his golf cart, and the gunny stood nervously at attention. When the president walked by, the gunny saluted and said, "Sorry, sir." Bush laughed. He'd been in the Navy and he saw the humor of it.

Whatever one's form of leisure, all the people at Camp David—the president, the First Family, their guests, and the crew—try to be happy campers. They often succeed, though every president has a different way of relaxing. And when the crew is invited to join the president at play, it is not exactly stress-free, as the hapless participants in Bush sporting events discovered. Marines and Sailors experienced this when they were invited to participate in a basketball game with Barack Obama. When the president got knocked to the floor in the midst of an aggressive scramble, everyone was concerned—except the president. There was never another basketball game with the crew, but that was likely due to security's nervousness, not Obama's choice. He liked a hard-fought basketball game. According to CO Keith Autry, early in Obama's administration, Reggie Love, his body man, organized two basketball matches at Camp David. The men who poured out of the van for the first game were young, fit, and as impressive as professional athletes. Watching them play, Autry thought, *This is a real game.* The second van of players Love brought onto the compound were quite different. The men were in their forties and fifties, double the age of the first group. Some had knee braces. They still played a pretty intense game.

Obama often worked out in the gym, and he was rigorous about it. He liked to tease CO Halsey, and one day he said to her, "The master chief was in the gym with me this morning. I didn't see you there."

Without missing a beat she replied, "I was there an hour earlier."

The highlight of Obama's visits from an activity standpoint was his annual birthday party, which he liked to celebrate at the camp by holding what was dubbed a "campathalon." CO Rang recalled how he'd bring up to fifteen friends, some going back to his early days in Chicago, and they'd engage in a two-day all-out competition. It included a home-run derby (using an automatic pitcher), a football toss, skeet shooting, bowling, pool, darts, and a finale of an intense three-on-three basketball competition. The CO was assigned to give the awards to the winners. "Obama won one year I was there," said Rang. "He had a very big smile when I gave him the award—a competitive guy."

By nature, those who achieve the highest office in the land are competitive types, and while they're not all physically high-powered, there has certainly been an emphasis on fitness among modern presidents. George Baker, a military aide during the Johnson administration and author of *The Making of a Marine-Scholar: Leading and Learning in the Bear Pit,* noted that during the Kennedy administration when there was a physical fitness craze, the Marines at the camp got into the spirit, going on fifty-mile hikes to show they were in sync with the president's fitness goals. Bobby

Kennedy got in the spirit too, once setting out on foot from Washington, DC, toward Camp David. He made it fifty miles. Baker recounted a visit during which Supreme Court justice William Douglas, Bobby Kennedy, Ethel Kennedy, and a few others went for a long hike. When the group returned to the compound, they realized that Douglas was missing. Apparently, the aging justice had gotten sidetracked looking for herbs and mushrooms. When Douglas finally found his way to the entrance, the guards had changed shift and didn't recognize him. They thought he was a stray mountain man and refused him entrance. Outraged, Douglas stormed off, vowing to walk back to Washington. When he heard what had happened, President Kennedy jumped into a car with a Secret Service agent, tracked Douglas down on the road, and persuaded him to return to the camp.

Camp David is designed to be a sanctuary and a place of relaxation for the president and his family. Here again, different presidents get different things out of it. It isn't exactly a vacation spot; every president has a preferred location for that—Hyde Park for FDR; Key West for Truman; Augusta National Golf Club or his Gettysburg farm for Eisenhower; Hyannis Port for Kennedy; the LBJ Ranch in Texas Hill Country for Johnson; a western White House in San Clemente for Nixon; Vail, Colorado, for Ford; the farm in Plains, Georgia, for Carter; Rancho del Cielo, near Santa Barbara, for Reagan; Kennebunkport for Bush 41; Martha's Vineyard or Jackson Hole for Clinton; the ranch in Crawford, Texas, for Bush 43; Hawaii or Martha's Vineyard for Obama. Camp David is not a family retreat in that sense; it's a *presidential* retreat, and its key assets are that the days are unscripted and protest- and press-free. (The camp of war protesters that was set up by Cindy Sheehan outside Bush's ranch in Crawford could not have happened at Camp David.) A president's schedule at the White House is completely scripted and divided into increments of fifteen minutes or less. At Camp David, there is, for the most part, no script. A wise president understands this distinction and its importance. CO Howe was very impressed that President Kennedy rarely spent a weekend in the White House. Howe thought that was an excellent idea.

Relaxing was not in Lyndon Johnson's DNA. For him, Camp David was a place to work, and that is mostly what he did there. But he did take up bowling. He had never bowled before coming to Camp David, and on his first try he knocked over seven pins. That only made him obsess about a perfect game, and he was never satisfied until he bowled a perfect strike. However, Johnson was a great multitasker. According to Baker, he didn't wait for his turn to bowl; he usually spoke on the phone during a game, and he would occasionally stride over, bowl a couple of frames whether it was his turn or not, then go back to his call. Some of those calls, according to Baker, were clearly with recalcitrant congressmen, and on one occasion the president returned to bowling crowing, "Just hook 'em and reel 'em in." He did everything with gusto, his six-foot-four frame looming over everyone with an intimidating force.

The bowling alley was a popular venue at Camp David. Guests gravitated there. During his 1959 visit, Khrushchev marveled at the automatic pinsetter. And Madeleine Albright got excellent coaching from President Clinton for her first attempts during the 2000 Middle East Peace Summit. Even Richard Nixon, who was not athletic, liked to bowl. This led to some uncomfortable moments for CO Dettbarn, who was the designated scorekeeper when Nixon and Pat bowled together. "The president wasn't much of a bowler," Dettbarn said, adding, "Scorekeeping could get complicated."

Always the loner, Nixon actually preferred to bowl by himself. This was a sharp contrast to Bush 41. Once, when visiting as vice president, he paged CO Rispoli to ask if it was okay if he went to the bowling alley. "Of course," said Rispoli. But after Bush had been there for a while, he paged Rispoli again.

"I'm down here bowling," said the vice president.

"Yes, sir."

"It's no fun to bowl alone. Do you bowl?"

"Yes, sir."

"Come on down."

Rispoli, who wasn't a particularly good bowler, joined Bush, and they had an enjoyable time. Bush later wrote him a thank-you note.

The Fords were a very sporty family, and they took advantage of all the opportunities Camp David had to offer. The president enjoyed swimming with the family dog, a golden retriever named Liberty, and the whole family liked bowling, playing tennis, and sledding. David Hume Kennerly took many photos that attest to the Fords' gift for relaxation. The crew always enjoyed having the Fords around. As America had learned, the Fords were very normal people who wanted to be treated just like everyone else. The president would introduce himself, shaking a Sailor's hand and saying, "Hi, I'm Gerry."

After recovering from the assassination attempt in his first months of office, Ronald Reagan was physically vigorous, but unlike the Bushes, he preferred a gentler form of recreation. Weather permitting, he and Nancy liked to go horseback riding each Saturday they were at the camp. At the time, the camp had a small stable and corral near the helicopter pad. (These no longer exist.) National Park Service horses were trailered up to the camp for the First Couple's rides. There were two horses specifically set aside for the Reagans, but there were five or six horses in the entourage, including one for a Secret Service agent, one for a military aide, and a couple more for the park police riders who brought up the horses. The president and First Lady dressed in riding clothes and high leather riding boots with spurs. They both knew their way around horses and enjoyed riding very much. Reagan once said that, honestly, he preferred riding at his California ranch because of the wonderful mountain views. At Camp David, he said, the woods blocked any view and it was more like riding through a green tunnel. Just the same, the Reagans enjoyed the rides, which took them out the back gate into the Catoctin Park grounds. The trail was completely private with no intersecting public roads or trails, much to the pleasure of the Secret Service. Marines were responsible for securing the riding routes ahead of time. They performed thorough sweeps and then stationed several armed Marines in camouflage dress (called gillie suits) to maintain control of the area.

One time a Marine asked President Reagan if he ever saw them while riding. He said no, he never did, but he appreciated the fact that they were there. Another security measure, unknown to almost everyone, including the Reagans, was the rubber-tired armored personnel carrier with a fifty-caliber machine gun mounted on a remote-controlled turret. Marines called it Gargoyle, and during the horse rides, it would be running and manned with a squad of Marines. Out of view, but on the job.

As they were with the Reagans, the security guards at the camp mostly stay hidden. During the Johnson administration, Commander Jones ordered the sentries to get out of sight if the First Family approached. One day Lady Bird was out walking with a foreign dignitary's wife, and the sentry ducked behind a large rhododendron bush. Lady Bird, whose love of flowers was well known, went over to the bush, took a large flower in her hands, leaned in to sniff, and immediately jumped back in alarm when she saw the fully armed Marine hiding there. The trembling Marine, who thought his goose was cooked, was surprised when the First Lady said warmly, "Oh, please forgive me. I didn't know you were here."

Camp David is an idyllic winter setting for outdoor sports, especially cross-country skiing and sledding. When Jimmy Carter took up cross-country skiing, it presented a challenge to the Secret Service. How could they stay close to the president? The solution was to purchase snowmobiles so the Secret Service could follow behind. They soon came in handy when Carter had a bad spill on an icy stretch and fell on his face. Agents following him hauled the bleeding, embarrassed president onto a snowmobile. Later, just before leaving the presidency, he had a second fall while out sledding with Rosalynn and broke his collarbone. Barbara Bush also had an unfortunate encounter with the snowy mountain. In 1991, she was sledding with her husband, grandchildren, and guests Arnold Schwarzenegger and Maria Shriver when her saucer-shaped sled began spinning out of control on the unusually icy hill. Despite her husband yelling, "Bail out! Bail out!" she clung to her saucer, hit a tree, and broke her leg. Fortunately, it was a minor break, and Bush 41 quipped, "No damage to the tree."

One of the things my wife, Michele, enjoyed doing during the lonely winter days was cross-country skiing on the trails inside the camp. The quiet and serenity were very calming and a great "reward" for the solitary lifestyle on the mountain. Fortunately, she never had any mishaps or hurt any trees.

Among the most popular presidential leisure activities was golf. Although Camp David doesn't have a golf course, presidents and their guests have often gone off-site to nearby courses. President

Eisenhower was well known to be a dedicated golfer. In fact, one of the first acts of his presidency was to set up a putting green on the South Lawn, and he often went out there to hit balls. Sometimes he wore his cleats into the Oval Office so he could pop out for a quick golf break. When he left office, there were hundreds of cleat marks on the Oval Office floor.

At Camp David, Eisenhower had a driving range built near the helicopter landing zone. He enlisted golf-course architect Robert Trent Jones, who had built the putting green outside the Oval Office, to design a three-tee green behind Aspen. Many presidents have chipped balls there. That's what Bill Clinton was doing one day during my time when the sprinklers went on. Obviously, someone had screwed up, because the sprinklers were supposed to be off for the visit. Clinton wasn't rattled. He just picked up his bag and went to a different area of the course. And the sprinklers went on there as well. Frustrated, Clinton threw his golf bag into Golf Cart One and sped off. Unfortunately, he failed to secure the bag and it fell off, spilling his clubs on the ground. I heard about it from the Secret Service agents who watched the whole thing. The next day at departure, I considered how I could use a little humor without overstepping. "I see you found our water hole," I said to the president, and he smirked.

Outside of chipping on the Aspen lawn, what President Clinton really enjoyed was going golfing at one of the municipal golf courses in and around Thurmont. Very often on a weekend he would head out with his guests and the detail of Secret Service agents; the president's doctor, nurse, and a Navy corpsman; a communications detail; our XO, John Coronado; and Command Master Chief Kevin Timmons for a day that was almost always relaxing and invigorating. Weather, of course, could wreak havoc on anyone's golf game, and the president of the United States wasn't immune to wind, rain, or bitter cold that he suffered for the sake of relaxation and wanting to get away. We were always happy in the camp when President Clinton golfed, as it seemed to highlight his comfort with us, the game, and the few hours he was able to spend away from it all (mostly).

George W. Bush liked to play golf out back, and he was often accompanied by the dogs Barney and Miss Beazley, who were on hand to retrieve balls out of the holes. Obama was also an avid golfer, which was one reason he limited trips to Camp David— there was no full golf course. "Whenever I could, I had conversations with the president about golf," said CO Autry, who loved the game. "One of my desires was to play golf with him." Unfortunately, it never happened.

Eisenhower's other passion was fishing. Like FDR, he enjoyed going to nearby Trout Run, off-site and slightly down the mountain, where this beautiful private campsite yielded a satisfying catch of trout. On at least two occasions during Eisenhower's presidency, newspaper articles told of his successful fishing efforts. Trout Run, of course, was initially made famous when FDR and Churchill fished there. FDR's initials are carved into a sign on the fishing bridge. It is stylistically so similar to Camp David that the hit TV show *The West Wing* used it as a stand-in for the presidential retreat for episodes that were supposed to be set at Camp David.

Another nearby fishing site in the Catoctin Mountains was Spruce Creek. Jimmy Carter loved to fly-fish there whenever he had a chance. Always sensitive to the appearance that he might be slacking off, he defensively told a press conference, "I have a rare opportunity to go fishing...to get out in the woods and swamps and in the fields and on the streams by myself. I really believe that it's not only good for me but for the country to be able to do that on occasion. I wish I could do it more, but I don't intend to ignore any opportunity to take advantage of a fishing trip when my own work permits it. And I hope the press will understand and the people will understand that I, like the average American, need some recreation, at times." It's unlikely anyone faulted him for it.

The Obama girls liked to fish, and the camp would use a well-stocked and private fishing hole on farmland owned by a local family. During my time, another wonderful family offered their private fishpond whenever we needed it. Over the decades, the camp has developed deep and meaningful relationships with some of its mountain neighbors, and these two couples were some of the best folks you'd ever want to meet. They always made their private properties available for the First Families or guests, and although usage was infrequent, we knew we could always count on them when we needed to. I've seen these families when I've gone to the Naval Support Facility Thurmont anniversary balls over the years, and I know that they greatly enjoy and appreciate their special relationship to the camp.

Hillary Clinton liked to work out in the Wye Oak gym. When Michele's father, Coach, was visiting, he happened to meet her and he introduced himself and wished her good luck on her campaign for senator. She was very nice about his words of encouragement and would always greet him with "Hi, Coach" whenever she saw him after that.

Mrs. Clinton also enjoyed biking alone along the paths at Camp David. One day while I was doing some chores in the driveway and garage at Cedar, she rode by on her bike. Later, while she was out on a trail, her bike chain came off and she had to walk the bike back to Aspen, where the crew provided her with a replacement. I hated when things like that happened outside my view, but I think Mrs. Clinton took it as a normal camping experience.

Like Bess Truman, Michelle Obama enjoyed bringing female

friends for the weekend, along with a chef to prepare healthy meals. She and her friends would work out pretty intensely — up to three times a day in the gym, with Marines holding the punching bags — and then relax by the pool, laughing and talking.

During their visits, the Obamas participated in one of the most normal family activities in the world: Dad gave his daughter driving lessons. The Secret Service closed the roads, and with the president playing instructor, Malia drove slowly around the camp, ending at the landing zone to practice three-point turns. In an earlier time, Bill Clinton had decided that Camp David was the perfect setting for him to teach Chelsea to drive. His wife wasn't so sure about the idea. "Outside of golf carts, the Secret Service never let Bill drive himself around, which was a good thing," Hillary Clinton wrote, trying to be diplomatic. "It's not that my husband isn't mechanically inclined, it's just that he has so much information running around his head at any given moment that he doesn't always notice where he is going." Fortunately, the driving lessons went off without any mishaps.

The staff too had its opportunities for downtime. As the CO family, my wife and I were always thinking of ways we could provide leisure opportunities and get-togethers for the people working at Camp David. We were also intent on ensuring a welcoming environment for the president's staff, which included a doctor, nurse, Secret Service agents, helicopter pilots, and aides. Sometimes we'd ask the camp culinary specialists (we called them mess specialists back then) to prepare us a great meal, which we'd pay for, just as if we were in a very fine restaurant. Other times we'd set up croquet games in the front yard or host dessert and cocktails. The crew and staff members appreciated it, and we got a chance to bond with them.

Serving cocktails, however, was a challenge at first. When we moved in, we weren't allowed to bring any beer, wine, or alcohol in our boxes; the movers wouldn't take them. So once we were settled, Michele went down to Thurmont to stock up. When she came back through security in the car, the guard told her, "Sorry, ma'am, you're not allowed to bring alcohol into the camp."

She hadn't heard about such a rule, and he clarified, "Only the CO is allowed to bring it in."

"Okay," she replied, "could you call and ask my husband to vouch for me?" Soon after, another change was made to camp protocols and policies for those living in Cedar.

Michele is a very friendly, sociable person, and she was eager to reach out to the spouses and children of the crew. Sometimes, when the president wasn't there, they'd come up to the camp and hang around the pool or use the grounds. The kids would play and pick berries. Michele always told the families, "Please stop by the house when you're up here. We'll have coffee or a drink." But nobody ever came.

At first Michele assumed it was because she was the commander's wife. Since I was the boss, she figured the other spouses might want to keep her at arm's length—an idea she hated. But the reality turned out to be much different. She soon asked one of the wives she was close to why no one ever visited, and she was surprised by the answer.

"We weren't sure we could be on your road," the woman said. "We'd like to come."

Michele was floored, but she understood that sometimes people tended to put the commander's family at an elevated remove. She calmly assured her that anyone was welcome at any time.

As previously noted, one of the leadership tasks at Camp David is keeping the crew motivated and on track. COs do what we can to provide them with community. The annual family day is one such event. Families come up from housing, mingle, swim, and have a barbecue. In the past, the single Marines and Sailors who lived at camp were not allowed to bring boyfriends, girlfriends, or other nonfamily guests. But this rule was eased during the Obama administration.

When the president wasn't at camp, the crew made good use of the facilities. The staff pool was always a popular and fun spot for the crew and families to gather during the summer months. During my time, the Marines were our lifeguards and gave swimming lessons to the children. It was a nice, relaxing place to hang out. Briana and Ryanne's favorite moments were when everyone was hanging out by the pool, having fun, picking berries, and acting like this was a "normal" community pool. Several years ago, the pool was covered so that it could be used year-round. It was a practical solution, but in my opinion, it lost some of its charm and appeal.

Sometimes the presidents and First Ladies tried to make things more casual for the crew, not fully appreciating the protocol of a military facility. On President Obama's first visit, when he was met at the landing zone by Reuning and others in full dress uniform, he told Reuning, "You don't have to wear those uniforms for me."

Oh yes, they did!

Driving the president in Golf Cart One, Reuning felt relaxed enough to ask him, "How do you like your job so far?"

Obama replied, "You know, Bob, if at the end of my administration I can get thirty percent of the people in Washington to march in the same direction, I'll be happy."

Michelle Obama also sought to make things more relaxed. Riding along the empty paths in the golf cart with Reuning, she asked, "Where is everybody?"

Reuning explained, "We keep out of sight to allow you your privacy."

"Oh no," she exclaimed. "We want everybody out. We want to *see* people." She also wanted to touch them. Michelle Obama, the crew found, liked to give hugs.

"When I came to camp I was preparing to meet Mrs. Obama for the first time," said Russ Rang. "I was standing outside Aspen waiting for her to arrive in a car, and Command Master Chief Mark Schlosser said, 'Heads up. She's a hugger.' I laughed. 'No way she'd hug a new guy.'"

The car drove up; Mrs. Obama hopped out and gave Rang the biggest hug ever. And it wasn't just a onetime thing. "Coming or going, there was always a hug — whether you were CO, crew, or a steward," Rang said.

Bush 41 also chafed at the ultra-privacy. While he was at camp as vice president, he paged CO Jim Rispoli one day. Rispoli went to a tree phone (there were no cell phones then) and called Bush.

"Is it okay if I play tennis today?" he asked with his typical deference.

"Of course," Rispoli answered.

"How about eleven o'clock? I've invited [tennis star] Pam Shriver to play with me. Can you meet her at the gate and bring her to the tennis court? She'll be driving a white BMW."

"Yes, sir." Rispoli went down to the gate, met Shriver, brought her to the tennis court to play with the vice president, and left them. Twenty minutes later Rispoli got another page from Bush. He found a phone.

"We're down here playing," Bush said.

"Yes, sir."

"There's no one here."

"Yes, sir. We're giving you privacy."

"Could you ask some of the crew to come down and watch?" he asked. "I think they might enjoy seeing Pam play."

The well-trained crew is only human, so it was always a special thrill when Arnold Schwarzenegger visited, which he did a number of times during Bush 41's presidency. The word would come down as soon as he reached the gate: "Terminator arriving." Off-duty Sailors and Marines began hanging out in the gym in anticipation of seeing Schwarzenegger. He'd usually make an appearance there, and he'd give them weight-lifting instructions and chat. One day he told President Bush that the gym was missing an important piece of equipment. "I'm going to send it to you," he promised.

A week later CO Berry got a call from a supplier. "I'm supposed to send you this weight-lifting machine from Arnold Schwarzenegger," he said. "Can you give me the address for delivery?"

Well, *that* was a problem — but they finally worked it out. The machine was delivered, and a small plaque crediting its famous benefactor was affixed to it.

There was an absolute rule that the crew was never to discuss politics or policy with the First Family. Seems obvious, but the presidents didn't always cooperate. John Dettbarn recalled the alarm he felt one day walking with Nixon as the president was brooding about critical decisions during the Vietnam War. Nixon turned to him and asked, "Commander, do you think I should mine Haiphong Harbor?" Dettbarn mumbled something noncommittal, but he was spooked.

Reagan particularly liked to chat with the officers and engage them in political discussions, so they were always on guard. "Did you hear what they said about [Secretary of State] George Shultz today?" he asked, trying to bait CO Rispoli into commenting.

Rispoli was tempted to reply, *George who, sir?* He felt trapped.

He nodded dumbly, hoping the president's staff would join the conversation, and he was relieved when they did. No CO wants to weigh in on policy or politics!

Camp David has not been without romance. When Lynda Bird Johnson was dating the movie star George Hamilton, the nation was transfixed by the details of their jet-set romance. In his memoir, Hamilton wrote, "I sensed that somewhere inside that bookworm there was a babe trying to get out." That's exactly what worried Lynda's parents, although they wanted their serious daughter to have a bit of fun. They were relieved when the relationship ended. Then she met Captain Chuck Robb—and Camp David played a role in their romance. Robb was the adjutant at the Marine Barracks in Washington and a social aide at the White House. Sometimes he accompanied the president to Camp David. Lynda and Robb had met at a White House reception, and there was definitely a spark. Later, on a visit to the camp, Lynda called the Marine command and told George Baker she was looking for a fourth for bridge—then casually asked if Captain Robb was available. It turned out he was on duty, but realizing what was going on, Baker arranged for Robb to be off duty, allowing him to join the bridge game. The relationship took off from there, and the couple was married in the East Room of the White House in 1967—with George Hamilton an invited guest. Afterward, the Robbs honeymooned at Camp David, bringing the leftover wedding cake to be enjoyed by the crew.

The only wedding to take place at Camp David was that of George and Barbara Bush's daughter Dorothy (Doro). It was her second marriage, and not only was the groom, Robert Petri Koch, a Democrat, he was the administrative assistant of Congressman Richard Gephardt. Still, George and Barbara Bush were thrilled. For them, happiness trumped politics every time. The wedding, at Evergreen Chapel, was beautiful and tearful; chaplain Jon Frusti officiated. Doro's two children stood beside her at the ceremony. The reception was a casual affair on the lawn behind Aspen.

As an example of the way the laid-back mood of Camp David could work a spell on the president, the father of the bride still hadn't given any thought to what he'd wear hours before the ceremony. Barbara told him a navy suit would be fine. He replied that he hadn't brought a suit, thinking the affair was informal. "How I love that man," she wrote when describing the incident in her memoir. "He thought it was informal. Wait until he gets his Scaasi bill!"

CO Joe Camp, whose job it was to coordinate the comings and goings of the one hundred and thirty guests, was pretty busy that day. "VIPs were coming out of our ears," he said. He was touched when the president stepped in to help with golf-cart traffic control. As always, he was very sensitive about the pressure being put on the crew.

Food is part of the joy of life, and no one believed this more fervently than FDR. Shangri-La was his culinary haven. Much has been written about the tyrannical White House cook Henrietta Nesbitt, who refused to serve him the foods he loved. This was on the order of Mrs. Roosevelt, who was concerned for his health and was also trying to cut costs. The result was a bland diet. Although the Roosevelts famously served hot dogs to King George VI and Queen Elizabeth when they made the first royal visit ever to the United States, their usual fare was the likes of creamed chipped beef, corned beef hash, poached eggs, and bread pudding. Mrs. Nesbitt's philosophy of food was simple: it should be plain and plainly prepared—completely at odds with the president's desires. "My God," he exploded to Grace Tully one day, "doesn't

Mrs. Nesbitt know that there are more breakfast foods besides oatmeal?" Later, he called her in to take dictation:

Corn Flakes! 13 ounce package, 19 cents!
Post Toasties! 13 ounce package, 19 cents!
Cream of Wheat! Two for 27 cents!

He continued the list through Rice Krispies, Wheaties, and Grape-Nuts Flakes, then sent it to Mrs. Nesbitt, but it's unclear whether or not she budged. Blanche Wiesen Cook, who authored a three-volume series on Eleanor Roosevelt, wrote that the First Lady's refusal to accommodate the president's culinary tastes and her support of Nesbitt "was one expression of her passive-aggressive behavior in a marriage of remarkable and labyrinthine complexity." Maybe so. But it's one reason FDR loved coming to Shangri-La, where he could have more control of the cuisine. In particular, whether at the White House or Camp David, Roosevelt loved cocktails, which he mixed himself. Having repealed Prohibition, he was delighted to introduce his guests to a perfect martini — two parts gin and one part dry vermouth, shaken with crushed ice, not stirred.

Dwight Eisenhower loved to cook, and Camp David gave him the opportunity — especially at the outdoor grill, where he would slap on the big steaks. Mamie, not a particularly good cook, was glad to let him do it. He also cooked more complex fare for his Camp David guests, including his special beef stew. Eisenhower was usually accompanied by his valet, John Moaney, an African American sergeant who had been with him since World War II and who would remain with him until his death, and then with Mamie until hers. Moaney was well versed in preparing steaks the way Eisenhower liked them—an unconventional method, which the president wrote down:

Get a sirloin steak two and a half to three inches thick. Roll the steak in a mixture of fine salt, black pepper and garlic powder. Throw the steak in the fire. After about 10 minutes nudge it over once and let it stay in the fire for a total of about 20 minutes. Take it out, brush off the ashes and coating of seasoning, and slice on the diagonal.

Not surprisingly, barbecue was served up by the Johnsons while they entertained guests outside Aspen and at the camp pool (this was before Nixon built the president's pool at Aspen). Spareribs, beef, country corn, coleslaw, and biscuits were heaped onto plates. George and Laura Bush also favored a touch of Texas at Camp David, and they were grateful to the crew for having their favorite Tex-Mex foods shipped to the camp.

Lady Bird Johnson confessed in her diary that one of her favorite indulgences at Camp David was the special Sunday breakfast. "We ate as if we were never going to have another meal," she wrote. "First came scrambled eggs and fried eggs, with home-cured bacon, thick and luscious. I had had my mind set on grits, and sure enough in came a big dish of them, followed by a dish of hot pancakes and more bacon, and syrup and melted butter. We threw discretion to the winds and had a banquet."

The Nixons' devoted valet Manolo Sanchez was in charge of their meals. Sanchez arranged for food to be brought from the White House when they came to Camp David, and it was prepared under Sanchez's ever-watchful eye.

The Reagans relied on their steward Eddie Serrano to be sure they got what they wanted to eat at the camp. Serrano would drive up and stop at supermarkets along the way to purchase the ingredients, choosing different stores every time for security reasons. Then he'd supervise the preparation of the meals. The Reagans liked to eat "ordinary" American food — pork chops, baked chicken, and the like.

When the Clintons moved into the White House, Hillary brought in Dean Ornish, the healthy-diet guru, to train the chefs there and at Camp David. She was interested in Ornish's ability to make the president's favorite rich foods using alternative ingredients, such as soy for milk. It worked, but only up to a point. On his own, Clinton was always on the hunt for his higher-fat Southern favorites. (In recent years, following severe heart problems, Clinton has become a vegan.)

"The Camp David cooks are Navy Mess... and they're great at fried chicken and a lot of other foods that we all like," Laura Bush told a CBS interviewer. "And so we can have sort of an American weekend in a beautiful setting with great American foods for heads of state."

Today's Camp David kitchen is staffed by Sailors who have been sent to culinary schools for certification. Most people agree that the food is quite good. It always surprises people that the First Family has to pay for their food at the White House, and they have to do the same at Camp David, so the menus tend to be to their liking. The culinary staff at Camp David prepared the Obamas' meals, but the menus were provided by the White House chef. Sometimes the valets would bring in the organic foods that couldn't easily be procured locally. In spite of Michelle Obama's reputation for healthy eating, what the crew most remembers are the pies brought from the White House and the wonderful cookies fresh from the oven.

The Thanksgiving and Christmas holidays are often occasions when the First Families and the crew come together. President and Mrs. Reagan traditionally shared the Thanksgiving meal with the crew in the galley. George and Laura Bush normally spent Thanksgiving with friends, but the year of 9/11 they chose to celebrate at Camp David. The menu was a Southern-style traditional meal: turkey with giblet gravy, corn-bread dressing, mashed sweet potatoes, green beans, cranberry relish, and pumpkin and pecan pies.

The Reagans normally went to California for Christmas, but during their second year, at the last minute, they decided to go to Camp David for a week over the holiday. "We feel bad about this," Reagan told a surprised CO Rispoli. "We know your crew made plans to spend Christmas with their families, and we hate to mess up those plans."

"We're here for you," Rispoli assured him.

"I know," said Reagan. "But we'd like to do something for the crew to express our appreciation." He later told Rispoli he'd decided to take a photo with the crew during the holiday.

"You don't have to do that," Rispoli said.

"Of course I don't," Reagan said, his eyes crinkling as he smiled. "I want to."

So Reagan arranged for a photographer, and Rispoli organized his crew into groups and sent them into Aspen for photos. It was a freezing day, and when the first group arrived, Reagan explained that he didn't want to do group photos but individual ones, with each crew member standing next to him outside the beautifully decorated front door.

Reagan took his time with each person, asking all of them questions about themselves and their families, and the photo session stretched on through the morning. After two hours, they'd finished only half the crew. "Let's break for lunch," Reagan suggested, "and continue this afternoon."

They reconvened after lunch and spent two and a half hours finishing the photos. "The president of the United States stood in that cold doorway for four and a half hours taking pictures," Rispoli marveled. After Christmas each person got a signed photo. It was some gift! Reagan liked the photo idea so much he did it another year, only this time there was a mishap. One roll of film with about a hundred photos got lost. Everyone was quite upset until Reagan proposed an easy solution. He'd just retake those photos with them the following weekend. And he did.

The Clintons and a large group of family and friends always came to Camp David for Thanksgiving, and the two holidays that I experienced with them were fun and enlightening. I met Senator Barbara Boxer, Hugh Rodham, Roger and Molly Clinton, and Dick Kelley, President Clinton's stepfather. If you have to work on a holiday, this is a pretty nice way to do it.

On Thanksgiving Day my first year, the president and some friends went down the mountain to golf at Maple Run in Thurmont. A chapel service was held at Evergreen at one o'clock, followed by a meal for the staff and their families in the galley. The president visited, chatted with the families, handed out little white boxes of presidential M&M's, and made sure, with our coordination, that people got their pictures taken with him. The selfless gesture went a long way with the Sailors, Marines, and families and was a highlight of the Thanksgiving weekend.

On Friday and Saturday nights that weekend, our niece Meghan babysat for the president's guests' children at Laurel. She was paid well and had some fun with the kids, who played president in the conference room, pretending they were Uncle Bill and Aunt Hillary.

The Clintons came again the next year, which was their last, again with a large group of guests. One of them spent seven thousand dollars on souvenirs at the Shangri-La gift shop and then gave a five-thousand-dollar donation to the chapel. All the guests sent us boxes of candy and thank-you notes afterward. Very nice to feel the appreciation that "ordinary" people have for Camp David.

During my first year, the Clintons would visit only one more time before Easter—and what a visit that was! There were a lot of moving parts—several guests and eight children, with various activities, including our camp Easter egg hunt on Saturday and golf on Easter Sunday. Plus my parents, having received permission from WHMO, were visiting us at Cedar.

The most notable guest was Chevy Chase, who came with his wife, Jayni, and daughters Cydney, Caley, and Emily. Chevy's first words to me when I greeted him in the rain outside Dogwood were "Go, Navy!" He was very friendly and he mixed well with the crew, playing pool and Ping-Pong with them, to their delight.

It was a rainy weekend but everyone had a good time. There were over one hundred people at Sunday services at Evergreen, with my family in our assigned front row across from the president. Mrs. Clinton approached my mother after the services and said, "You must be Mike's mom!" Mom was a little shy about talking to the First Family, although she did quietly tell Mrs. Clinton, "You've done a wonderful job raising Chelsea."

Mrs. Clinton smiled warmly. "You couldn't have said anything nicer," she said.

The Clintons didn't normally spend Christmas season at Camp David, but during their final year in office they made an exception. It was the first time they had seen the camp's decorations, which were quite spectacular. Preparing for the visit, I went to the White House and met with the ushers and florists. I learned that there was to be no live tree in Aspen due to allergies and that Mrs. Clinton liked blinking colored lights. I left the White House with a few decorations to add to our effort, including special ornaments for the tree in Aspen: golf clubs, Arkansas and Stanford ornaments, and one depicting Buddy. They liked it so much they had the White House photographer take pictures.

The entire Bush family gathered at Camp David for Christmas for all four years of Bush 41's term and all eight years of Bush 43's. The crew laughingly referred to it as "the twelve days of Christmas" because it was such a major undertaking. Bush 41 was always leading the festivities and leaving wrapped gifts in all the cabins, and he continued this tradition when his son was president. One day the phone in CO O'Connor's office rang. "Skipper, it's the president— forty-one," said the voice on the other end of the line. "The old guy." And then he discussed the Christmas arrangements.

Every CO who served under Bush 41 and Bush 43 agreed: the Bushes made Christmas a very special time at the camp. Christmas Eve was carefully choreographed and rehearsed. It included a stirring church service that started in complete darkness; the candles were then lit one by one until light filled the chapel, and the choir began to sing the beautiful music. It was tremendously moving. But the high point of the service was the annual Christmas play put on by the camp kids. The Bushes found this charming and entertaining. They smiled, laughed, and took pictures as the tiny Mary, Joseph, shepherds, and Wise Men said their lines. Bush would get up and pose with the kids during the final scene. One year he picked up the littlest kid—an angel—and her wing batted him in the eye as he held her. There were also Christmas carols at Laurel with the First Family passing out cookies to the crew and their families.

The family meal on Christmas Day was traditional: roast turkey with corn-bread dressing, green beans, sweet potatoes and mashed potatoes with giblet gravy, spinach salad, cranberry sauce, rolls, and pumpkin and pecan pies for dessert. The Bushes were very sensitive to the fact that the crew preparing their Christmas meal at Laurel had to be away from their own families. One Christmas, the cooks were shocked when Barbara Bush breezed into the kitchen and sent everyone home. "I've cooked a lot of meals in my life," she said. "I'll take over. You go be with your families."

Chapter Five

THE SPIRIT OF CAMP DAVID

*I hope the spirit of King David will prevail at
Camp David.*
—Anwar Sadat before the 1978 peace talks

NIKITA KHRUSHCHEV WAS uncertain and even suspicious when he received an invitation from President Eisenhower to visit Camp David during his U.S. tour in 1959. In his mind, a camp was a place you put undesirables. His staff set him straight, and he was charmed by the rustic atmosphere. The visit was historic; both Eisenhower and Khrushchev were engaged in a delicate effort to ease the tensions between their two countries—something that had eluded them so far. Eisenhower was well aware of the chasm that existed between their ideologies and principles. On what basis could they possibly achieve common ground? He was determined to try, believing that the future of the planet was at stake if the two powers did not come to a mutual understanding about nuclear arms.

Although Roosevelt had welcomed Churchill, neither he nor Truman had ever invited an adversary to the camp. But Eisenhower had seen the mellowing effect that Camp David had on its visitors. The mountain air, the reflective environment, the recreational emphasis, all came together to melt the hard lines that existed between people—and he hoped it would have that effect on Khrushchev. Khrushchev actually stayed at Aspen with Eisenhower, as did the Soviet minister of foreign affairs Andrei Gromyko and U.S. Secretary of State Christian Herter—in remarkably close quarters, given the circumstances.

At one point Khrushchev told Eisenhower that he was fond of American Westerns—a pleasure he and the president shared. Happy to find even the smallest commonality, Eisenhower showed him a list of movies available at the camp, which included *High Noon, Gunfight at the O.K. Corral,* and *Big Country,* and the two leaders watched Westerns together. They also dined on all-American fare circa 1950s. The menu for Saturday night is on file at the Dwight D. Eisenhower Presidential Library:

Broiled Half Grapefruit
Broiled Loin Strip Steak
Chopped Broccoli with Hollandaise Sauce
Buttered Roasted Bread
Corton-Bressandes Red Burgundy
Assorted Green Salad with French Dressing or Cottage
  Cheese
Pol Roger 1952 Champagne
Vanilla Ice Cream—Cookies
Maple Syrup
Demi-Tasse
Mixed Nuts—Mints

Of the visit, Eisenhower wrote that sitting alone, talking about their hopes and concerns, the two leaders were able to establish a personal connection that had not been possible at international conferences or across the wires. Khrushchev seemed to agree, writing, "I remember a conversation I once had with President Eisenhower when I was a guest at his dacha at Camp David. We went for walks together and had some useful informal talks." Khrushchev wrote that he told the president, "Part of my reason for coming here was to see if some sort of an agreement would come out of these meetings and conversation."

Afterward, Khrushchev would speak of "the spirit of Camp David," and it briefly looked as though a breakthrough was possible. But it was a short-lived détente; it collapsed after an American U-2 spy plane was shot down over the Soviet Union. Goodwill dissolved. However, Eisenhower's outreach to Khrushchev reinforced Camp David's status as a site where world leaders could meet to work through the most troubling issues of the day. This is the remarkable dichotomy of the presidential retreat, where tennis, biking, and bowling can seamlessly intermingle with high-stakes diplomacy.

The first major summit, and the one that would decisively put Camp David on the diplomatic map, occurred nearly twenty years later, in 1978, when President Jimmy Carter brought together Egyptian president Anwar Sadat and Israeli prime minister Menachem Begin for thirteen days in an effort to resolve the Middle East conflict.

Achieving peace in the Middle East had been Carter's most cherished goal since the beginning of his administration. He frequently shuttled to the Middle East, establishing working relationships with the nations. He was instrumental in brokering an unprecedented event in 1977 — a visit by Sadat to Jerusalem. That visit gave him hope that an agreement between the two nations was possible, an event that would, in turn, serve as a gateway to further agreements with other countries. In July 1978, while walking along a wooded path at Camp David, Carter turned to Rosalynn. "It's so beautiful here," he said. "I don't believe anybody could stay in this place, close to nature, peaceful and isolated from the world, and still carry a grudge. I believe if I could get Sadat and Begin both here together, we could work out some of the problems between them, or at least we could learn to understand each other better and maybe make some progress."

In his initial invitation to the two leaders, Carter deferred the final choice of location to them but suggested Camp David as a setting that would allow them, along with their respective advisers, to "work together in relative seclusion." Maximum direct contact between Begin and Sadat was of the utmost importance, he wrote. That Camp David was able to provide that seclusion would ultimately prove to be more important than Carter might have realized. The Carters had also invited Sadat's and Begin's wives to attend, believing that they could ease the tension and distrust between the two men. At the last minute, Jihan Sadat was unable to be there because one of her grandchildren was ill. But Aliza Begin joined her husband.

If President Carter hadn't already been well versed in the political and personal fault lines complicating the chance for peace between Egypt and Israel, a telling moment that occurred before the first meeting on day one might have hinted at what he was up against. The president and First Lady met Sadat and Begin outside Aspen, and the three leaders greeted one another at the cabin's threshold. The Carters then proceeded inside. Begin and Sadat, though, hesitated at the door. Who should enter next? Neither moved. An awkward jostling threatened to ensue. "You? Me?" "You go." "No, no, really, after you." Both men laughed, and Sadat insisted that Begin go first. It was an apparent moment of goodwill that the president and Rosalynn observed through a window. Carter later decoded it for his wife: Prime Minister Begin would never have gone ahead of Sadat. Proper protocol dictated the order: president above prime minister.

It was indicative of the tone of the next thirteen days; protocol vied with politics, and awkwardness and inviolable error seemed always to lurk in the wings. In the midst of historic negotiations, the delicate potential for peace could be destroyed by the large intractable issues or some small but potent misstep.

For the crew and diplomatic corps, the organizational challenge of hosting the peace talks was enormous. Sadat was assigned to Dogwood, and Begin to Birch. More than one hundred people were accompanying the leaders, so there were substantial housing and dietary issues. In her memoir, Rosalynn Carter described the complexities of the food arrangements. President Sadat, whose diet was restricted for health reasons, brought his own chef; he prepared his simple meals of boiled meats and vegetables and honey-flavored mint tea. But the camp crew also had to prepare kosher meals for Begin and his staff. It was decided that all meals for the principals would be prepared in Aspen's kitchen, separating an area with special dishware and cooking pots for the kosher meals. Meals for the staff and crew would be prepared and served at Laurel — although Begin and his wife often caught everyone off guard by choosing to eat at Laurel. "When the cooks saw them walk by on the way to Laurel at mealtime, they would have to put together more kosher food quickly, load up the golf cart with it, and hurry down to the big dining hall," Mrs. Carter wrote. Sadat preferred to dine alone in Dogwood.

Then there were the challenges of accommodating guests of this caliber for such a long time. National security adviser Zbigniew Brzezinski later recalled how he'd been quite ready to leave

Camp David by the time the negotiations were finished, because he'd been sharing a room with Hamilton Jordan and "we measured the passage of time by the size of the pile of the dirty laundry in the middle of the room."

It was tight quarters, but that's just what Carter wanted, as he wrote in *Keeping Faith*. Camp David "had not been designed to accommodate so many people, especially when they came from three different nations and represented three distinct cultures.... Sadat, Begin, and I had private cabins within a stone's throw of each other. None of the other cottages was more than a few hundred yards from us, and all of them were packed to the limit with people." But, the president added, "the close proximity of the living quarters engenders an atmosphere of both isolation and intimacy, conducive to easing tension and encouraging informality."

Carter chose Holly cabin as the setting to begin face-to-face negotiations, wanting an intimate mood. On the second full day the principals moved the discussion to Aspen while their teams continued at Holly. Working in the bedroom, Rosalynn could clearly hear the shouting matches, and the president later complained to her, "The meeting was mean. They were brutal with each other, personal." Sometimes he made a point of taking notes, she recalled, "looking down at his pad so they would have to talk with each other instead of to him. Sometimes when their words became too heated he had to break in." The negotiations quickly descended into bitter acrimony. Carter wrote, "All restraint was now gone. Their faces were flushed, and the niceties of diplomatic language and protocol were stripped away. They had almost forgotten I was there."

By the end of the second day, Sadat was convinced that they had reached a stalemate. He declared that there was no reason for the discussions to continue. Both men tried to leave the room, and Carter stood in the doorway to block them.

Though Sadat and Begin reluctantly agreed to continue, they left that day without speaking to each other. They maintained their silence the next day, and Carter eventually began to negotiate with each leader separately. The ensuing days would see Carter shuttling between Dogwood and Birch, determined to keep the whole thing from falling apart.

All wasn't hostility, however. The relaxed setting of Camp David afforded some moments of levity and calm, including an amiable dinner on the Jewish Sabbath. "Everybody at the dinner was in a very good mood," Rosalynn Carter wrote. "I think because it was the Sabbath. Begin told me they always observed the Sabbath with rejoicing and singing because the Bible said that you cannot serve God with sadness. They all sang during dinner, and laughed, and it was a good evening."

When they weren't locked in negotiations, the principals and their staffs took advantage of the pleasures Camp David had to offer. Every morning, like clockwork, Sadat, dressed in a jogging suit, took off from Dogwood for a three- or four-mile walk. He also enjoyed playing chess with Brzezinski. The movie projector was running twenty-four hours a day. The fifty-eight movies that were viewed over thirteen days included *Dr. Zhivago*, *The Thomas Crown Affair*, *Sleuth*, *Hawaii*, and *Return of the Pink Panther*. There was also bicycling, jogging, tennis, and swimming. Even the Carters took their usual walks and played tennis.

The children were active too. Zbigniew Brzezinski, who'd brought his daughter Mika (now cohost of *Morning Joe*) to camp to keep Amy Carter company, wrote in his memoir that Mika and Amy "narrowly escaped ramming into Prime Minister Begin while out driving [in a golf cart]. Only the quick action of Amy's Secret Service guard saved the Prime Minister from injury and the Carter and Brzezinski families from embarrassment."

Ultimately, it proved beneficial for the parties to be able to retreat to separate quarters that were still close enough for Carter to travel from one to the other as negotiations continued. Cooler heads were able to prevail. Camp David's proximity to significant Civil War sites was also an advantage. Sadat was well versed in the history of the area and the battles fought there, and Begin was an admirer of Abraham Lincoln, so Carter arranged for the leaders to visit the nearby Gettysburg battlefield, which he hoped would remind them of the need for peace. In the limousine traveling to Gettysburg, he sat between the two men and dictated that there would be no discussions of their negotiations on the trip. It was a much-needed break, and Carter was surprised by how knowledgeably—and almost reverently—Sadat and Begin talked about the American Civil War and the importance of Gettysburg.

Probably the biggest advantage Camp David conferred upon the negotiations was the way it shielded Sadat and Begin from outside influences. Camp David's relatively modest size limited the number of aides either leader could bring along. And, most notably, Carter prohibited the press from the meetings. He worried that open and honest dialogue between the leaders would be impossible if they had to worry about how they might be represented in the press or how their positions might be framed to their countrymen back home. It proved to be a vital and prescient decision. Especially when, two days before the scheduled end of the conference, September 17, the sides came to yet another acrimonious impasse. This time, Sadat called for a helicopter and announced that he was leaving. To back down from such a stance would have been all but impossible had it been done in public. Instead, Carter was able to privately convince Sadat that U.S.-Egyptian relations would be irreparably harmed if he left.

That night Carter had trouble sleeping. His mind was full of concerns about Sadat's advisers, some of them hard-liners not entirely on board with the peace process. Suddenly worried about Sadat's safety, Carter rose at four a.m. and spoke with Brzezinski and the Secret Service about putting greater security around Dogwood. It was an eerie premonition; on October 6, 1981, Sadat would be assassinated by his own military in large part because of the Camp David Accords.

Reflecting later on the peace process, Brzezinski said, "What I remember well is the President's tenacity—unwillingness to yield, his determination. There were moments when he was very low and distressed that the whole thing might fall apart. But, it was his tenacity and outward serenity that, I think, held the process together and eventually led to success." That stamina was tested again and again, right up to the final day of the conference, when Begin once again balked at some language in the agreement. It seemed to Carter that peace might elude them at the last minute. Earlier, photographs had been taken of Begin, Sadat, and Carter, and Begin had specifically requested that Carter autograph them for his grandchildren. Carter's secretary suggested that she get the actual names of the grandchildren to make it more personal. Now, feeling nervous and exhausted, Carter walked over to Begin's cabin with the photographs. He found Begin sitting on the porch of Birch looking dejected.

When Carter handed him the photographs, Begin glanced down and saw his granddaughter's name on the top photo. Then he looked at the other photos, and his eyes filled with tears as he mouthed their names. He spoke quietly to Carter about each child, and they were both feeling quite emotional. Carter returned to Aspen, still experiencing the weight of impending failure. But the personal gesture had broken the impasse. By the end of the afternoon, Begin was back on board.

With a thunderstorm rolling in over the mountaintop, the three men boarded the helicopter to return to the White House for a signing ceremony.

Despite all the tension, animosity, and potential dead ends, when Carter, Sadat, and Begin left Camp David that day, they had a historic blueprint for peace between Egypt and Israel. Camp David would become synonymous with the hard work of diplomacy, and the negotiations would provide a benchmark for future leaders.

They had achieved the impossible at Camp David. But the impossible wasn't enough. In retrospect, it might seem naive that such great hope for peace in the region came from the small agreement between Israel and Egypt when Israel's greatest foes remained defiant. In particular, the Palestinian issue would only grow and expand, with Palestinians drawing support from most Middle East nations. Twenty-two years after the Camp David Accords, another president sought the spirit of Camp David to bring the Israelis and Palestinians together over their extremely contentious territorial disputes.

ON JULY 5, 2000, President Clinton announced at the White House that he had invited Israeli prime minister Ehud Barak and Palestinian Authority chairman Yasser Arafat to Camp David for a conference beginning July 11. In his statement, Clinton declared that despite all previous efforts, the two sides were at an impasse. "Movement," he said, "now depends on historic decisions that only the two leaders can make." In hosting the summit at Camp David, Clinton was sending a clear signal that the best chance for such historic decisions was at the retreat synonymous with diplomacy. "I hope that the setting will help to inspire them and to inspire us. I hope we'll all be inspired by it. But it's also a great place for us to be, because it gives us a reasonable chance to work in quiet and without interruption and to observe the necessary discretion that, without which, we won't be able to move forward."

A negotiation with even higher stakes and more volatile flashpoints than those of twenty-two years earlier, the 2000 summit was playing out in a more media-centric age, subject to greater scrutiny and with any number of parties hoping for failure. The issues involved were at the very heart of the long-standing Middle East conflict. Nothing could be left to chance.

As the CO, I was initially stunned by how little time we had to prepare, but in the end that might have been a good thing. I had learned the simple fact that when humans are given too much time to study or prepare, they will redo things, be inefficient, not keep focus, and even turn on one another. In the Pentagon we used to say that any meeting will expand to fill the time allotted. This is called Parkinson's Law: work expands to fill the time available for its completion.

Because of the short notice, friends of ours from Coronado and one of their two young daughters were already booked to visit us that first week. I knew that the adults would not be allowed in camp, but I did receive permission from WHMO for the older daughter, one of Briana's best friends, to visit if she wanted to. Similar to what CO Rispoli had arranged many years before, the key issue for approval was that she was a child under ten years of age. The family decided to let their daughter visit, but the others would lose their airline tickets. I called the airline to plead for a refund for the tickets. I was not successful. I distinctly remember telling the supervisor who denied my request, "Certainly, you've never heard *this* excuse before!" She admitted that she hadn't, but she still said no. Michele stayed at camp and kept the girls entertained for the first week of the summit. One day they went to Hershey Park, and they also went to the Thurmont fair and won those goldfish that my wife assured security were our dinner. Briana, her friend, and Ryanne were all scheduled to go to camp in Pennsylvania, and Michele drove them to Breezewood to meet her dad and make the transfer. After the drop-off, Michele returned to camp to witness from the sidelines the attempt to forge peace in the Middle East.

Hillary Clinton, in full campaign mode for the New York senate race, was on the trail in advance of the September primary, but Chelsea joined Bill Clinton at Camp David, as did Mrs. Clinton's assistant Huma Abedin, an American Muslim who had grown up in Saudi Arabia and spoke Arabic.

In addition to working very diligently with WHMO, the Department of State, and the White House press pool to prepare for the summit, I called former CO Ralph Cugowski, the 1978 camp commander who was long retired from the Navy and living in Florida. I asked him how he and the crew had prepared for the visit then; much like us, he'd had very little notice and didn't know how long the parties would stay. His advice was consistent with a common theme in the military: sometimes you go forward with the best plan that you have at the time and figure it out as it goes. We were embarking on act two of a play he'd produced in 1978, and he wished me the best of luck.

One of the most important guiding tenets of my job was never to do anything that might somehow embarrass the president. Plus, it was imperative that the Israeli and Palestinian delegations felt they were treated equally in terms of the types and number of guest cabins, number of golf carts and bicycles, appropriate meals, and worship facilities. No easy feat, especially since Arafat considered the whole summit a trap and a ploy against him and the PLO. So I was constantly on my guard, trying to anticipate any pitfalls.

Prior to opening day, the White House press pool visited camp and we went over protocols, security procedures, and how they and other world media would enter and depart the camp on July 11. We rehearsed where the three principals would walk for the opening sequence and where we would all stand and watch. It went off without a hitch, Clinton, Barak, and Arafat walking down the leafy path toward Laurel, with the cameras clicking away. Clinton, between the two others, had his arms spread in a loose embrace, and all of them were smiling. "How's it going?" called a reporter.

Clinton laughed. "We pledged to each other we would answer no questions, offer no comments," he said. "So I have to set a good example."

"Shake hands...shake hands, please," the reporters called. That didn't happen. A handshake at that point would have implied too much. When the three reached Laurel, Clinton preceded them inside, and then, in a jockeying reminiscent of 1978, Barak and Arafat performed the little dance of "you first." In the end, Barak preceded Arafat.

That evening, after initial discussions, there was a dinner at Laurel for the delegations, about forty people. The president, Barak, and Arafat sat at one table with about fifteen of their aides. Secretary of State Madeleine Albright hosted a second table, and national security adviser Sandy Berger hosted a third. The menu was tenderloin of beef with sun-dried tomatoes, fillet of salmon with Thai curry sauce, roast baby Yukon potatoes, steamed green beans with almonds, a mixed garden salad, fresh fruit, and assorted desserts. It was a lighthearted evening with few signs of the troubles to come.

At the camp, Barak was assigned to Birch, Arafat to Dogwood, and some of the Palestinian staff to Rosebud, right across the path from Cedar, our home. Prior to the summit opening, and being respectful of cultures that frowned on the display of certain parts of a woman's body, the State Department gave me the guidelines, and I discussed with Michele and the girls that although it was July, they should not wear bathing suits, shorts, or tank tops around the house or yard. This was a no-brainer and a sign of respect, but the edict didn't work both ways. The first morning, Michele went outside to water her geraniums. Across the street at Rosebud, several Palestinians were walking in the front yard with open robes and nothing else. So she went back in, closed the blinds in the sunroom and the living room, and kept the girls busy inside.

Rosebud was certainly a challenge during the summit. There were frequent calls to the command duty desk about flies and insects inside the cabin. This was the result of windows being left open, the air conditioner left running uncontrolled, and food brought into the cabins and left uncovered. There was also a near-catastrophe.

One late afternoon our resident fire department, manned by military service members trained in structural and aircraft firefighting, responded to a fire alarm in Rosebud. Our command duty officer also responded, as is the protocol, and was concerned when she observed the Palestinians nervously flushing papers down the toilets and throwing them into the lit fireplace. She sensed that maybe they felt they were being attacked and were concerned about their private and possibly classified papers falling into the wrong hands. Already in a delicate and sensitive situation just by coming to Camp David to negotiate the elusive peace agreement, the Palestinians might have seen the arrival of the fire crew and duty officer as an aggressive act by the United States. It certainly wasn't, but I was concerned enough to hurry over myself. I assured the nervous Palestinians that our diligent and well-trained fire department was responding only to the fire alarm, which was apparently set off by the lit fireplace or by the hookah they were using in residence.

About that hookah. At the end of the summit, the cleaning crew found that it had been left behind in Rosebud. Its return was not requested, so I donated it to Buckeye, home of the Marine Security Company, with specific instructions that it belonged to no one and was to remain in camp at all times. More than ten years later on a visit back to Camp David, I asked about it and was told that no one recalled or knew about the hookah.

Another issue was renegade golf-cart driving. I assumed that most guests were driving golf carts for the first time, but I wasn't fully prepared for some of the cultural differences in how people relate to their infrastructure. That is, our roads weren't always the preferred path of conveyance, and our nicely manicured lawns, flowers, and bushes were frequently leveled and torn up with screeching and turning tires, especially in wet weather. Our grounds crew was quietly getting miffed and concerned about bringing the camp back to the norm when the summit ended, but as always, the crew members handled themselves with perfect politeness and respect.

Prior to the start of the summit and under the expert lead of our Navy chaplain Bob Williams, we made an effort to accommodate the different faiths that would be represented. Bob obtained a Torah and some prayer rugs from Washington, DC, to use in Evergreen Chapel. The Jewish delegation did make use of the chapel, and Barak, who loved to play piano, came by several times to use the instrument. One Israeli guest visited Evergreen, looked at the Torah with Bob, and explained some of the inscriptions and meanings. But the Palestinians did not use the chapel, viewing it as a place for Christians and Jews. Since the pews were fixed to the floor, there would not have been space for them to worship. Rather than using a larger area like the hangar, they worshipped in their cabins.

My job, and that of the crew, was to make sure the wheels turned smoothly on the outside, even though turmoil was great on the inside. The meetings were intense—and tense. Madeleine Albright wrote in her memoir, "We worked day and night; and night and day the lovely countryside was enshrouded in a suffocating fog like a biblical plague." Still, as long as they were talking, Clinton believed that progress was being made.

Not knowing how long the summit would go—and hoping the parties would stay until an agreement was reached—Clinton chose to leave on July 21 for a long weekend to attend the G8 Summit in Nago, Okinawa Prefecture, Japan. This particular G8 Summit was the first for Russian president Vladimir Putin and the last for Clinton. Global health was one item introduced at this session. Before he left, Clinton instructed us and Secretary Albright to keep things going until he returned, telling Albright she should "not let them kill each other."

That evening, we waited outside Aspen for the president. A storm prevented a Marine One departure, and Clinton would be taking a motorcade to Andrews Air Force Base to fly to Japan. We stood there for about five hours in the cool summer night, light rain occasionally falling through the dense forest canopy, the smell and sense of a summer rain and history hanging in the moist air.

Eventually, Chelsea came out of Aspen, full of apologies. "I'm so sorry, Commander, my dad's running late," she said, and she offered me her hand. I have a picture of this moment as we shook hands, snapped by a White House photographer.

"No problem," I said, amused by the apology. After all, her dad was only working on peace in the Middle East. What I observed that evening was President Clinton shuffling between Aspen, Birch, and Dogwood, personally talking to, and probably pleading with, Barak and Arafat over whatever points they were stuck on, much as Carter had done twenty-two years earlier with Sadat and Begin. All this complicated ancient history of the Middle East and another attempt by a U.S. president to broker a peace, and, like many things in life, it principally came down to interpersonal relationships. These three adult men each had their own strengths and weaknesses, successes and failures, aspirations and fears. For me, watching Clinton roll up his sleeves and work the personalities was a striking example of leadership. I was more than willing to wait for that!

The light rain turned torrential overnight, and Secretary Albright was left with a summit barely holding itself together. Not wanting everyone to just sit around and wait for Clinton to return, she encouraged informal discussions and activities, such as basketball games and movies. Albright noticed that Barak was growing increasingly unhappy. She sought ways to please him, and when he asked if he could visit Gettysburg, she agreed, in spite of the president's edict that no one leave the camp while he was gone. He made the request on Friday, so the trip was scheduled for Sunday, after the Sabbath.

Albright realized that she needed to offer Arafat a similar field trip, and she asked him if he'd like to visit her family's nearby farm on Saturday. He said yes, although she warned him that her children, her grandchildren, and their friends would be there. "That will make it even better," he said.

But when they arrived at the farm, Albright wondered if she'd been out of her mind to suggest the visit. Right off the bat, she wrote, "My two-year-old grandson Daniel, waking from a nap, took one look at Arafat with his stubble and kaffiyeh and let out a piercing scream." But the visit went well after that. Arafat genuinely enjoyed watching the children at play around the pool. The following day, Barak had a good time at Gettysburg as well, bringing along a photographer to take pictures that would later be broadcast on the nightly news in Jerusalem.

On Monday Clinton returned, and the two sides met late into the night. But by the next day, Arafat had rejected all of Barak's overtures, refusing to accept anything but total sovereignty over the disputed territory. It was over. The parties tried to put a good face on the failure, talking about seeds being sown that would one day flower. But it was a huge blow to Clinton. In his memoir, he recounted that later Arafat told him, "You are a great man," to which Clinton replied, "I am not a great man. I am a failure, and you made me one."

THE TWO MIDEAST summits are irrevocably linked with Camp David, but in 2012 President Obama decided to perform his own version of mountaintop diplomacy—minus the rancor.

G8 "made my tour," CO Wendy Halsey said of the 2012 gathering of world leaders President Obama organized at the camp. The Group of Eight, composed of eight industrialized nations—

France, Germany, Italy, the United Kingdom, Japan, the United States, Canada, and Russia—meets once a year to discuss critical global issues. This was the thirty-eighth summit. Originally scheduled to take place in Chicago, the meeting was moved at the last minute, giving Halsey and her crew three months to prepare for it. "I thought it was a lot of time," she said—until she was introduced to the phenomenal organizational effort involved in having eight world leaders, their staffs, and multiple other guests land on the site for two days. As an additional complication, four African leaders were scheduled to arrive on the second day for a conference on food security.

One reason Camp David was an ideal site was that there were enormous security concerns surrounding such a high-powered international gathering. In 2012, the Occupy movement was targeting the conference, and Occupy Chicago had been planning a massive protest for the summit. As it was, the towns down the mountain from Camp David were preparing for an onslaught of protesters. Thurmont hung WELCOME TO THURMONT banners and prepared to host visitors from around the world, but the public officials and police were readying for protests. Fewer than two hundred arrived during the summit, many from Occupy Baltimore, and Thurmont police closed public parks at ten p.m. There were no real incidents, but every room in Thurmont and the surrounding towns was booked for the occasion. No one could get close to the mountaintop retreat. The Secret Service shut down all access to the Catoctin Mountain Park; it was a federal crime to trespass.

Press for the event was tightly restricted, with most journalists corralled at Camp Round Meadow, a dormitory a little over a mile away from Camp David. For special events, they were brought in by bus to Evergreen Chapel. Photos and tapes were strictly forbidden unless explicitly allowed. For many in the media, this was the first time they had been to Camp David, so the temptation to snap a photo or two was almost irresistible. But a French journalist who succumbed to the temptation was immediately ordered to delete the photos.

The G8 leaders began arriving over a seven-hour period on May 18, with President Obama arriving last. CO Halsey was on hand to meet every leader, and she recalled it as a heady experience. "Each time I got to say, 'On behalf of President Obama, welcome to Camp David.'" She greeted French president François Hollande, German chancellor Angela Merkel, British prime minister David Cameron, Canadian prime minister Stephen Harper, Japanese prime minister Yoshihiko Noda, and Italian prime minister Mario Monti. Vladimir Putin was not present—which some people considered a snub to Obama. In a line that resonates today, the *Atlantic* noted, "The Russian leader's decision not to attend the major diplomatic event could be a bad sign for Obama's 'reset.'" Russia was represented by Prime Minister Dmitry Medvedev, but no one knew for sure whether Medvedev would truly be speaking for Putin.

A dinner was planned for the first evening at Laurel. President Obama stood at the door and greeted the leaders as they arrived. "François," he said to Hollande as he approached, "we said you could take off the tie." Hollande was sharply dressed, in contrast to the rest of the guests, who wore open shirts and slacks. "For my press," Hollande replied, but by the time he reached the table, he had removed his tie.

A small panic had erupted earlier when CO Halsey learned it was Prime Minister Noda's fifty-fifth birthday. But the chefs were up to the task and whipped up a cake. "Actually, we made two cakes," Halsey said. "Just to be sure." After dinner, the Japanese prime minister was presented with the chocolate birthday cake, and it was a welcome moment.

Behind the scenes, the crew was tasked with framing photos of Obama and the various leaders so they could be arranged on the wall near the entry at Laurel when the group reconvened the next morning. That same morning, Hollande had met Obama at the White House, so aides arranged to have a photo from the meeting flown up to Camp David and displayed. It was a nice touch.

Not surprisingly, the matter of cabin assignments was somewhat tricky for the summit that Reuters called "a sort of VIP sleepover." Both the State Department and Halsey were concerned about word leaking out about the assignments, concerned that people would start making comparisons and drawing conclusions. There was no way to disguise the fact that some of the cabins were not as fancy as others. For those in the know, the two top-tier cabins, Birch and Dogwood, were occupied by Hollande and Medvedev, respectively.

Everyone was on high alert for any possibility of perceived slights. In some cases the White House and the State Department were at cross purposes. For example, the White House wanted made-in-America-labeled items in the cabins, but the State Department was concerned about making any changes in the linens, towels, and other items that had not already been switched to American vendors. Halsey contemplated cutting the labels off the pillowcases but finally let them go as they were. "I did, surprisingly, spend a lot of time on this," she said. "I never thought pillowcases would be my issue." But actually, water pressure and water power were the biggest problems. The large contingent, with every available cabin in use, stretched the limits of the camp's hardworking facilities.

There was also a golf-cart shortage. Most of the attendees either walked or waited patiently for a cart. In fact, the only complaint Halsey remembered came from a staff person who was indignant that he didn't have his own golf cart. When Halsey politely explained that there simply weren't enough carts, he shouted, "Do you know who I am?"—a response that left her momentarily speechless. Maintaining her calm, she apologized and then walked off, marveling that at such a high-level gathering—not to mention the *president's* retreat—a staffer could feel that he was the only one who was special.

On the second day of the summit, four leaders from African nations joined the group for a discussion about food security. The meetings were serious, but in the afternoon, many of the participants crowded into Hickory to watch the Champions League final soccer match on the big movie screen. A photo of the spectators' faces, by turns agonized and ecstatic, hangs in Hickory as evidence that commonality can always be found in a human moment. It was a lesson Camp David would teach again and again.

Chapter Six

THE LONELY SENTRY

He likes to be left alone.

—Bob Haldeman, speaking of President Nixon

S OME NIGHTS, LONG after my wife and daughters had gone to bed, I'd step outside our cabin into the cool, pine-crisp darkness and just let it all surround me. It's unbelievably quiet at Camp David. The airspace is restricted, so there's not even the sound of an occasional airplane passing overhead. In the summer there are crickets and owls. Sometimes I could hear the squirrels scampering through the leaves on the ground or the wind rustling in the trees. But mostly it was the silence that struck me, so dense and thick it was like awe itself. The history and immensity wrap around you and muffle everything else.

These times of loneliness happened often at the camp and were usually known only to me and Michele. As I slowly walked the dimly lit asphalt roads and golf-cart paths, the calm and serene canvas of the still and surreal setting would be painted with questions like *What am I doing here?* and *How did I do today?*

Alone with nature in such a beautiful part of camp year-round, covered by a canopy of leafy boughs in the summer and ice-encrusted, dormant branches in the winter, I found the loneliness penetrating. I heard only my footsteps and saw only the moonlight; there was no light from neighbors' houses because we didn't have any neighbors. At these times, my thoughts tracked back to the events of the day, the ups and downs of a recent or current visit, the constant effort to make life more normal and happy for my family. Yards away from the people who loved me most, I could still feel a sense of loneliness that comes from command.

I suspect that most commanding officers, executives who have led their organizations, and anyone who has been responsible for a mission and people have had times of loneliness. The reality of "It's lonely at the top" hits you, and it's not a bad thing, although there's a temptation to fall into dark, introspective periods of self-doubt, self-criticism, and self-evaluation — and these can consume your psyche. I tried to resist these and focus on what I could do to make things better the next day or week. But I couldn't resist reflecting on the loneliness that our primary guest, the president, experienced as a constant of his job.

I think what many people don't realize, and maybe don't care to realize, is that the president is a person like you and me, as far as psychological and emotional makeup go. This president, this normal person, has likes and dislikes, favorite foods and games, might enjoy napping on the sofa or throwing a ball in the yard just like anyone. For the president, there aren't many places to do that other than at Camp David. And our job is to make sure that the chief executive gets those moments whenever needed.

If I sometimes felt like a lonely sentry at Camp David, I knew that the president, too, was a lonely sentry, except his oversight

Holly cabin in the winter, shrouded in white. (Courtesy of Michele Giorgione)

Old friends FDR and Churchill fish at Hunting Creek and plot the course of the war. (Franklin D. Roosevelt Library)

Cedar, the place we called home on the mountaintop. (Courtesy of the author)

On a typical morning, Briana, backpack in tow, waits in the golf cart to be driven to the gate to catch the school bus. (Courtesy of Michele Giorgione)

Eisenhower and Khrushchev arrive at Aspen for one of the first attempts at Camp David diplomacy. Later Khrushchev would speak of "the spirit of Camp David." (Dwight D. Eisenhower Library)

Caroline Kennedy rides Macaroni while JFK and John John stroll beside her on a Camp David trail. (John F. Kennedy Library)

Gloria, John Jr., and Jim Dettbarn feed Apples, the camp's pet deer. (Courtesy of the John Dettbarn Family Collection)

Richard and Pat Nixon on a stroll at Camp David with their three dogs, Pasha, Vicky, and King Timahoe. (Richard Nixon Presidential Library)

President Carter contemplates life, seated on the well-worn log bench by Aspen pond. (Jimmy Carter Presidential Library)

CO Bill Waters escorts the Reagans to the helo pad after a weekend in late summer 1981. In the background is Agent Tim McCarthy, who was wounded protecting the president in the March assassination attempt. (White House Photograph)

Ryanne hugs Buddy, a frequent visitor to Cedar. (Courtesy of Michele Giorgione)

Barbara Bush says good-bye and thank you to CO Joe Camp on her last Christmas visit, in 1992. (White House Photograph)

The dedication of Evergreen Chapel was a magnificent occasion. (White House Photograph)

The author's family with Presidents 41 and 43 after the ten-year chapel rededication ceremony. (White House Photograph)

After Gorbachev got a ringer on his first try at horseshoes, President Bush presented him with the horseshoe on a plaque. (White House Photograph)

President Clinton loved singing in the choir on Sunday mornings. "He has a marvelous voice," chaplain Bob Williams said. (White House Photograph)

The Clintons, laughing and relaxed as they arrive at Camp David for a little downtime after being welcomed by CO Joe Camp. (White House Photograph)

President Clinton with the author's family during his annual Thanksgiving visit to the Camp David galley. (White House Photograph)

The author meeting Yasser Arafat at Laurel for a historic summit at Camp David. (White House Photograph)

On their final Sunday at Camp David, the First Family is presented with a chapel gift by Michele Giorgione and Ginger Williams. (White House Photograph)

Laura Bush takes the wheel in a golf cart. (White House Photograph)

President Bush's "war cabinet" assembled for a high-level meeting in the woods (left to right): Condoleezza Rice (partly visible at left), Dick Cheney, the president, Colin Powell, Donald Rumsfeld, and Paul Wolfowitz. (White House Photograph)

The lonely sentry. CO Bob Reuning approaching the hangar in dress whites on a foggy night. (Courtesy of MC1 Williams, USN)

Ready to ride? The kids' bikes are assembled outside Hickory during the Obama era. (Courtesy of MC1 Williams, USN)

The author accompanying the First Couple to the landing zone for their flight back to Washington. (White House Photograph)

President and Mrs. Bush complete their first weekend at Camp David
with their special guests, Prime Minister Tony Blair and his wife, Cherie
(not pictured). (White House Photograph)

President Obama liked to joke with CO Wendy Halsey and especially enjoyed causing her to burst into laughter during formal occasions. (White House photograph by Pete Souza)

CO Russ Rang accompanies President Obama from Marine One. (Courtesy of MC1 Rachel McMarr, USN)

During our farewell at the Oval Office, President Bush describes a tree that he and Laura planted in the Rose Garden. (White House Photograph)

We were happy at Camp David. The author with Michele, Briana, and Ryanne under the iconic sign. (Giorgione personal collection)

spanned the nation and even the world. My mind often travels back to images of the solitary figure of FDR sitting on his screened patio at Shangri-La working on his stamp collection, alone with his thoughts — and what thoughts they were! Grace Tully recalled the drive up to Shangri-La with FDR on the day of the invasion of North Africa, one of the critical turning points of the war. She did not know it was happening, but she observed that the president was preoccupied. Throughout the day, others noticed that the president seemed to be on edge, as if he was waiting for something. "Finally, a call came from Washington — from the War Department," Tully remembered. "The Boss' hand shook as he took the telephone from me. He listened intently, said nothing as he heard the full message, then burst out: 'Thank God. Thank God. That sounds grand.'" The Allies had landed in North Africa. "We are striking back," he told those assembled in his cabin.

Away from the intense, noisy swirl of the Oval Office, reflection is possible. Eisenhower felt the unrelenting buzz of activity was a distraction. "When does a man get a chance to think around here?" he complained. When Harry Truman called the White House "the great white jail," he might also have been referring to the clamor.

Regardless of the personality of a president, a sense of loneliness comes with the job. It stems from the weight of responsibility for decisions only he or she can make, the need to keep at a remove from others in order to properly weigh advice and requests. When I was at Camp David, I was often struck by the isolation of the president, even when he was with his wife and children and friends; he always seemed to be standing apart. When I spoke to the other commanders, they told me how certain presidents visibly brought the burdens of the office to camp to contemplate them on their own.

It is interesting that President Kennedy's first visit to Camp David came at one of the loneliest moments of his presidency — the time when his heart was most heavy. He wasn't there to relax. Soon after the catastrophic Bay of Pigs invasion, which was less than three months into his term, Kennedy was at a loss. He admitted that the invasion had been a mistake, and he even worried it could end his presidency. So he called Eisenhower and asked him to come to Camp David for a private conference. Eisenhower agreed. When Eisenhower's helicopter landed, President Kennedy was there to meet him. They walked solemnly along the paths, Eisenhower pointing out various features of the camp that Kennedy was unfamiliar with. But mostly they sat together in Aspen and talked about Cuba. Eisenhower offered some sharp criticism in a gentle manner as well as some solid advice. Kennedy, who hadn't thought much of his predecessor before that day, listened intently. Looking back, this seemed to be a moment when a full awareness of the weight of the presidency settled on Kennedy's shoulders. It was also a bonding, a point when Kennedy realized that only presidents knew the full extent of how hard the job was. After that, he often sought Eisenhower's counsel. As Nancy Gibbs and Michael Duffy revealed in their wonderful book *The Presidents Club,* in the presence of those few who are truly peers, the president might find that his solitary load feels a little less heavy.

For Johnson, who preferred his Texas ranch for respite, Camp David was mostly a working site. He filled it with advisers debating the most troubling issues of his administration, including the one that would be his downfall — the Vietnam War. Arguably, one of the most critical meetings of his presidency took place at Camp David in July 1965. On the table was the urgent question of whether to continue the war. At this meeting Clark Clifford, who had been a key adviser to both Truman and Kennedy before

Johnson, placed his seasoned hand on the table and warned Johnson that an escalation of the war would surely lead to a "quagmire.... It will ruin us."

Arguing with equal force for escalation was Robert McNamara, who said withdrawal would make America look weak and that the war could be won with the nation's superior military might.

The discussions and debates continued into the next day. At last, Johnson retreated for some time alone and walked around the grounds, his heavy shoulders bent. And when he finally made his decision, he sided with McNamara. The war would be escalated (and indeed, it did result in a quagmire). The nation watched as Johnson seemed to sag, his long face and haunted eyes evidence of his sleepless nights.

Lady Bird often woke in the night to find him sitting up in bed, his eyes wide open. She was grateful for the small relief Camp David offered. "What a glorious night of sleep!" she wrote in her diary during one visit. "I treasure it for Lyndon as I would a four-carat diamond on my finger."

In April 1968, after he had announced that he would not seek reelection, Johnson gathered his key military and diplomatic advisers at Camp David to try once again to hammer out a formula for peace talks. In *The Vantage Point,* published after he left office, Johnson described the way Camp David could work on his mood:

On the evening of April 8, I flew by helicopter to Camp David. It was a relief to get away from the noise and carbon monoxide of downtown Washington. At the Aspen Lodge I changed into more comfortable clothes and sat in the living room talking with Walt Rostow [special assistant for national security affairs] about the problems we would be discussing the next day. Finally, I dozed off in my chair until dinnertime. The next morning, I drove to the helicopter pad to greet my visitors from Washington.... We went to the lodge and over breakfast, talked about Vietnam and discussed the latest exchanges with Hanoi. We later moved outside to enjoy the sunshine and continue our discussion.

In an obituary for Richard Nixon, Tom Wicker wrote in the *New York Times* of his "incurable loneliness." For him, it wasn't caused solely by the burdens of the office; it was a central aspect of his character. That loneliness was on display at Camp David even when he was accompanied by aides. In *Breaking Cover,* the White House military aide Bill Gulley wrote about how Nixon kept his closest advisers at arm's length. "When Nixon went to Camp David...he would choose to eat alone. He never asked Haldeman or the others to join him for dinner; they would eat their meals separately. None of the camaraderie existed among them that you might have expected. Nixon told me one time that he didn't believe in socializing with his staff, and he meant it."

During his first year in office, Nixon spent many days at Camp David, and when the press asked what the president was doing, Bob Haldeman told them bluntly, "The man knows the value of contrasts, and he's entitled to be wherever he chooses. Besides, he likes to be left alone, and getting out of Washington is the only way he can be alone, really alone."

Bob Haldeman and John Ehrlichman governed Nixon's visits like "Doberman Pinchers [sic]," wrote George Baker. John Dettbarn, who was commander for nearly four years during Nixon's presidency, concurred. "Haldeman was a tough guy who seemed all-powerful and full of disdain for everybody not in the inner circle," he said, although he found Ehrlichman to be somewhat nicer. His impression was that they pulled the strings for the president who was in the shadows.

In *President Nixon: Alone in the White House*, Richard Reeves described this characteristic in evidence at Camp David: "In the mountains, Nixon was forever plotting, planning revolutions great and small, sometimes to build a better world, more often just coups against his own staff and cabinet. He saw himself as a man of ideas, and of surprise moves, his real work done alone with his yellow pads or with Haldeman and Ehrlichman, his agents of control and organization whom he saw as his two arms."

One thing Nixon did enjoy was ruminating about his fellow politicians. Kenneth T. Walsh, the chief White House correspondent at *U.S. News and World Report*, wrote of Nixon's political musings at Camp David, noting that Nixon once opined of the governor of California, "Reagan is not one that wears well." For Walsh, this was an example of Nixon's fundamental blindness to a basic reality: Reagan was likable; Nixon was not. He might have had more depth on the issues than Reagan, but he didn't see the distinctions between knowledge and personality that Americans grasped intuitively — and that were often reflected at the polls.

The only person who could break through Nixon's isolation was his secretary Rose Mary Woods, a frequent guest at Camp David who occasionally even dined with the president. Once, Nixon summoned Woods during the night to take dictation using a tape recorder. The next morning, in another one of those eerie omens that occur at Camp David, she went to transcribe the tapes and found they were blank; the recorder seemed to be faulty. The device was immediately replaced, although technicians couldn't find anything wrong with it. "Someone's going to have to tell the president," said Woods. "And it's not going to be me."

By the time Watergate took hold and consumed the presidency, Camp David had the aura of a presidential exile. Nixon often retreated there alone or surrounded by close family members, brooding about the assaults delivered daily in the press. In April 1973, more than a year before the end, he dealt the fatal blow to Haldeman and Ehrlichman not in the White House, but at Camp David. There was almost a Shakespearean quality to the firings. First Nixon summoned Haldeman to Aspen. The president shook his hand, which, according to Haldeman, he had never done before, and asked him to step outside and look at the fresh tulips blooming. Nixon described how, as he'd said his prayers the previous evening, he'd hoped he wouldn't wake up. Yet he had — and now he faced the terrible duty of asking for Haldeman's resignation. He repeated the process with Ehrlichman, again relating his prayerful wish of the previous night, and then he started to cry. Later, as Haldeman and Ehrlichman boarded a helicopter at Camp David for the last time, Nixon saw them off. It felt like the end, but the end would drag on for the next year.

During the Watergate hearings, the crew at Camp David saw the pain of the First Family. "Mrs. Nixon, Julie, Tricia — they were in tears," said Dettbarn. "It was hard for us because we *knew* them."

On August 8, 1974, before the resignation was official, Gulley was told to pack up some items from Aspen that Nixon wanted, including a dozen Camp David highball glasses.

In spite of Jimmy Carter's success with the Camp David Accords, his time at Camp David in the last years of his presidency was defined by two words: *malaise* and *hostages*. In July 1979 he retired to Camp David alone for weeks, filled with a pessimistic spirit about the American way. His goal was to craft an important speech that would inspire the nation. Instead, the result of all this deep reflection was the "malaise" speech, delivered on July 15. Carter sounded like a disappointed parent as he chastised the nation for its shortcomings and told its citizens they needed to do better. This perhaps more than anything else set up a contrast with Ronald Reagan that the governor of California would exploit in the coming election. The Iran hostage crisis, which began on November 4, 1979, when fifty-two Americans were taken hostage at the U.S. embassy in Tehran, underscored Carter's weakness — and his isolation. Instead of going out on the trail to appeal personally to the American people, he remained sequestered and grim while Reagan's sunny personality captivated the country.

Presidents, as I've said, are human beings, and as anyone would be, they are tormented by the fear that they have let down the nation and the people they love. George Bush 41 agonized at Camp David over the decision to launch the Gulf War after Saddam Hussein's invasion of Kuwait. Once he'd decided, he was resolute, but haunted. It was a more sober Christmas at Camp David that year, and on New Year's Eve he sat alone and typed a letter to his children:

Dear George, Jeb, Neil, Marvin, Doro,

First, I can't begin to tell you how great it was to have you here at Camp David. I loved the games (the Marines are still smarting over their 1 and 2 record). I loved Christmas Day, marred only by the absence of Sam and Ellie. I loved the movies — some of 'em — I loved the laughs. Most

*of all, I loved seeing you together. We are a family blessed;
and this Christmas simply reinforced this. I hope I didn't
seem moody. I tried not to.*

*When I came into this job I vowed that I would never
[w]ring my hands and talk about "the loneliest job in
the world" or [w]ring my hands about the "pressures or the
trials." Having said that, I have been concerned about
what lies ahead. . . . When the question is asked, "How many
lives are you willing to sacrifice"—it tears at my heart. The
answer, of course, is none—none at all.*

Surrounded by a family who loved him, President Bush was
still, at that moment, the loneliest man in the world.

IT'S AT TIMES of great national crisis that the citizens of this nation
feel as if we are really in it together. The barriers dissolve as we
grapple with our shared emotions and fears as Americans.

Such a time was Kennedy's assassination. Hank Howe, now
sixty-six, is still unable to talk about that period without choking
up. It was a formative experience for him, one shared by most
Americans, but especially intense for him because these were
people he felt close to. "I remember we were sitting in class when
President Kennedy got shot," he said. "They came in and told us
and we were all stunned. We couldn't grasp it."

At camp, Hank's father, CO Howe, was just returning from
lunch at Cedar when he got a call to turn on the television. As he
watched in horror, he fielded a couple of calls from the White
House warning him that it could be a conspiracy, and there might
be additional incidents. So he and his crew did everything they
could to make sure the camp was secure. And then they did what

every other American was doing: they sat and waited. When the announcement finally came that the president had died, Howe went down to the barracks and assembled the troops. They lowered the flag to half-mast and said a prayer. Everyone was heartbroken. They had come to enjoy being with the president, who was always optimistic, friendly, and full of humor and energy. And they felt protective and loving toward Jackie and the kids. Now, in an instant, it was all over.

"My parents were very religious," Hank said, "and the afternoon of the day Kennedy was shot I went out in the woods and wandered around crying. When I came back, still crying, I said to my mom, 'Why...why...why?' She told me, 'Hank, it's because God gave man free will. He can't control everything, but He'll be there every day to deal with what happens, and He'll help us all go on.'"

Jackie and the children never returned to Camp David. Their possessions were packed up and sent to Washington. Howe had the crew remove all the pictures Kennedy had chosen, and, not knowing what the new president, a westerner, would like, he replaced them with Russells and Remingtons. Hank didn't see Jackie and the children again, but his recollections are as fresh as if it were yesterday. Lady Bird Johnson indicated that she always felt as if Jackie's shadow loomed over her. She was at Camp David in 1968 when she learned Jackie had married Aristotle Onassis. "I feel strangely free," she wrote in her diary. "No shadow walks beside me down the halls of the White House or here at Camp David...I wonder what it would have been like if we had entered this life unaccompanied by that shadow."

September 11, 2001, was another tragic and momentous occasion for every American. At Camp David, CO Mike O'Connor had just completed his first presidential visit and was looking forward to an easy week. The morning of September 11, O'Connor received a call from his wife, Elizabeth, at the front gate. "Julia is refusing to go to school," she said. O'Connor was annoyed; his wife argued with Julia, to no avail, and finally gave up. Julia was allowed to stay home that day, and no one understood why she was so adamant about not going to school.

Soon after, O'Connor's personnel chief walked into his office. "Turn on the TV right now," he said. They stood and watched reports of a plane flying into the North Tower of the World Trade Center. Like many other people, they assumed it was a small plane, and as Navy pilots themselves, they found it quite bizarre. How could a plane inadvertently hit a building on such a beautiful day? There was a lot of confusion in the reports. But then they heard that a second plane had flown into the South Tower.

At that moment, their pagers erupted. The next report was that another plane had just hit the Pentagon. Someone said there were rumors of a fourth plane in Pennsylvania, and it might be headed their way. There were clear blue skies over Camp David, and the trees made it nearly impossible for anyone to find the camp from the air. But no one was in the mood to take chances. O'Connor ordered the emergency fire trucks to head to the north end of the camp, and he went to the south end. Later they would hear of United Airlines Flight 93 crashing near Shanksville, Pennsylvania, 117 miles northwest of the camp. No one would ever know for sure where it was headed.

Soon O'Connor received word that Vice President Cheney would be arriving. (Only recently has it been revealed that Camp David was Cheney's secure location.) He and his team went to meet the helicopter, and moments before it landed, a four-point buck walked across the landing zone, giving everyone a chill.

Cheney landed, and a photo was snapped of O'Connor

greeting him. Later, the *Washington Post* would publish the photo, captioning it "An unknown sailor greeting Vice President Cheney." O'Connor didn't mind being called an unknown Sailor. After all, his job was to stay in the background.

When O'Connor was coordinating Cheney's visit with the White House, he asked which cabin Cheney should be put in. He was told Aspen.

O'Connor was confused. "Aspen is the president's cabin," he said.

"The president said to put him in Aspen."

So he did. When the Bushes arrived on September 15, the president walked into Aspen and barked at O'Connor, "Who's been sleeping in my bed?"

O'Connor explained that he had been following the president's orders to locate Cheney there. Turns out the president had not ordered any such thing. O'Connor realized he'd been misled by Cheney's people, and from then on, whenever he heard the words "The president said," he double- and triple-checked. I learned the same lesson with both presidents I served. Sometimes the people around the president—I call them the handlers—have their own agendas. I had to learn how to ignore, work around, or filter some of the things they instructed me to do.

Bush's arrival the Friday after 9/11, following a tour of the World Trade Center site on Thursday, signaled an intense period. His first remark after he landed was to O'Connor; he took him to task for allowing the bright pathway lighting. He thought they made the camp a target. "If you don't get those lights off by morning, you'll be running laps around the camp," he said. Turning off the lights was easier said than done. O'Connor eventually had to send the crew out with wire cutters to shut them off.

The president was accompanied by Laura as well as a large

team of advisers, including Secretary of State Colin Powell, Secretary of Defense Donald Rumsfeld, national security adviser Condoleezza Rice, Treasury Secretary Paul O'Neill, attorney general John Ashcroft, FBI director Robert Mueller, many generals, and "more Secret Service than you could shake a stick at." They arrived that day and on Saturday by road and air. They sequestered themselves for meetings. "George was convening a council of war," Laura Bush wrote in her memoir.

Saturday evening before dinner at Laurel, John Ashcroft sat at the piano playing hymns as the group gathered round and sang. He then accompanied Condi Rice as she sang "His Eye Is on the Sparrow." Rice later wrote about the powerful moment. "The comforting song proclaims God's eye is on the sparrow 'and I know He watches me,'" she wrote. "It was a deep, mournful moment. At dinner, the President asked me to say the prayer. 'We have seen the face of evil, but we are not afraid,' I prayed. 'For you, O Lord, are faithful to us.'"

The high point of a painful and somber weekend was the Sunday service. Navy chaplain Bob Williams brought the president and the congregation to tears with his words, which included this note of enduring hope: "I believe I shall see the goodness of the Lord in the land of the living."

When it came time for the passing of the peace, Elizabeth O'Connor walked over to President Bush and they embraced and kissed. Everyone was filled with such emotion that the normal distances between presidential family and crew evaporated. In his book *Decision Points*, Bush wrote of how the "late summer light streamed through the serene woods and into the chapel" during the service. He called Williams's sermon "touching and comforting. He asked the questions so many of us had struggled with: 'Why?... How could this happen, God?'

"Bob said the answer was beyond our power to know," but he counseled, in a quote from Saint Ignatius of Loyola, "Pray as if it all depends upon God, for it does. But work as if it all depends upon us, for it does." President Bush later used some of the chaplain's remarks at his press conference.

"It was a time when people were hurting," Chaplain Williams said. "Across the country they were standing in line at churches, caught up in a need for community and prayer. Whatever practice of faith they walked in with, they found what they were looking for that weekend."

My family and I were at my new duty station in Hawaii on 9/11, and the girls were quite upset, especially Ryanne, who peppered us with questions. She was very worried about the O'Connors' daughter Julia, and she was also concerned for the president, with whom she'd developed a sweet relationship. She wanted to know if her "buddy" was okay. She didn't really understand that the attacks hadn't been at Camp David. On September 13 Ryanne wrote President Bush a letter:

Dear President Bush,

I am so glad you are safe. I was so worried about you, Mrs. Bush, Spottie and Barney. Mommy let me call my friends at Camp David so I would know they were safe. I wanted to call you but she said you were very busy trying to find the bad guys and are working to keep us safe. I was so happy when I saw you talking on our neighbor's TV (our things aren't here yet). That's when I knew you were okay! Are Barney and Spottie scared? Mom says that Mrs. Bush and Mr. Dale are giving them extra huggs [sic]. I'm glad you are going to camp a lot because our Marines will keep you safe.

*Hawaii is fun. I like my school. I am taking surfing les-
sons and hula lessons. I have fun snorkeling and hiking. Our
house is in a neighborhood with lots of kids. You were our
only neighbors at camp. I wish you were still coming to
Hawaii. I miss singing for you on Sundays!*

Love
Your friend,
Ryanne Giorgione

On November 2, Bush wrote a response by hand:

Dear Ryanne,
   *Thank you for your letter. I am glad to learn you are
doing well. Hawaii sounds like a great place.*
   *I miss seeing you at Camp and at Church. You always
made me smile. And these days I need to smile. Give your
Mom and Dad my best. Say hello to sister.*

Your pal,
George Bush

The buildup to the war was a difficult time for the camp commander. Most of the Navy guys at camp were pretty senior and
already had several deployments under their belts, but the young
Marines and Sailors longed to be at the front. They wanted to go
in the worst way and were totally unafraid of what might happen
to them at war. Elizabeth O'Connor had gotten close with some of
them, and she'd come home shaking her head. "They want to go.
They say, 'Don't worry, I'll be okay.'" O'Connor tried to deal with
their frustration by instituting high-speed training, bringing
Navy SEALs and Secret Service on-site to work with them. It was
in part to distract them from their desire to join the fight. But the

primary goal was to keep them alert and motivated—to remind them that their very unique mission was important too.

For a president, crisis can sweep in without warning, as it did on September 11, 2001, and again on February 1, 2003, a lovely day at Camp David. O'Connor was getting ready to go for a run with President Bush and his chief of staff, Andy Card. They were standing around chatting when a military aide tapped Card on the shoulder and asked if he could speak to him for a moment. Card stepped aside, listened, and then came over to Bush. "Bad news," he said. "The space shuttle *Columbia* just exploded over Texas."

Suddenly the laughter stopped, and they stood for a moment, shell-shocked. Bush looked tortured, in pain, and everyone thought the run would be off. But then he said grimly, "Let's get this run going."

Reflecting on the moment, O'Connor said, "He needed to get his thoughts straight—that was now the purpose of the run." Bush let the inspiring setting speak to him, and when he came back, he had found the words to address the nation.

"In the skies today we saw destruction and tragedy," the president said somberly. "Yet farther than we can see, there is comfort and hope.... The same Creator who names the stars also knows the names of the seven souls we mourn today. The crew of the shuttle *Columbia* did not return safely to Earth; yet we can pray that all are safely home."

Watching at Camp David, O'Connor and the crew were once again moved to tears.

Chapter Seven

An Unusual Duty

Undoubtedly, the happiest and the most challenging
moments as a CO involve the crew.
—CO John Heckmann

THERE'S A LARGE log, about two and a half feet in diameter and five feet in length, at the fishpond in front of Aspen with a generous cutout to make it a bench. The original log-bench was placed there so FDR could sit and fish. Occasionally, wear and tear has required it to be replaced. One day as commander, I was walking around the grounds; in a reflective mood, I stopped at the pond and put my boot on the edge of the seat—and broke off a chunk of it. I froze, my boot in midair. "Oh my God," I said, "I just broke the presidential log." I gently picked up the piece and stuck it back in, but it no longer fit right. I decided I needed to get a new log-bench before the next presidential visit, which was no easy task. It had to be cut, had to be aged, had to look very much like the original. What a headache. I walked away worrying about how much history I'd just demolished.

At Camp David, the profound and the mundane occur on a daily basis. Every single thing that happens has tremendous significance. When you're a member of the crew—from the commander to the freshest recruit from boot camp—you get that message pretty quick.

The most important thing to say about working at Camp David is that it's very much a team effort. Quite simply, the Sailors and Marines at Camp David are extraordinary men and women, and every commander, including me, will tell you what an incredible honor and privilege it is to serve with these inspiring and motivated professionals. They are humble patriots, experts in their fields, and they come from across our nation, drawn by the call to duty, although the camp is certainly an *unusual* duty.

The NSF Thurmont command hand-selects the crew through an extremely rigorous interviewing process, background check, and security-clearance protocol to ensure that we can trust and depend on them to serve around the president. The Sailors we recruit ourselves; the Marines are handled by Marine Barracks Washington, DC, and assigned to the command. The Marine Security Company reports to NSF Thurmont, and together we operate, maintain, and guard the retreat, always ready to host the president, First Family, friends, guests, and the world's leaders in this most unique assignment. Assigned to Camp David, we all find that it is nothing like anything we've experienced in our military careers. All COs value the camaraderie of the crew and their families, and most of us continue close friendships with them long after we leave camp.

Originally, during Roosevelt's time, the only nonsecurity military crew was from the presidential yacht. It wasn't such a heavy lift, as the camp was open only during the summer months, and no one lived on-site. Once Camp David was winterized, during Truman's presidency, that changed, and in the early 1950s, the first Seabees were assigned to the camp. Seabees are the nation's naval construction force; the term *Seabee* is derived from the abbreviation of Construction Battalion—CB. At Camp David, the Seabees maintain the cabins, roads, utility systems, grounds, and other facilities, and they represent about 60 percent of the Navy crew.

"Those also serve who operate rock quarries, build roads, construct runways and keep Camp David running," wrote Julia Robb in the *Frederick News-Post,* referring to the job of a Seabee. Her article featured one Seabee in particular, Ted DePaolis, who was operations chief (in charge of maintenance) at Camp David during Nixon's and Ford's terms and also briefly during the Carter administration. DePaolis came to the camp after two tours in Vietnam; among other duties there, he had been in charge of setting up at a remote rock quarry near the village of Phu Loc, with Vietcong artillery attacks happening on a regular basis. Mortar fire killed six of his men. At Camp David, he was highly motivated to do a good job because he felt that the president's well-being depended on it. "Mr. Nixon would come in looking like an old man and when he left he would be rejuvenated," he said. Most of the Seabees I worked with felt the same way.

The balance of the enlisted Navy crew, in addition to the Seabees, are fleet Sailors: aviation boatswain's mates, culinary specialists, damage-control men, electrician mates, enginemen, electronics technicians, hospital corpsmen, interior communications electricians, information systems technicians, logistics specialists, mass communications specialists, counselors, religious program specialists, ship's servicemen, and yeomen. The most senior enlisted leader at camp is the command master chief (CMC), a third of what the Navy calls the leadership triad: commanding officer, executive officer, and the CMC. As I mentioned, I had the privilege of working with Kevin Timmons and George Havash, two of the eighteen CMCs who have faithfully served at camp and have been the link between the officers and the enlisted. As of this writing, Joe Maioriello fills that role, coming a long way from his fresh start in the Navy as a grounds maintenance crew member at the camp when I first reported in 1999.

The wardroom, or commissioned officers, at camp become every CO's family. Most of the officers are from the Navy's Civil Engineer Corps (CEC), and in 1963 CO Chuck Howe was the first such officer as the camp commander. The CEC officers include the CO, XO, public works officer, assistant public works officer, and the readiness and electronics security officer. In addition, there is a supply officer from the Supply Corps and a chaplain from the Chaplain Corps. The Marine Security Company CO and XO were also in the wardroom, as were the officer in charge of the WHCA unit and the Civil Engineer Corps contracts officer from WHMO who worked at camp and resided in Foxville Gardens.

Beyond the traditional command wardroom, I was also a member of a more ad hoc WHMO wardroom; this included those who traveled with the president whenever he visited Camp David. This was another opportunity to roll out the welcome mat for my fellow servicemen and servicewomen.

Michele and I occasionally invited people for hors d'oeuvres and dinner at Cedar, and sometimes we'd host a dinner in Holly or have folks over for dessert and games. Because most military personnel can connect almost immediately anywhere in the world, this felt like home for many of us, and I found it made life a little more normal. I know that many other COs have continued the tradition.

Being assigned to Camp David was a great entry on crew

members' military records for promotion, but it also opened up other professional opportunities, ones that were often quite unique. Naval recruitment literature, seeking the best and the brightest, offers a tantalizing list of possibilities; for example, if you're assigned to Camp David, you might have the opportunity to attend the Starkey Culinary Arts School at Fort Lee. Additionally, there are various in-camp training opportunities with the Naval Supply System Command corporate chef and master chefs from the Culinary Institute of America.

Thus trained, the culinary staff is top notch, and some presidents use the camp staff instead of bringing their own chefs — the highest form of praise. Many of these cooks are young enlisted men and women, but they quickly become sensitive to the likes and dislikes of their presidential guests. George and Laura Bush were always thrilled when the culinary staff surprised them by shipping in some enchiladas from Texas and their favorite Blue Bell ice cream. "These were young kids just out of cooking school, with amazing talent, and they had the instincts to bring a little bit of home to the First Family," said CO Bob McLean.

Logistics specialists and ship's servicemen are other positions at Camp David. They are responsible for a multitude of operations, including the management of a multimillion-dollar budget, warehousing, and contracting. They also serve as managers at Hickory during presidential visits, supervising the lounge, game room, and Shangri-La bar. Working with these crew members, other crew personnel operate and maintain the theater, bowling alley, horseshoe pits, driving range, putting green, bicycles, and trails and provide an assortment of recreational gear. The Marines operate and maintain the Wye Oak fitness center, the Leatherwood basketball court, the staff swimming pool, and the skeet and archery ranges.

Although the president's private physician and nurse accompany him to Camp David, there is also a medical dispensary in Eucalyptus managed by our hospital corpsmen to handle the everyday needs of the crew.

A newer unit under WHMO, the Joint Presidential Weather Support Unit, serves as the weather forecaster for the retreat. Weather is *always* an issue at Camp David. CO Berry recalled that when the Reagans were at camp, every Saturday night after the movie, Mrs. Reagan would ask what came to be known as the W question—weather. "Commander," she would say nervously, "what's the weather going to be like Sunday?" Berry said everyone knew that Mrs. Reagan was a bit nervous about helicopter flying, so no one wanted to respond to her question; they all kind of stepped back and left Colonel Mike Glynn, CO of the presidential helicopter squadron, to answer. "Mrs. Reagan," he usually said, "it looks like a beautiful day for flying." If the forecast changed, he'd deal with that the next day, but for the time being she could get a good night's sleep. But he, like other commanders, felt some pressure to get the weather right. Problem was, the wind could change at any time. So the best answer to the weather question was always "Wonderful" until nature proved otherwise.

Weather wasn't just a flight issue. As previously noted, it could play havoc with the mission of keeping things pristine. Remembering my own battles with snow, I was sympathetic to Russ Rang's description of "hiding" the snow after a massive storm during his first winter at the camp. The snow-removal crew trucked the heavy snow to the camp's industrial area, where it rose three stories high—out of public view. This solution did have one advantage: Rang's kids immediately ran down to the snowbank to build forts and play king of the mountain.

Although not a department of Camp David, a fellow WHMO unit that resides in camp is the White House Communications Agency. Every CO works on welcoming and including the WHCA personnel and their families, as we all support the same mission.

Arguably the most important job at Camp David is security. Before 1957, the Marine security came and went with the president, but in 1957, the first full-time Marine detachment arrived at the camp. The Marine Security Company, assigned from Marine Barracks Washington, DC, was typically commanded by a Marine Corps major or captain, with a captain XO, first sergeant, and two gunnery sergeants. The bulk of the company was composed of first-tour, brand-new Marine Corps lance corporals in their first assignment, which was far from the traditional Marine Corps duty they had enlisted for.

Guard duty can be lonely and cold in the winter. On the 8th & I reunion site, there are stories from Marines who served on these posts back in the day. According to Ed Crogan, who was sergeant of the guard in the 1950s, the gate sentries tamed a skunk by feeding him rations. One night a new sentry was on duty, and he'd not been informed about the sentries' "pet." He called Crogan at midnight to report, hysterically, that a skunk was trying to get into the gate shack. The sentry screamed to Crogan that he was going to shoot the skunk. Crogan warned him to do no such thing and said he was on his way. "I jumped in the guard jeep and broke the speed limit on the short drive to the gate," Crogan recalled. "As I screeched to a halt and hastily disembarked, I saw one of those scenes that make you wish for a camera. The sentry, who shall remain anonymous in defense of his dignity, was perched, standing straddled, atop the small desk with one foot on the windowsill and the other on the edge of the desk. He was in the firing position with a forty-five clutched in both hands and aiming at the poor confused skunk sniffing at the door, who was only looking for his accustomed night rations."

After giving the skunk a bologna sandwich and the sentry a firm talking-to, Crogan went back to bed. The incident was never recorded in the log.

In May 1989, Camp David had a literal gate-crasher. According to CO Berry, a woman who lived down the road wasn't always in her right mind, and occasionally, she would walk barefoot to the main gate and take her blouse off in front of the Marines. One night she drove her car right into the gate as fast as she could. Naturally, Berry worried that the camp was under attack, but the gate was barely damaged, and they instantly recognized the gate-crasher. Berry sent corpsmen down to administer first aid and called for an ambulance from town. The story made it into the press, and the deputy White House press secretary B. Jay Cooper reported, "The heavily reinforced vehicle gate was not damaged. The auto, a 1989 Fiero, was extensively damaged and the driver was injured." That's the last time this particular strange visitor was seen at Camp David.

There are separate barracks at the camp for single male and single female crew members. The married families, with the exception of the commander's family, live down the hill, some at Foxville Gardens, now privatized military housing, and most others in communities in southern Pennsylvania and northern Maryland. Foxville Gardens is a beautiful complex with nice houses and a park and playground for the children. During our time at camp, Foxville Gardens was not privatized, and we, like most other naval commands, managed the housing assignments, maintenance, and services. Families *wanted* to live there; the sense of community, the support, and the friendships were incredible. That's why Michele frequently took the girls there just to hang out, so they'd have normal playmates in a normal setting and she would have other spouses to talk with. Michele often joked that she lived out of her car. It's a common need and tendency when you live alone.

To work at Camp David is to learn the art of doing the impossible. CO Berry recounted an incident early in his tour that occurred while the Reagans were vacationing in California. With the president safely elsewhere, it was time to do some serious upkeep, including a major fence relocation. Unfortunately, while drilling for a fence post, one of the crew hit the camp's main power line. The damage was assessed, and the crew consulted with the power company, and it estimated that it would take several weeks to get full power restored. Berry started to worry. The Reagans were scheduled for a visit over Labor Day weekend, just two weeks away. Berry's boss, WHMO director Jim McKinney, was with the president in California; Berry advised him of the situation and said, "We may not be ready for Labor Day."

"Oh yes, you will," McKinney stated emphatically.

Berry replied, "Yes, we will." And they were. "I learned we could move mountains up there," he said.

I had a similar experience at camp when we had a water-main break three days before an arrival. This occurred only a few weeks into Bush's presidency, when he was planning to come to camp for the second time. Heather Wishart (you'll remember her from the pool-cover incident) was sitting in her office when she overheard a couple of Seabee utilities men talking about a problem with the reservoir losing water. Poking her head out the door, she asked, "How *much* water?" It turned out to be a lot. This was a serious issue. There was a leak somewhere, but where? The hunt was complicated by the fact that snow was covering the ground. After a thorough search failed to uncover the problem, a consultant was hired—and he couldn't find it either. "We tried everything but a divining rod," Wishart said. A few hours into the task, they finally located the general area of the leak and started digging between the chapel and the pilot's cabin. Everything that could go wrong did. Among the problems was a massive tree sitting right in the way. They had to take the tree down. Then a valve they needed couldn't easily be procured from a local supplier who had every size but the one they specified. By this point, Wishart was nearly forty-eight hours into the task. Most of the camp was without water, and the galley had been closed. Around two in the morning before the visit I came over to see how they were doing.

"Should I call the White House and tell them not to come?" I asked.

"Sir, I know we can do this," Wishart said.

I hesitated. The implications if we couldn't fix it were grave. "Are you sure?" I asked.

"I *know* we can do this," she repeated forcefully.

"Okay," I said, and left her to it.

By seven a.m. the situation was under control, and all that remained was to place new asphalt, despite the cold temperatures, and, of course, do the cleanup, which in part involved bringing in snow to cover up the site. She was surprised when two chiefs came by and invited her to have breakfast in the chief mess, which was considered a high honor. She was pleased and flattered, thinking they wanted to acknowledge her hard work. But in truth, they just didn't want the crew to see her. "I was a hot mess," she said.

An addendum: Wishart left the Navy after her Camp David service, but she returned to camp with her husband and three children in 2016 at the invitation of Command Master Chief Joe Maioriello. "My family was excited to see the historic places at the camp," she said. "I was excited to see the site of the water-main break and the pool, which was now enclosed."

CO Heckmann supervised the renovations of some of the cabins during his time at the camp, fixing the exteriors and updating the interiors from their vintage 1980s style. Laura Bush was closely involved in the finish work and used a consultant to help her find just the right antiques and artifacts to create a lovely look without compromising the essential rustic feel. There were also upgrades at Aspen, including a new HVAC system for temperature control, the installation of which was a difficult task. Shades of LBJ — it was a process of trial and error. "He liked it cool; she liked it warm," Heckmann said of the Bushes, describing a classic clash that most married couples will find familiar. But he finally taught the Bushes how to control the system — and then left them to debate the ideal temperature between themselves.

Like Reagan, Bush 43 was at the camp so frequently that the crew was at the top of their game. However, getting the big jobs done — such as one project to repave all the roads — was a challenge. Those tasks had to wait for times when the Bushes were in Crawford.

After a visit to Idaho, Bush got hooked on riding a bike on single-track trails, and he asked Heckmann if the crew could create some at the camp. Not knowing much about single-track trails, Heckmann initially "made the mistake" of asking the Secret Service for advice. They favored nice, wide trails with lots of room for security vehicles; a single-track trail was just the opposite, a narrow path that was no wider than a bike's tires. The president won that battle. Heckmann gathered a few Seabees, Marines, and tools and proceeded to blaze some new trails for the president. Since the

Secret Service could not easily follow in a vehicle, some of the agents had to get up to speed and bike along. Marines joined them to help with straggling guests once they were deemed fit enough to bike with the president without embarrassing the camp. This was serious business in Bush's "survival of the fittest" mode. "To see our riders congratulated by the president at the end of the ride while splattered with mud was inspiring," Heckmann said, remembering his pride.

WHILE I WAS commander, a typical day in the life of the camp began with a seven-thirty staff meeting at Poplar, the command office. On Mondays we'd plan what was going on that week. If there was a visit scheduled, we'd have a kickoff meeting where everyone was represented — the communications team, the Marines, and all the department heads. That's where we would share information on who was scheduled to come. Sometimes the social secretary didn't have the specifics, and it was frustrating not to know who we were preparing for, how many cabins were needed, how many guests we'd have, how much food was required. It was on my head to figure it out. Visit prep means checking and double-checking that everything is running — making sure the bikes are good, the water fountains are working, the tennis courts are clean, and all those types of things. That's where the senior leadership of the camp has to learn the delicate art and skill of effective delegation and management. You want everything to be perfect but natural. And you rely on the crew to do all of this, although as the commander, you feel the heat when it's not perfect and you get the praise when it is. If the bed corner is not flush or someone drove over the flowers and they have to be replaced, it's harrowing. Be accountable; take the hit or pass on the praise — that was another critical part of leadership COs learned in this high-risk, high-yield mountaintop environment.

One of the perks of serving as the CO at Camp David during my time was that I was given a visitor's pass to the White House that did not require me to have an escort. The pass could get me into most of the common areas, but not the residence (for that, I had to be escorted). Because of the pass I could visit the grounds superintendent, Dale Haney; the florist; the ushers' office — Gary Walters was head usher at that time — and other staff that the camp shared a common work bond with. In the White House, I met ushers, Navy valets, Sailors, and others who supported the First Family behind the scenes, much as we did at Camp David.

Occasionally, I would invite the groundskeeper, the florist, and the chefs to Camp David to observe and advise us. For dinners with heads of state at Camp David, the White House chefs and butlers were sometimes sent to camp to preside over the event, which made total sense to me, and we worked well together.

There was definitely a sense that we were all on the same team — supporting the president. Early in my time at Camp David, Gary Walters invited me to the White House so we could share thoughts and insights, and he very graciously gave me a personal tour that included the residence upstairs, the only time I ever saw the space. It was intriguing to see where the Clintons watched TV, worked puzzles (the Clintons loved puzzles), got snacks from the kitchen, and slept. Almost like a regular family. Almost.

Haney, the grounds superintendent, was particularly warm and friendly, and we would share stories about flower-bed care, golf-green maintenance, and the presidential dogs, which he and his staff, like the crew at Camp David, would sometimes take for walks or keep company.

I always felt the two staffs had much in common, and yet the nature of our encounters with the First Family were markedly different. The White House staff lived the daily grind of the presidency, while at Camp David we usually saw them in a more relaxed mood. However, we all felt that same constant pressure and sense of responsibility.

It was the norm to have periodic WHMO commanders' meetings at the White House. During President Bush's administration, those meetings were monthly. Coordination with the other WHMO units was an important part of my job. Camp David personnel never traveled with the president, and because these trips were when most of the WHMO units and personnel really bonded, I felt I had to work a bit harder to forge and maintain relationships with them whenever I had the opportunity. Once a month, I would get to check in with my boss—the director of WHMO—the deputy director, and the other WHMO units, such as HMX-1, the Presidential Airlift Group (which includes Air Force One), the White House Communications Agency, the White House Transportation Agency, the White House Medical Unit, the Presidential Food Service, and other offices. The military aides were not an official WHMO unit, but they were great to see and talk with. During the time that I served under President Clinton and President Bush, each had five military aides from the U.S. Army, Navy, Air Force, Marine Corps, and Coast Guard. During any visit to Camp David, one military aide would always be with the president, and he served as my primary link for information on how the president was feeling that day, what mood he was in, and what he might want, or not want, to do. Together, the military aide and the First Lady's social secretary gave me the best view of how a visit was going to go.

People have often asked me if it takes a special kind of person to be a Camp David commander. Part of the vetting to be the commander has to do with temperament. I think a balanced, non-ideological personality helps, as does a strong respect for the crew and its mission. One of my key principles of leadership, which served me well at the camp and that I use to this day, is the importance of going behind the scenes and experiencing what the crew experiences. It's a form of empathy, I suppose, and it's the best way to understand the challenges on the ground. It's also great for employee morale.

On occasion at the camp I did a routine similar to the show *Undercover Boss*, though obviously without the secrecy. I really wanted to understand what my crew dealt with during a normal week. I would spend a whole day with grounds maintenance weed-whacking the hill known as Big Bertha and working flower beds. I'd spend a day with the Marines walking the patrol. I'd spend a day in the galley cooking meals and serving them to the crew. I'd spend a day at guest ops cleaning cabins and making beds. I'd spend a day cleaning out the shredder and doing all those other behind-the-scenes tasks. It gave me some perspective on why it sucks to weed-whack that big hill, why you need a CamelBak of water and new boots and a lot of thread to run the machine. I saw firsthand what my people dealt with day in and day out. I heartily recommend the exercise. If you do it genuinely, it builds respect; the crew members will think, *Hey, the CO's out here weed-whacking with me, and he's not here just for a photo op, he's here all day.* I enjoyed walking in their shoes. I was always very much out and about. Sometimes I would catch things that needed to be fixed, but that wasn't really my job. My job was to inspire, support, and motivate the crew in a genuine, caring way. They were giving it their all, and I was right there with them.

CO Joe Camp shared those leadership principles when he was at Camp David. "I'm a people person, as comfortable out of uniform as in uniform," he said. "Biggest thing I still practice: Never have the troops do anything I wouldn't do. Walk the walk as well as talk the talk." Or as CO Russ Rang used to tell his crew, "Give me the dirtiest job." They would reply, "Yes, sir, go over to Big Bertha and whack weeds for four hours."

CO Camp learned right away that he was in the presence of excellence when he came on board. "These were the best troops I'd ever worked with. It was sometimes tough to stand in front of them as their leader." One day a female yeoman first class was in his office for a discussion. Just after she left, he remembered something else he wanted to tell her and he called her desk phone, thinking he'd leave a message. She answered the phone—already back at her desk. "How did you get back there so fast?" he asked in surprise.

"Sir," she replied, "I'm a happening unit."

"The biggest difference at Camp David is the level of detail," said CO Berry. "Everybody is looking at every small detail. It's a quality crew, self-motivated, smart, extremely responsive." Sometimes to an extreme. President Bush 41 once grumbled to Berry, "Everybody wants to please us so much. If I ask for a rowboat, don't give me an aircraft carrier."

CO Autry acknowledged the stress of a visit, where everyone is supremely focused on one person—the president. But he abided by the same philosophy I had: "Let your people do what they're there to do." Much as I had learned on my first day in command.

On occasion, though, there is the opportunity for training, especially for the younger members of the crew. CO Berry recalled an incident during a picnic at Camp David when a very large group was invited. There weren't enough golf carts for the guests that day, so when General Colin Powell asked where his golf cart was, the lieutenant on duty had to tell him that the guests were not being offered carts. "What about that cart right there?" the general asked. "That's my cart, sir," the lieutenant replied. Hearing about the incident later, the wardroom gave the lieutenant an "award" for refusing to give a four-star general his golf cart.

At Camp David you never know when something new will be expected of you. In January 2007, CO Heckmann was outside Hickory shoveling snow when President Bush stopped by to practice his State of the Union speech. He asked Heckmann to come inside and listen so he'd have an audience. Heckmann went in with the president, but since snow was continuing to fall outside, he was distracted by the noise from the snow-removal crews. He was so worried that the loud sounds would disrupt the president's rhythm that he barely paid attention to what he was saying. To his chagrin, at the end, the president asked him what he thought about the speech, and he felt silly for not listening more attentively.

The camp crew must be prepared for any eventuality. Heckmann remembered a time when President Bush was scheduled to take a short trip from the camp to make some remarks at an event. He'd invited a camp guest to accompany him. At the last minute, the guest realized he didn't have a dress shirt on hand, and he asked the guest steward if he could help. The steward reached out to the supply officer, who began frantically looking for a shirt the man could borrow. Heckmann, waiting at the landing zone, heard about the urgent need and sent word to his wife to find one of his shirts to loan the guest. When the guest finally arrived for the flight, he looked embarrassed and uncomfortable. Heckmann assumed it was because he was late—but it was really because the sleeves on his dress shirt were way too short.

Also in the context of unusual duty, during the 2012 presidential campaign, the Camp David hangar was taken over for prep for the third and final presidential debate, on foreign policy. With Senator John Kerry (who would become secretary of state in Obama's second term) playing the role of Romney, Obama hunkered down in the hangar for Debate Camp.

As I said before, there is a fair amount of downtime at Camp David—by which I mean days when the president isn't there. While the maintenance load is great, every commander steps up during those occasions to hone the skills of the crew. During my years there, we'd have well-choreographed practice visits where people dressed up as the president and First Lady and the crew went through the entire visit, start to finish, just to stay sharp. Of course, nothing beats the real thing.

I had a particularly trying spell during President Clinton's last year when we had five months between visits. Sure, we did a lot of training and maintenance, had a lot of sports competitions, and took a few professional field trips, but it doesn't take too long for the leadership challenges to rise. We all want to do our mission— that's what the Sailors and Marines come to camp for—and when you hit these gaps, it can be taxing. The COs during the Reagan, Bush 41, and Bush 43 presidencies never caught much of a rest, but many other COs have had to deal with these long absences.

I can tell you that from the first visit of President Bush, in February 2001, and for the next eight years, the COs and crews had no time for sports competitions and extracurriculars. The mission went high and right, and while that's what we love, it too has its challenges. Some of the crew caught in the transition from

Clinton to Bush had some trouble adjusting to more frequent visits.

So what does the CO do when there's downtime? In addition to the assorted activities, you pretty much have to keep talking with your crew, reminding them why we all serve and that our job is to always be ready. Sometimes you just have to hunker down, suck it up, and be strong. During those times I told the crew, "Our fellow Sailors and Marines are doing hard things in hard places around the world, and while many of you may want to be with them, our place is here and now. This is *our* mission."

When Chuck Howe was CO, during the Kennedy and then the Johnson years, he had forty-nine enlisted Navy people, representing all different trades, on the crew. He had a White House communications group that ran the switchboard, and that was probably a dozen people. Then he had a platoon of Marines that rotated through the camp; today it's a company. On an off-visit night, Howe decided to test their readiness. He went down to the hangar, took out a barrel, put some paper in it, and set it on fire. Then he put in the call that there was a fire in the hangar.

Next thing he saw was the big fire truck chugging up through the cold winter night. It had a bunch of Sailors on it, but they were hanging from the vehicle. The truck came rumbling through the forest down to the field, and he was concerned that somebody was going to get killed. So soon after, he went to the military command and asked to shore up the emergency services. There needed to be at least one person who was an aviation-crash-rescue expert, in case of a helicopter accident. And the Sailors needed firefighting training. This was done.

During my time, all crew members took firefighting training when they came aboard. Today, the camp has modernized the facilities and the personnel, and while it still conducts training for the crew, there is a permanent civilian fire chief from the Federal Fire Service.

As we've seen, every commander brings his or her special background, personality, and family configuration to the camp. Traditions get broken as times change. For example, it is the traditional role of the commander's spouse to provide a support system for the crew spouses, which my wife did. In addition, your spouse can be your eyes and ears with the crew and families, often seeing and hearing things that a CO might not catch or be exposed to. When Wendy Halsey was commander, that role changed a bit. Her husband, Mark, didn't attend spouses' meetings, but he did coach the Army-Navy softball team. It took a little getting used to for some people. Once, when the Halseys came into camp, the guard at the gate said, "Welcome back to camp, sir," assuming Mark was the commander. Wendy Halsey laughed about it. They'd know soon enough!

She actually found her dual roles as mom and commander easier at Camp David than elsewhere. Work-life balance was smoother because she was always close at hand and had dinner at home every night. Joe Camp had the same experience. "When the leaves fell, I could wave at my wife from my office," he said.

Camp described his selection as Camp David commander as an example of "hard work meets opportunity. You don't ask for the job. They ask you." He kiddingly told people, "Commander Camp is going to be camp commander."

Reflecting on the experience, he said, "I gained a lot of self-confidence. If I could survive working for the president and not get fired, I must be doing something right." He also felt a certain awe. "It's corny, but real—me, a boy from the cornfields of Ohio, working for the president of the United States. During one visit,

President Bush called me on the phone. 'This is George,' he said. I jumped up and stood at attention for the length of the call."

As a young boy in western Pennsylvania, I got into a fistfight with one of my best friends because he taunted me that I could never be the president since I was born overseas. Well, I can't and won't be president, but I got about as close to the president as possible. It was special. But CO Heckmann said it best: "The president made being at camp special," he observed. "But the crew made it a fulfilling experience every day."

Chapter Eight

PEW ONE

Evergreen Chapel is the president's little church in the country.
—Chaplain Bob Williams

O N SUNDAY MORNING, January 12, 1964, a motorcade of black cars wound down the mountain, then continued on south through Thurmont to a small historic Episcopal church called Harriet Chapel. A month and a half after the assassination of John F. Kennedy, his successor, Lyndon Johnson, was at Camp David for his first visit as president, and he wanted to go to church. The congregants, fewer than fifty people, were shocked when the president entered their church and dropped into a pew. After the service, he lingered to shake their hands as they left.

According to the late Thurmont historian George Wireman, Harriet Chapel probably dates back to Revolutionary War times and was reestablished as an Episcopal church in the early nineteenth century.

Johnson would return there several times over the years, including one notable Father's Day visit when he was accompanied by his Camp David guests Australian prime minister Harold Holt and his wife. Wireman reported that after that service, the president and Holt spent time with the congregants. At one point Johnson picked up a four-year-old girl and kissed her, and the prime minister bounced a three-year-old boy on his shoulders and told him, "Today is Father's Day and this is the day you must be nice to us fathers."

While the local congregants down the mountain probably enjoyed having the president share a pew with them, one man with ties to Camp David was distressed that the camp did not have its own place of worship. Kenneth Plummer, a contractor and member of an old family from nearby Chambersburg, Pennsylvania, had been doing work at Camp David for twenty-five years. In fact, he was at the camp on the day of Kennedy's assassination. As he and his fellow workers sat in shock, Plummer wished desperately that the camp had a place where they could pray and seek comfort from one another. That was the kernel of an idea—to build a chapel.

He vowed to make it a reality, but he could not do it yet. It would have to wait for his retirement. Meanwhile, presidents continued to worship locally or, more often, bring pastors to the camp to hold services in the hangar or in one of the cabins. By the time Mike Berry became CO, in 1988, Plummer had retired and was actively pursuing his dream. He had written a letter to President Reagan offering to raise the funds for the chapel and build it, and Reagan approved the project and gave a donation. Plummer figured they'd have to get a million dollars in private donations, money that would come mostly from interfaith groups and organizations.

On July 26, 1988, the first day of turnover from CO Broaddus to CO Berry, there was a ground-breaking ceremony for the chapel with the Reagans in attendance. While the construction would not begin for another year, when the money was raised, it was a shovel in the ground for Plummer's dream. Now sixty-six and semiretired, he was all in.

Berry was delighted that he would be the CO overseeing the construction. His faith was important to him and he embraced the idea of building a chapel at Camp David. He found a kindred spirit in Plummer. The two men divided up the work: Plummer was in charge of organizing a multidenominational chapel board, raising money, designing the structure, and getting it built; Berry coordinated with the Navy and White House and worked on obtaining a chaplain billet, selecting a Navy chaplain, and organizing a program to hold services with guest chaplains until the chapel got built.

Almost immediately, the camp started holding Sunday services for the crew and visiting staff, beginning with Protestant services in Hickory led by the Marine Barracks chaplain; after that, there was a rotating list of chaplains. "I drafted my wife, Dee, to be the pianist," Berry said, although the piano was a challenge. It had been taken from the presidential yacht, *Sequoia,* so it was smaller than a regular piano — in fact, it was missing two full octaves. They made do.

The Reagans didn't attend these services, preferring to worship privately at Aspen. In his memoir Reagan wrote that although he missed his regular church attendance while at Camp David, "I prayed that God would realize that when I was out in the beautiful forest I felt as if I was in his temple."

When the Bushes came aboard in 1989, Bush 41 was more inclined to worship with the crew. On the Bushes' first visit to Camp David after the 1988 election, Berry met with them to discuss how they wanted the camp to run and find out if there were changes they wanted to make. "The chapel was on my list of things to discuss," Berry said, "but I never got a chance. One of the very first things the president told me was 'I want there to be a church service every Sunday that we are here, and I want you to invite the crew to attend with us.'" Berry was happy to hear it. "He was singing my song!" he said.

President Bush's personal assistant Tim McBride was Catholic, so Berry worked with the base commander at nearby Fort Ritchie to bring a Catholic priest to the camp every week, something Kennedy had done during his presidency. The Catholic Mass was held before the Protestant service. Once again, Berry drafted Dee to play the piano, and he went to both the Catholic and Protestant services because in the beginning there were so few attendees. He joked to the priest that he and Dee should be made honorary Catholics since they attended Mass so regularly.

Later on, a Navy chaplain was assigned full-time to the camp, but prior to that Berry had to contend with a rotating list of chaplains, so he was constantly having to explain all the special rules of Camp David. At first, his instructions to the clergy involved only logistics, directions, schedules, security issues, and the admonition that their sermons not be political. But over time, as difficulties and confusion were encountered, he added to the list of directives, eventually developing what he called the Thirty-Nine Thou Shalt Nots.

One of the thirty-nine prohibitions was that the chaplains were not to preach on the parable of the prodigal son. This had made it onto Berry's list after three different chaplains over three consecutive weeks had chosen that passage for their sermons. After the third Sunday, Barbara Bush commented to Berry on the way out of chapel, "Well, I think we've covered that one pretty well."

With the Bushes at services, attendance increased rapidly.

Another big draw was that the Bushes invited special guests from time to time; among them were the Gatlin Brothers, Jimmy Dean, Moe Bandy, and Sandi Patty. The president and Mrs. Bush usually hung around outside for a few minutes after each service, visiting with the crew and their families and shaking hands just like any other congregants.

When the camp finally got a permanent chaplain, Jon Frusti, Berry gladly retired his Thirty-Nine Thou Shalt Nots. It made a tremendous difference for the camp to have its own chaplain, not just for services, but for other activities. One of Frusti's first initiatives was the chapel choir. The president even invited its members to a "hoedown" with Moe Bandy in Laurel one evening.

Meanwhile, the construction of the new chapel was coming along nicely. President Bush was very interested in its progress and often went to the site to check out how it was going. It was decided by the board to name the chapel Evergreen, in keeping with the tree theme of the cabins and because evergreen is a symbol of the eternal nature of life.

A chapel bell with a historic distinction was procured for the chapel. It came from the USS *Endicott,* a Navy destroyer that was launched in April of 1942, the same month Shangri-La was designated the presidential retreat. The *Endicott* was used as an escort ship in the convoy carrying President Roosevelt to the Yalta Conference during World War II.

Since the chapel was nonsectarian, there would be no cross or Star of David. A Torah scroll and Jewish prayer books were donated by the Jewish Chaplains Council, and the stained-glass windows, mentioned earlier, were designed to reflect different faith traditions. This was spelled out in a memo from the windows' creator, Rudolph Sandon. The medallions in the Tree of Knowledge included

Sheaf of wheat, symbolic of the bounty of God;

Seven flames, as seven gifts from the wisdom of God;

Presidential seal, the symbol of strength and glory;

"We the people," the American pledge under God;

The dove, a universal symbol of peace;

Lamp with flame, the lamp of knowledge.

The medallions in the Tree of Life included

The sea, to symbolize the waters of life;

The anchor, a symbol of hope;

Mountains, to symbolize the faith of humanity and its
eternal quest;

Abstract of God, to symbolize love, goodness and beauty;

The globe, with the Greek word *oikoumene*, meaning
ecumenical;

The book, symbolizing the teaching of life.

Evergreen Chapel was dedicated on April 11, 1991, in front of a large interfaith crowd. Prayers were read by an archbishop of the Greek Orthodox Church, a rabbi, a Catholic priest, and Protestant bishops, as well as by laypeople and members of the First Family.

It had been foggy and drizzling all weekend, and the day of the ceremony was pouring rain. That meant the planned dedication at the front doors had to be changed to a dedication inside the foyer. The crew and guests were all seated in the chapel. "The weather was dreary, but the spirit inside that chapel was not dampened in the least," said Dee Berry. "It was wonderful!"

The Christian-music singer Sandi Patty was invited by President Bush to sing. She'd given a concert in Chicago the night before but she arrived at the camp to participate. She sang "Love in Any Language" and "America the Beautiful" and then led the gathering in "God Bless America."

At the service, President Bush rose to accept the chapel on behalf of the government of the United States and the office of the president. Wiping tears from his eyes, Bush said, "I accept with joy and gratitude this magnificent gift on behalf of those who shall use this chapel, and extend my profound thanks to God and to all those whose generosity and labor have made this possible. May the hopes of those who envision this building as a house of prayer for all peoples be fully realized."

I can definitively say that Evergreen Chapel enhanced the character of the camp. And one of the high points of my time at the camp was the chapel's ten-year-anniversary rededication ceremony. It was a big event, requiring a lot of preparation, and George and Laura Bush were closely involved. I often went to Aspen or Laurel to meet with Mrs. Bush and carefully plan the events of the day.

The rededication, held on June 3, 2001, was a beautiful service, with both Bush families present. Laura and Barbara Bush both did readings, and President Bush 43 performed the dedication rite. But perhaps the most moving part of the service was the "act of presentation" by Ken Plummer, now seventy-seven, whose vision had resulted in this glorious chapel. His words that day were inspiring for all of us.

We present the Camp David Chapel to the government of the United States for use by presidents, their guests, and all who advise and attend them. This is a house of prayer for peoples of every faith where petitions and praise are offered, where divine guidance is sought, and where strength and wisdom are gratefully received.

After the service, people gathered on the flagstone patio, and the culinary staff brought out a big cake. President Bush 43 was handed a knife to cut the first piece in a ceremonial way. With all the children standing around him, he continued to cut and plate the cake until Michele noticed and hurried over. Reaching for the knife, she said, "Mr. President, let me take over the cake-cutting."

He grinned. "Yes, please."

Michele realized that he'd thought it was his job to cut the whole cake. It was charming, but not what was intended for the president of the United States! Michele remembered an admonition we'd received in the beginning: "You need to make the president look presidential." Cutting the entire cake was definitely not presidential.

Laura Bush invited our family and Chaplain Bob Williams and his family to brunch after the service, which was a very nice gesture. We were honored. In fact, it was one of the best events of our life. We got to really talk with George and Barbara Bush and the Bush daughters.

At the table next to ours, Briana and Ryanne sat with Barbara and Jenna, a big thrill for them. They were awestruck by these attentive young women who seemed to know exactly how they felt about the strange parameters of their life. I sat next to Bush 41. The conversation was easy, light, and funny. I told him that outside my office at the Pentagon there was an oil painting of him being rescued from a life raft by the USS *Finback* after he was shot down in the Pacific in World War II. He replied that someone had taken a video of the painting and given it to him. I enjoyed our conversation. For a brief time, it was just two Navy guys telling stories, me mostly listening, and I was the recipient of Bush 41's famous common touch.

*   *   *

THERE IS NO denying that Camp David can have a spiritual impact in the broadest meaning of that word. Its designation as a presidential *retreat* connotes a monastic, contemplative quality that is apparent once you step through the gate. As such, it is a getaway with a purpose, where the silent nights and mountain air can settle the weary soul of the leader of the free world. It is this atmosphere, so difficult to capture in words but so visceral to anyone who has visited, that sets Camp David apart.

I think this is the reason that presidents and their families — even those who don't regularly attend church services — gravitate to Evergreen Chapel. "In many ways the chapel is the glue that holds the community together, the regular drumbeat," former chaplain Bob Williams said. It's more than just the Sunday service. The chapel is involved in community activities such as the harvest festival and Easter egg hunt. Everyone, religious or not, is invited. The emphasis is on *community*. "I wasn't there to be preacher to the president," Williams said. "The chapel pastor is for the Marines and Sailors assigned to Camp David. There's Sunday school, choir, children's choir, and Bible study. I don't change things when the First Family comes to camp."

The chaplain is also the historian for the camp, responsible for compiling the history and heritage. This is a transient community of people who move every couple of years. The chapel is the stabilizing keeper of historical memory.

In Pew One, the president and the First Family have a chance to worship in the presence of a real congregation without the fanfare that accompanies their visits to more public churches. Whenever a president takes office, there is always a great deal of interest in whether he will choose a home congregation. This is a difficult decision, as most presidents are sensitive to the disruption that accompanies the chief executive whenever he is in a public setting. For this reason, modern presidents, even if they are devout, mostly stay away from church services in Washington.

Months after President Obama took office, *Time* magazine reported that he had decided to make Evergreen Chapel his home congregation. The article generated a great deal of publicity, especially for the Evergreen chaplain at the time, Lieutenant Carey Cash. Cash had some cachet of his own. A great-nephew of Johnny Cash, a former Citadel football star, and an Iraq War veteran, he was the subject of much interest — and he despised the attention. Fortunately, soon after the *Time* article, the White House announced that it was not true that Obama had chosen Evergreen as his home church. In reality, though, Obama often attended services at Evergreen when he was at camp. He just chose to be private about it.

Privacy is hard to come by for presidents, even when it concerns their faith practices, but Camp David does its best to shield them from the gawkers. On Easter weekend in 1993, following the burial of Mrs. Clinton's father, Hugh Rodham, the Clintons came to camp. The First Lady was grieving, and she didn't want to be out in public, but she welcomed the supportive community and the inspiring Easter service at Evergreen. "Jackie Kennedy Onassis had encouraged me to shelter my intimate family life in this protected retreat, surrounded by a forest preserve in Maryland's Catoctin Mountains," she wrote in her memoir *Living History*. "Her simple, pragmatic advice, as always, had proved invaluable." She recalled that Easter Sunday after her father's death: "I sat in my pew and thought of how my father used to embarrass my brothers and me with his loud, off-key hymn singing. I share his tone deafness, but that morning I sang out, hoping the discordant notes might reach the heavens."

This warmth and familial sense were typical of the Clintons when they were at Evergreen. After services they would often stay to have coffee and muffins and talk—and they seemed to relish being just like ordinary congregants.

Early in his presidency, Clinton made it known at Camp David that he wanted to be in the choir. "He had a marvelous voice, and being in the choir really made him part of the community," Williams said. The other choir members were glad to have him, and they thought it was pretty special that the president was singing in their midst. Clinton asked to have the sheet music delivered to Aspen on Saturday so he could dutifully review it before the service. And then on Sunday he'd show up early and stand around with the others drinking coffee. He treated the crew like old friends, and he told them a secret one morning about his strategy with the congressional leadership: "I'll go to bed and wake up at two a.m. and call 'em—make 'em think I've been up working all night." The other choir members loved hearing these little inside details told in Clinton's expansive, charming way.

And the choir had a great leader. Wayne Wold was the choirmaster, organist, pianist, and pageant director for many years. Wayne also taught at nearby Hood College, in Frederick, and was an extraordinarily talented, friendly, and crucial member of our chapel community. He was family, like the crew, and we thoroughly enjoyed having him lead our musical programs every Sunday.

Bush 41 had a strict rule: Chapel attendance was mandatory for guests. No exceptions. Once when Arnold Schwarzenegger was visiting, he was not at chapel when the First Family arrived. The president, not seeing Arnold, told CO Berry, "Go get him."

Berry hopped on his golf cart and headed to Birch, worrying all the way about how he was going to drag the Terminator to church. Fortunately, one of the officers had overheard the president and asked the switchboard to ring the cabin. By the time Berry arrived at Birch, Schwarzenegger was coming out the front door. "Show me to the chapel," he ordered, and Berry invited him aboard the cart. "I'll take you there."

Several times during his administration, Bush 41 invited the cabinet up for the day, and their meetings always began with a prayer service at the chapel. Again, everyone was expected to be there *on time*. Once, CIA director William Webster was running late, and he arrived at the gate in a sweat and explained to the guards putting him through the usual paces that he couldn't afford to be late for Bush's prayer service. "Get me to the church on time!" he begged.

One Sunday morning Berry's son, Ken, was running late for church, and Mrs. Bush in her golf cart stopped to give him a ride as well as a talking-to about not having a coat on in the cold weather. Since he was with Mrs. Bush, Ken, by definition, made it to church on time.

When I was CO my family always attended services with the president, but it was our second service of the day, because we attended Catholic Mass earlier. It was one of our concerns when we first came to the camp, whether our young daughters could sit still for two services. It seemed like a lot to put them through. Mostly, it worked out, but sometimes the girls grumbled a bit about what they thought was an excess of services. One day, a year in, Briana came to us and asked, "Are we getting extra credit for going to two Masses? Can we skip going to Mass when we live somewhere else?"

But it turned out that Evergreen was a positive place for them. Briana took piano lessons from Wayne Wold and one night there was a big piano recital and dinner in the mess hall. That was a special memory. She and six other camp children received First Communion at the chapel, with a party afterward in Laurel. Bob Reuning's daughter Hannah also received First Communion at Evergreen. "We picked the date of Jenna's wedding [for Hannah's First Communion] because we knew the Bushes wouldn't be at camp that day," Reuning said.

One of Briana's favorite moments was singing a solo in front of the Bushes one Sunday. Both girls sang in the children's choir, and in a sweet way, that's how Ryanne bonded with President Bush 43. Sometimes during a sermon, the president would play a winking game with Ryanne—first he'd wink at her, then she'd wink back at him.

John Heckmann's daughters also sang in the choir. They practiced on Thursday evenings while the adults played dominoes. Like my family, the Heckmanns attended both services on Sunday.

The children's choir is a favorite feature at Evergreen; the singing is so lovely that guests of one CO asked if they'd brought a professional choir to the camp to sing for the president.

CO McLean found church service very stressful, as any parent with an infant and a toddler can appreciate. "The question was *when*, not *if*, my son and daughter would be disruptive and I'd have to put them in the nursery," he said. One day during the sermon, little Callum burst out into loud laughter. McLean grimaced with embarrassment—until he looked over and saw that President Bush was playing peekaboo with his son. The chaplain, realizing that he'd lost his audience, wrapped up the sermon quickly. McLean reflected that it was another example of the president, who bore the weight of the world, reaching out for a moment of levity. It was one of Bush's greatest, and perhaps most underrated, gifts.

Chapter Nine

GUESTHOUSE TO THE WORLD

I like the gaiety of Camp David.
—Soviet leader Leonid Brezhnev to President Nixon

TRICIA NIXON ONCE said of Camp David, "It's like a resort hotel where you're the only guest." However, Camp David has hosted a rotating cast of world leaders since its inception. Not only does the invitation to Camp David confer a certain prestige, but a president knows that his counterparts appreciate the chance to get away from the hot lights of scrutiny that follow them to meetings with the American president.

"Camp David is a far more intimate setting than the White House," wrote Laura Bush. "It is a place where you can get to know another leader without the crush of a roomful of a hundred or so invited guests....A visit to Camp David is more like a visit to someone's weekend place. And it cements a different friendship than simply having a fancy event amid gleaming silver and glittering chandeliers."

Nearly every president since Roosevelt has brought world

leaders to camp for high-level sleepovers or even just lunch meetings. Some of these are friendly, others chilly, but all allow fascinating personal views.

Camp David, as we've seen, has a way of imposing its mood on the people who visit. Whether playing horseshoes or driving golf carts, these usually sober leaders let down their guard for a moment, and the result is a revealing glimpse behind the curtain. This is clearly apparent at high-level summits, but it also exists during one-on-one meetings. The underlying purpose of inviting a foreign leader to Camp David is always diplomacy, but an invitation to Camp David is more significant than an invitation to the White House, which is why it is not extended that often. In the scheme of things, except for large summits, relatively few foreign leaders have had the opportunity to visit the presidential retreat, and they don't often get much coverage because the press is held at bay. For example, while Khrushchev received a lot of attention when Eisenhower took him to Camp David in 1959, less note was given to two important visitors with related concerns—Harold Macmillan in March 1959 and Charles de Gaulle in April 1960. Macmillan, who was at the camp to talk to President Eisenhower about the Soviets and Berlin, nonetheless was given a little downtime. No doubt the two men reminisced about their time in the war, after which they watched what Macmillan later described as "inconceivably banal" movies from Eisenhower's list of Western favorites. (These were the same movies Khrushchev would eagerly ask for during his visit a few months later.)

In his book *Silent Missions*, Lieutenant General Vernon Walters described the sixty-nine-year-old Charles de Gaulle's "aura of aloofness and mystery that he felt was absolutely necessary for greatness." Yet at Camp David, in the company of Eisenhower, de

Gaulle softened. The two men took a side trip to Eisenhower's farm in nearby Gettysburg, where they strolled through the Civil War battlefield, and later on they hunkered down at Camp David and discussed how to end the Cold War. During his final days in office, Eisenhower was increasingly focused on that goal. On Sunday morning they drove down the mountain to attend church at the Trinity United Church of Christ in Thurmont.

More than a year after being elected president of France, de Gaulle was critical of both the Soviet Union and the United States, so the discussions were blunt. But the two men, who had been sparring since World War II, understood each other.

The opportunity for personal diplomacy is one of the hallmarks of Camp David, and that diplomacy was most actively pursued with the Soviet Union and then Russia. Eisenhower's charm offensive with Khrushchev was one for the history books, but it didn't crack the shell of resistance. In the coming decades, Camp David would play host to several Soviet and then Russian leaders, although the freeze hardened after Khrushchev's visit and stayed that way for a long time. Johnson tried to get Khrushchev's successor, Alexei Kosygin, to Camp David in 1967, but the Soviet Union leader declined. He did, however, invite Johnson to Moscow, and the president accepted, only to cancel the trip after the Soviets invaded Czechoslovakia. The freeze continued. It wasn't until June 1973 that another Soviet leader, Leonid Brezhnev, accepted a U.S. president's invitation; Nixon invited Brezhnev to a weeklong summit in the White House and then a visit to Camp David after the meetings. Unbeknownst to the Soviet leader, Nixon taped their conversations, which were unusually friendly and mild. At one point Nixon commented on Brezhnev's cigarette box, which had a special timer that allowed him to retrieve a cigarette only at intervals. "That's a way to discipline yourself," Nixon said admiringly.

When Nixon asked Brezhnev if he'd like to go to Camp David, he replied, "Anything you suggest, I'm happy to go along with. I like the gaiety of Camp David"—although *gaiety* was an odd word choice in reference to Camp David. He probably meant the chance for relaxed discussion and a break from closed-door meetings.

"Diplomacy is not always an easy art," Nixon wrote of the occasion in his memoir, and Brezhnev's visit to Camp David was literally a bumpy ride. Trying to court the Soviet leader, Nixon presented him with a gift—a dark blue 1973 Lincoln Continental that had been donated by the Ford Motor Company. Brezhnev was delighted. He immediately suggested they try out the vehicle. As Nixon recounted, "He got behind the wheel and motioned me into the passenger seat. The head of my Secret Service detail went pale as I climbed in and we took off down one of the narrow roads that run around the perimeter of Camp David.... At one point there is a very steep slope with a sign at the top reading, 'Slow, dangerous curve'... Brezhnev was driving more than 50 miles an hour as we approached the slope. I reached over and said, 'Slow down, slow down,' but he paid no attention." At the bottom, brakes squealing, Brezhnev made the turn, and Nixon, hanging on for dear life, said, "You are an excellent driver. I would never have been able to make that turn at the speed at which we were traveling." One can easily imagine the scene—a nervous, even terrified Nixon, frantic Secret Service men, and a gleeful Brezhnev. When the car finally arrived safely at the bottom of the hill, Nixon was relieved, but he also might have glimpsed a reckless side of the man he was trying to charm. Indeed, at a summit in Washington the previous year, Nixon had been caught off guard by Brezhnev's style, when he shifted so easily from good humor to rage — like Dr. Jekyll and Mr. Hyde, Nixon thought.

A tape released by the Richard Nixon Presidential Library in 2013 shows that the two men got along well at Camp David and perhaps shared their grievances over being misunderstood. In April Nixon had fired Haldeman and Ehrlichman, and the Watergate threat was pressing in on his presidency. In one memorable exchange between the two leaders, Brezhnev expressed his disdain for the critics who tried to thwart the efforts of strong leaders like himself and Nixon. He said, "Now, there are some people who keep throwing in this idea of there being two superpowers in the world who are out to dictate their, as they say, dictate their will, to foist their will upon others, and so forth. Now, but, are we to blame for being big? Are we to blame for being strong? What can we do about it? That is the way it is. I mean, what do these people want us to do . . . turn ourselves into some kind of Guinea, or a country like that?" But in spite of their common view of their critics, the president and Mr. Brezhnev did not reach the détente Nixon was seeking.

Achieving a breakthrough in relations with the Soviet Union became one of the central endeavors of the Reagan presidency, but he never brought Mikhail Gorbachev to Camp David, although the two men had several summits after Gorbachev became general secretary in 1985. Nevertheless, the Soviets were much on Reagan's mind at Camp David, especially during a visit by British prime minister Margaret Thatcher. The visit was Thatcher's idea. After Reagan won reelection in 1984, Thatcher wrote that she was planning to be in Peking in December, and if the president was going to be in California, she'd like to visit him on the way home. He responded that he'd be at Camp David, and she asked if she could visit him there.

Normally Reagan didn't like to entertain world leaders at the camp, seeing it more as a private retreat for himself and Nancy, but Thatcher was considered a close friend — almost like family — so he invited her to lunch at the camp on December 22.

Thatcher's advisers suggested she dress casually, as was fitting for the camp, but when Reagan met her at the landing zone in his golf cart, she was wearing her typical tweed suit. She got in beside the informally dressed president, and they took off for Aspen. As they passed Cedar, Reagan saw CO Rispoli's kids playing in the driveway; he leaned over to point them out to Thatcher, and he almost smashed into a tree. Fortunately for all concerned, he corrected course, and they continued on their way.

Finally, having safely arrived at Aspen, the two leaders had lunch and their important conversation about the SDI — Star Wars — mentioned earlier.

"He was at his most idealistic," Thatcher wrote in her memoir. "He stressed that SDI would be a defensive system and that it was not his intention to obtain for the United States a unilateral advantage. . . . He reaffirmed his long term goal of getting rid of nuclear weapons entirely." By the time he left office, Reagan had made some headway on that vision, but things were about to change once again.

In 1990, soon after Gorbachev became president of the Soviet Union — the first to hold this position — President Bush invited him to Camp David. The visit of Mikhail and Raisa Gorbachev was a huge event for the camp crew. CO Berry hosted several setup visits by the White House advance team, the USSR advance team, the KGB, the USSR communications team, the press advance team, and the White House chefs.

All the regular phones were taken out of the cabins and the Soviets installed their own. While the camp phones were high-tech and encrypted, the Soviet phones looked like holdovers from the 1950s — big, black, rotary-dial contraptions. The camp transport garage was cleared for Soviet communications, and when they started broadcasting to Moscow, they jacked the power so high that it interfered with the American communications. "We were hearing Russian," Berry said. "We had to ask them to tone it down."

The original plan was for Bush and Gorbachev to arrive in separate helicopters, but Gorbachev refused to fly in a U.S. helicopter unless the president was with him. This caused a change in protocol, as the president would usually be at camp first to greet his guest at the landing zone. Berry remembered the dramatic arrival ceremony, with both presidents coming down the steps of the helicopter, all smiles.

Each side had a full complement of officials — thirteen for the Soviets and fifteen for the Americans, including Vice President Quayle, Governor Sununu, Secretary Baker, Secretary Cheney, and General Colin Powell.

As the president and Gorbachev headed to the golf cart, Bush asked, "Do you want to drive?" Gorbachev motioned Bush to go ahead. They climbed in and Bush announced, "Here we go!" and they headed to Birch, where the Gorbachevs would be staying. Mrs. Bush and Mrs. Gorbachev got into a separate golf cart, with Mrs. Bush driving. Later the two women took a stroll around the grounds, the First Lady in her signature pearls and wearing sneakers.

President Bush was always a gracious host who put other leaders at ease, Berry observed, and the same was true of Gorbachev. They toured the camp, their ties off and relaxed. When they came to the horseshoe pit, one of Bush's favorite spots, Gorbachev said he'd never played the game, so Bush asked him if he'd like to. The

Soviet leader got a ringer on his first shot, impressing everyone, including himself. Bush had the horseshoe mounted by a camp Seabee and then presented it to Gorbachev at dinner that night. Raisa Gorbachev also played horseshoes with Barbara Bush.

At the end of the visit, Bush gave the Gorbachevs personalized Camp David jackets with their names embroidered on the front. The press was at camp to witness the departure, and they saw the golf cart approaching with Gorbachev at the wheel and both men laughing and joking.

Few could guess during that visit that the Soviet Union was in its final death throes. On Christmas Day of 1991, the Soviet Union collapsed, and less than a month later, the new Russian president, Boris Yeltsin, was at Camp David with President Bush. Yeltsin was accompanied by his wife, Naina.

The press was allowed in to witness the arrival. CO Joe Camp remembered the big crowd of security and translators. Bush and Yeltsin jumped into a golf cart, the cameras flashing, and sped off. Camp noticed that Mrs. Bush and Mrs. Yeltsin were left standing there with no ride. Horrified, he quickly brought his cart around and took them to Aspen.

Barbara Bush and Naina Yeltsin would become friends during that visit. The First Lady was impressed by Naina's warmth. When the Bushes' daughter Doro walked into Aspen and gave Mrs. Yeltsin a big hug, no one thought it odd. "Mrs. Yeltsin is that kind of person; you want to hug her," Barbara Bush wrote.

After their meeting, the two leaders proclaimed a new era of friendship and partnership, and for a time it seemed as if the age-old conflicts had finally ended. But in the coming years, as Russian leaders, old and new, jockeyed for power and prominence, the relationship went through many difficulties. President Clinton attempted to form a close relationship with Yeltsin but was often sidetracked by Yeltsin's unpredictable nature.

President Bush 43 thought he could work with Vladimir Putin, the president who had replaced Yeltsin in 2000. One of Bush's fondest goals was to achieve a reset with the Russians, something that had eluded every president before him. With so much to divide the two countries, he hoped that they could find common ground. After their first meeting in Slovenia in June 2001, Bush had said, "I looked the man in the eye. I found him to be very straightforward and trustworthy. We had a very good dialogue. I was able to get a sense of his soul; a man deeply committed to his country and the best interests of his country." When Putin expressed support after 9/11, it looked as if the two men were on solid footing.

In spite of Putin's opposition to the war in Iraq, Bush invited him to Camp David in September 2003. Bush hoped that the spirit of Camp David would have a positive effect on the Russian president.

President Bush was at the camp to meet Putin when he arrived in a convoy of two helicopters accompanied by a large entourage. A caravan of fifteen golf carts made its way to the residence. Soon after, CO Bob McLean received a call from the steward. President Putin had forgotten his bedroom slippers. One of the crew was sent to Walmart to purchase a new pair.

At a press availability, Bush welcomed "my friend" Vladimir Putin and said, "For decades, when the leaders of our two countries met, they talked mainly of missiles and warheads, because the only common ground we shared was the desire to avoid catastrophic conflict. In recent years, the United States and Russia have made great progress in building a new relationship. Today, our relationship is broad and it is strong." But in spite of its auspicious start, Bush's reset never took hold.

Later Bush would describe a telling clue to Putin's style. Relating how the Russian president sniffed derisively on meeting Barney and later introduced Bush to his *real* dog, a Russian Labrador, Bush said, "I learned a lot about Putin then. 'My dog is bigger than your dog.'"

Having foreign dignitaries at camp is always stressful, but not every guest is involved in high-risk diplomacy. Nixon made it a practice to send foreign dignitaries to Camp David before or after meeting them in the White House. In February 1970 Camp David hosted French president Georges Pompidou for a visit prior to a meeting at the White House. Nixon wasn't at camp and President Pompidou and his wife, Claude, stayed at Aspen. A formal dinner was planned at Aspen for the evening of their arrival. CO Dettbarn was thrilled when he and his wife, Gloria, were invited. The White House sent a culinary crew to prepare and serve the dinner, and there would be fourteen people seated.

This created an immediate challenge for Dettbarn, since Aspen did not have a large enough dining table to accommodate that many people. So the Seabees took two existing tables, pushed them together, and put a one-inch-thick piece of plywood on each table to cover the split and provide a stable surface. On top of that, they placed the appropriate pads and a tablecloth.

A Department of State official sitting at one end of the table was a large and gruff guy who tended to put his elbows on the table and pound it during a fun and exciting dinner. Dettbarn, seated at the midpoint where the two pieces of plywood met, felt the pieces shifting every time the official banged the table. Dettbarn fearfully imagined the calamity of the table tipping over and shattering the fancy White House china and crystal. He spent most of the dinner with a steadying hand on the connection point; fortunately, the makeshift table survived the meal.

After dinner there was a movie—or part of one. Pompidou had been watching the newly released movie *Patton* on the plane, and he wanted to finish viewing it. Drinks and cigars were passed around, and despite Madame Pompidou's insistence that she and her husband should go to bed, the last reel of *Patton* was started. She left the room.

About fifteen minutes later, Madame Pompidou reappeared in the living room in a housecoat with her hair in curlers. She lightly scolded her husband for watching the movie and said he had to come to bed, as there was an early meeting at the White House the following morning. Pompidou reluctantly got up and shuffled down the hallway; the movie was stopped and everyone left, leaving Dettbarn to reflect that most homes weren't all that different from one another.

As noted, foreign dignitaries didn't visit much during Reagan's presidency, but in 1981 he hosted Mexican president José López Portillo for an elaborate barbecue behind Aspen that would feature country-western singer Janie Fricke. The day before the barbecue, Nancy Reagan summoned CO Bill Waters to Aspen. Deer on the compound had eaten the flowers on the patio. Nancy told him, "I want the area festooned with flowers"—introducing Waters to a new word. The crew scrambled to find replacements, and on the day of the barbecue everything looked beautiful—and festooned.

The barbecue was a huge event, with a Who's Who of Washington invited. Waters remembered walking down the road with the chief justice of the Supreme Court, the vice president, congressmen, and members of the cabinet "like we were buddies." Reagan clearly felt very warmly toward Portillo, and in a toast at the pool that evening he promised a continued friendship with America's good neighbors.

During George W. Bush's presidency, British prime minister Tony Blair and his wife, Cherie, visited Camp David several times, the first time in February 2001, shortly after Bush's inauguration and during my term as CO. We planned an elaborate visit that included bringing twenty-four members of the press to camp to cover the Blairs' arrival. There would be two additional press events that day. We positioned the press on the grass in front of the flagpole. The Bushes arrived first and an hour later the Blairs landed in a helicopter dubbed State One. We provided the typical military cordon—ten Marines, ten Sailors, and a six-member color guard. The hatch popped open and for the first time, the Bushes met the Blairs. The Bushes escorted them to Birch.

Before the weekend Mrs. Bush had been a little bit nervous about meeting Cherie Blair. As she recalled in her memoir, she knew how close the Clintons and the Blairs had been, and the British press had been scathing in advance of the visit. One typical headline read "Frosty Forecast as Our Modern Mum Meets Bush's Little Woman." The characterization stung. But the two women hit it off over a private lunch at Aspen—"Rather like two busy mothers catching up over coffee," Mrs. Bush wrote. Indeed, the relationship between the two couples would become the closest of Bush's presidency.

One humorous, although embarrassing at the time, incident for me was the departure ceremony for the Blairs. The departure would again include an honor guard with the two national flags and our Sailors and Marines in full dress uniform forming the cordon down the walkway to the helicopter. About thirty minutes prior to the scheduled departure—and President Bush was *always* on time — I heard chatter over the radio that the president and prime minister were already at the landing zone. "Oh, crap, you've got to be kidding me!" I yelled at Michele, as she was standing next to me in Cedar. Fortunately, I was already dressed. I flew out the side door, jumped in my golf cart, and peeled out of the driveway to the landing zone.

Arriving there, trying to be cool but not dismissive, I quickly noticed that the two world leaders and Mrs. Bush were standing together, chatting and in a good mood, but Mrs. Blair was not present. Thank God. The president actually chuckled when he saw the concern on my face, and said, "Don't worry, Mike, Cherie's not here yet." Turns out she was shopping in Shangri-La, and she arrived a few minutes later. Departure went off very well, the Bushes were pleased with their first head-of-state guest visit to camp, and the crew went back to the normal business of the weekend.

Another part of effective leadership is learning from your mistakes and adjusting fire. While the nearly delayed departure ceremony with the Blairs ended up being a light moment, we certainly didn't want to run the risk of disappointing our president. Thus was born the Thirty-Minute Bush Rule. From then on, the crew and I would be ready and in place thirty minutes prior to every arrival, departure, meeting, meal, and event.

Blair's third camp visit, in March 2003, was a sober meeting to discuss the progress of the war. A press conference was planned in the hangar. When Blair came off the helicopter, he asked CO O'Connor, "Do you have anyone on your staff who can press trousers?"

"Of course," O'Connor replied. He found a crewman who knew how to iron and sent him to Birch with an iron and an ironing board. He knocked on the door and Blair opened it and welcomed him in. While the crewman set up his board, Blair took off his pants right there and then sat in a chair in his boxer shorts, chatting while his pants were ironed.

President Bush's second head-of-state visitor to Camp David was Prime Minister Junichiro Koizumi of Japan on June 30, 2001. I think that, as he did with Blair, Bush wanted to reach across the ocean and invite the newly elected prime minister and one of our key allies. Once again, it was fascinating to watch from the sidelines.

We welcomed the president's guest with an honor guard, and we were thirty minutes early for arrival and departure! President and Mrs. Bush attended, dressed casually, as had been scripted between the delegations, and former senator Howard Baker, now the ambassador to Japan, was also present; he and the president greeted the prime minister coming off the helicopter.

The one-day visit focused on economic ties, trade, the environment, and baseball! At the press conference afterward, the president and prime minister playfully tossed a baseball back and forth.

Both leaders remembered the day in very positive tones. Prime Minister Koizumi said, "I would be able to give my frank views [to President Bush] and . . . to speak from the bottom of my heart." Similarly, President Bush said that he admired Koizumi's frankness and noted that he was a "courageous leader" who took the challenge "not to avoid but to lead."

My leadership takeaway from watching President Bush engage Prime Minister Blair and Prime Minister Koizumi was quite simple: build relationships before you need them.

Some of the most colorful visitors during Bush 43's time were

Sheikh Mohammed bin Zayed, the crown prince of Abu Dhabi, and, in a separate visit, Sheikh Mohammed bin Rashid, vice president of the United Arab Emirates, both of whom were accompanied by entourages. In each case, the guests bought out the Shangri-La gift shop, and they left some gifts too. At the end of one visit, they left two large suitcases at the command office full of special-edition watches — one hundred of them — to show their thanks to the crew. What to do? CO Reuning researched the matter and learned that the watches had to be appraised by the GSA, and if anyone wanted to purchase a watch, he or she could do so at the assessed value. "My watch was appraised at twenty-seven hundred dollars," Reuning said. "I took a picture of it."

In March 2015, Secretary of State John Kerry hosted Afghan president Ashraf Ghani for a "strategic dialogue" at Camp David, capping meetings at the White House with President Obama. A large advance team arrived the night before to do reconnaissance for the visit. As always, there was a lot of hard work going on behind the scenes. CO Rang told the crew that the goal was for everything to go smoothly and for the guests to have the "camp experience."

There were a couple of close calls in setting up for the visit. The supply officer lighting a fire at Holly, where the meeting would take place, forgot to open the flue and practically burned the cabin down. The smoky air smelled terrible, so the crew gathered a bunch of scented candles and lit them. "Now Holly smelled like a burned candle," Rang said. Better, but not ideal.

And then there was the snow. A few weeks before the visit, there had been a big snowstorm, and the temperatures had remained cold, so the snow hung around. This worried Rang because old snow gets dirty, and the place looked terrible. Just as he was seriously contemplating a radical solution to restore the winter white—spray paint, perhaps—the temperatures rose and the snow melted. One more crisis averted.

THE HIDDEN NATURE of Camp David makes it an ideal location for high-level planning outside the view of the press and the public. In August 1990, during the buildup to the Gulf War, which was tightly under wraps, President Bush brought General Colin Powell, General Norman Schwarzkopf, and key military and civilian advisers to Camp David. CO Berry did not know the meeting's full purpose—no one did, including, it seemed, some of the principals.

Berry met Colin Powell's helicopter and saw that the general was struggling to carry a large covered chart. Berry instinctively reached out to help him. Powell quickly pulled back, giving Berry a warning look that said, *Don't you dare touch that.*

On that day, after the full briefings in the Laurel conference room, the senior political leadership asked the military to leave so they could confer privately. Bush walked Schwarzkopf outside and asked Berry to take the general on a tour of the camp. As Berry drove Schwarzkopf around, the general, in a somber mood, sighed. "Here I go to CENTCOM for my twilight tour, and now all hell breaks loose," he said. A twilight assignment is traditional for a person nearing the end of his or her career, something quiet and low pressure. That was certainly not to be for the general.

Before the start of Operation Desert Storm, which launched with an invasion of strategic targets in Iraq on January 17, 1991, everything was top secret. Some of Bush's own people didn't know the plan. Seeking to throw everyone off the scent, Bush scheduled a normal visit to Camp David. Berry's only hint that something was afoot was a call from the president's personal secretary asking him to have Marine One ready in case the president needed to get back to Washington quickly. Bush did everything he could not to raise suspicions or alarms — secrecy essential for the success of the mission. "It was good OPSEC," said Berry. Once the bombing started, Bush left Camp David for the White House. As the helicopter rose up above the trees, the president might have felt a sense of regret that he was leaving a place of such peace to become a wartime president.

Chapter Ten

DOWN THE MOUNTAIN

May all those who enter as guests leave as friends.
—Sign at the Thurmont Super 8

O NE OF THE certainties of an assignment at Camp David is that you'll drive up and down the mountain literally hundreds of times during your tour. Especially if you have kids, which all of the commanders I spoke with did. It's a strange juxtaposition between the elevated seclusion of Camp David and the small-town Americana that greets you in Thurmont. Camp David doesn't have an actual address, and the name it's officially listed under, Naval Support Facility Thurmont, also doesn't have an address because it's Camp David. If you're confused, you're not the only one. When we first arrived and registered Briana in school, Michele gave Naval Support Facility Thurmont as our address, only to receive a call from the principal, who could find no such location. *"Where* do you live?" she asked a bit suspiciously.

The town itself, however, is very real. I wasn't familiar with Thurmont before I came to Camp David, but it would become a touchstone of ordinary life while we were at camp. It's where we had a post office box for mail delivery. It's where my daughters went to school. It's where the military housing was. It's where Michele brought the girls to play with their friends in military housing. And it's where we shopped at the local Food Lion, got gas at Sheetz, and could have an ordinary dinner out at the Mountain Gate Family Restaurant or get fried chicken at the Cozy Restaurant. And like most people who have served at Camp David, I became very comfortable at the Super 8 in Thurmont. It's the humble lodging where I stayed before my first visit and interview in 1998 and where my extended family stayed during my change-of-command ceremony. The night before, we gathered to eat at Jennifer's Restaurant in nearby Frederick, known for hearty meals—pasta, steak, and burgers. Jennifer Dougherty, the proprietor, was elected Frederick's first female mayor in 2001. At dinner we made toasts and offered our thanks. Michele spoke of my career, my dreams of command, and read a poem from her mom on success. It meant a lot to me. Everyone felt completely at ease down the mountain—and a little nervous though excited about what awaited us above.

And so, in a book about Camp David, I wanted to step aside and credit this place that is *not* Camp David for the role it plays in the life of the camp.

Mike Berry's wife, Dee, kept a diary while Berry was CO. A notable feature in it is the dizzying descriptions of her many trips up and down the mountain. Not only was she the mother of two teenagers, but she also took a part-time job as a fifth-grade language arts teacher in the Frederick County School District. Back and forth she went, dropping off the kids and picking them up from sports, gymnastics, playdates, and jobs, not to mention going grocery shopping at the Food Lion and visiting the library. A trip up or down the mountain can take twenty minutes, depending on the weather, and that's not including the process of getting in and out of the gate, so you don't want to be in a position of realizing you forgot to buy milk on your return. But working and living at Camp David means becoming an honorary citizen of Thurmont and the surrounding towns.

In many ways Thurmont is the foundation of all that goes on above. Yet with the exception of those who live in military housing, few people there will ever see inside Camp David. They might raise their eyes to the sky at the sound of helicopters or stop and watch when a motorcade turns up Park Central Road to enter Catoctin Mountain Park, but otherwise, the inhabitants go about their lives with barely a passing thought for Camp David — unless there's a big summit, when the commotion can be a bit tough to miss.

Over breakfast at the Mountain Gate, the locals mostly stick to discussing neighborly gossip, town government, and goings-on at the senior center, the Thurmont Lions Club, and the farmers' market. The annual Colorfest, a big fall event, has been a highlight of the year since 1963. There's an abundance of local activity, as in most American towns.

Just as Camp David is not a luxury resort, Thurmont does not try to be an elegant vacation destination. It wears its history and proximity to greatness casually; walking around town, you'll see little overt evidence of the role it plays in what goes on up the mountain. Yet Thurmont is a destination of its own. Just twenty-one miles from Gettysburg, it is part of a historic corridor named by the Federal Highway Administration the Catoctin Mountain Scenic Byway. Sleepy in winter, it springs to life in the summer as a popular destination for campers, hikers, fishermen, history buffs, and antique hunters. There is much history to be found here, including the historic Catoctin Furnace, in which slaves and

European immigrants made bombshells during the Revolutionary War and which also supplied the area with iron products—an early example of American industry. Until the twentieth century, Catoctin Furnace was a company town, with iron-ore pits, houses, slave quarters, an Episcopal church, a school, and a company store. Today it is a tourist site maintained by the Catoctin Furnace Historical Society. There's the original structure, Isabelle, the second furnace, and buildings from the early village. Visitors might be able to sample old-time johnnycakes along with their history lesson.

Thurmont, which celebrated its 265th anniversary in 2016, was called Mechanicstown when it was originally incorporated in the early 1700s. In addition to iron ore, there were many industries, especially after the Western Maryland Railway came through. One example of an inventive spirit was Jacob Weller, a blacksmith, who created the first strike matchsticks, originally called lucifers, in the early 1800s. (His home and workshop, called the Old Match House, is still standing.) Weller never believed his invention was worth patenting, so he didn't make the fortune that was surely his due. But he earned a place in history.

The railroad opened the area to a thriving tourist population, as people sought to escape the hot, humid cities for the cool mountain air. But as the local historian George Wireman told the story, the name Mechanicstown became confusing with the arrival of the railroad. As Wireman explained, up the road from Mechanicstown was Mechanicsville, and then Mechanicsburg, and unless you were listening closely when the train conductor called out your stop, you might be left stranded in the wrong town—a pretty serious problem in the 1800s. In 1894, the town fathers decided to change the name. There were two finalists: Blue Mountain City and Thurmont. The townsmen voted for Blue Mountain

City, but the choice was rejected by the U.S. Post Office as too cumbersome, so Thurmont it was. Thurmont, a combination of German and French root words, meant "gateway to the mountains." The name change was made official on January 18, 1894, by the Maryland legislature.

To this day, the town of Thurmont proudly bears the moniker Gateway to the Mountains. But the second choice got some credit in a 2014 documentary called *Almost Blue Mountain City: The History of Thurmont, Maryland.* The film, produced by Chris Haugh, traced the town's roots from the early German settlers, and it features colorful interviews with longtime Thurmont residents, including George Wireman. Until his death in 2012 at ninety-one, Wireman was the epitome of a local sage, his wiry energetic posture defying age. He was a fixture in Thurmont, and he wrote a book called *Gateway to the Mountains,* which is alive with the history of Thurmont. In *Gateway* he takes readers inside an essential American story where patriotism, industry, determination, and faith fueled a revolution and then a humble prosperity. "*Gateway to the Mountains* is a true story of achievement and invention as well as a story of marked progress by the many citizens who helped to build this historic little community, nestled in the foothills of the beautiful Catoctin Mountains of Western Maryland," he wrote in the introduction.

Sadly, Wireman didn't live to see the finished film. Other residents were featured as well. One, an elder named Louise Rover, reminisced about the days when Jackie Kennedy came down to Thurmont if she needed something at the drugstore. "Of course," Rover said, laughing, "she wouldn't have been interested in a dress shop."

Jackie Kennedy helped bring one piece of Thurmont history to the White House, something Wireman described in colorful detail in the film and also in his book. It had to do with scenic wallpaper. In 1961, during the first year of the Kennedy administration, Gertrude Rowser Stoner, the widow of the former mayor William Stoner and part of a prominent Thurmont family, decided to sell the family home, which dated back to 1838. It was set to be razed, and as the demolition began, a Washington, DC, antique dealer named Peter Hill visited the house and was struck by the unique and stunning wallpaper from France, called Scenic America, that had hung in the hallway for a hundred and twenty-five years. The panoramic wallpaper was printed from multiple woodblocks and featured scenes of Boston Harbor, West Point, Niagara Falls, and other classic American settings. Hill purchased the wallpaper for fifty dollars. The question was how to remove it in the three days before the house came down. Hill brought a putty knife, a razor blade, and a sprayer filled with water and went to work. He removed the paper slowly and carefully, strip by strip. Then he took the paper to a friend of his at the Smithsonian and found out it was a very rare pattern. His friend, who knew of Mrs. Kennedy's restoration plans for the White House, sent Hill to the White House curator, who showed it to the First Lady. She loved it and envisioned it providing a dramatic backdrop in the Diplomatic Reception Room. The National Society of Interior Designers purchased the paper from Hill for $12,500 and presented it to the White House as a gift. Today, guests at state dinners can look at this beautiful piece of art, which dominates the room.

Until it closed in 2015, the Cozy Inn, which was opened in 1929 by Thurmont native Wilbur Freeze, was the most significant point of connection between the town and Camp David. It began as a three-cabin lodging for those passing through and was the original housing for the Secret Service who protected President Roosevelt while he was at Shangri-La. In 1933 Freeze added a lunch counter and then a dining room. (The Cozy Restaurant closed in 2014, a year before the inn.)

The presidential retreat put Cozy on the map, as it began to play host to impressive dignitaries — not only Winston Churchill, as previously mentioned, but European royalty, presidential aides, cabinet members, and famous reporters.

After Wilbur Freeze died, in 1961, his son Jerry took over and began expanding the site, promoting its history and connection with Camp David. In 1967 a rustic waterwheel and covered bridge were added to the outside grounds. A beautiful mural by artist Andrew Charles Colley interpreted the colorful history of the Cozy, depicting characters from the Freeze family and the presidents going off to vacation at Camp David. At its peak, the Cozy Inn had seventeen rooms and five cottages, some featuring fireplaces and hot tubs and some named in honor of the presidents, with reproduction furniture and artifacts. The Roosevelt Room included hangings purchased from the Roosevelt Museum in Hyde Park. The Eisenhower Room was decorated in Mamie's favorite colors, pink and green. The Kennedy Room contained a canopy bed, a reproduction of JFK's rocker, and a bidet — a French item Jackie Kennedy introduced to America. The Johnson Room was in a western style, with a large spindle bed similar to the bed at Johnson's ranch. The Nixon Room contained artifacts from the Richard Nixon Presidential Library. The Carter Room had a Georgian theme. The Reagan Cottage, which had a western theme but some luxurious accoutrements, was one of the most popular.

The Cozy Restaurant, where my family and I dined on occasion, had seating for two hundred and fifty people — a far cry from the original lunch counter. A huge bearskin rug on the wall was the centerpiece. The bear was said to have been shot by Herbert

Hoover on a hunting trip to Alaska and given as a gift to Wilbur Freeze.

Wireman wrote that millions of people had dined at the Cozy Restaurant over the decades, eating jumbo crab cakes, fried chicken, and a full menu of comfort food, including homemade root beer. On a busy day, the restaurant might serve as many as eight hundred diners. "Through the years Cozy Restaurant has retained its homey relaxed atmosphere, quite untouched by any desire for splurge or grandeur," Wireman wrote.

In 2005 the Freeze family introduced the Camp David Museum in the Cozy Village complex. It was open during restaurant hours and featured Freeze's large collection of pictures and memorabilia, along with a gift shop. Jerry Freeze and his father before him had collected these items from a long list of dignitaries, reporters, presidential staff, and other visitors, making the museum a one-of-a-kind trip down memory lane of the presidential retreat.

Cozy was also distinguished as a press hangout, since it was nearly impossible for reporters to get close to Camp David. Camp David has always had an uneasy if not dismissive attitude toward the press. According to the late Helen Thomas, who was a regular at Cozy, as she staked out Camp David for many years while the First Family was at the camp, "Wire service reporters assigned the 'body watch' were escorted to a duck blind. It was a three-sided, wooden affair that had two telephones, and we spent many hours in all kinds of weather just watching and waiting for helicopters from Washington to land. Will someone please remind me how glamorous my job is?"

Thurmont became a central gathering spot and respite for the press, especially when big events were happening up the mountain. During the Camp David Accords in 1978, townspeople rubbed elbows with the likes of Walter Cronkite, David Brinkley, Barbara Walters, Sam Donaldson, and Helen Thomas.

Joe Reynolds, a well-known angler who claimed Hunting Creek as one of his favorite fishing locales, recalled heading there one day during the peace talks to find a CBS news team filming a segment with Walter Cronkite. "It was 'Lights, camera, action' right out there in the woods," he marveled.

Daily briefings for the Camp David Accords were held at the American Legion Hall in Thurmont. Every morning reporters drove up from Washington and settled in for a vigil. On the last day, they waited eagerly for news of a signing, expecting to be ferried to Camp David or a nearby location where they could witness history being made. Late in the afternoon the word came: the signing was on, and it was to take place in ninety minutes at the White House. At that moment the principals were preparing to helicopter out of Camp David.

"Everyone made a mad dash to their cars," wrote reporter Thea Rosenbaum. "We got out of that little town as fast as we could. On the highway we hit speeds of 90 miles an hour so we could report on the signing in the East Room."

Because of the town's proximity to history, Thurmont's citizens felt a certain closeness to the brokers of Middle East peace. After the assassination of Anwar Sadat, Robert Kinniard of Kinniard Memorials took a stone from Hunting Creek, carved it into a smooth rectangle with lettering referencing Camp David, and sent it to Egypt.

For those Camp David residents and guests who are in danger of getting swelled heads from being so close to the power of the presidency, Thurmont offers a solid counterbalance. With Cozy gone, the Super 8 remains the main hotel in town. This is where potential commanders being vetted up the mountain will park their bags, where visiting families will stay during change-of-command weekends, where overflow guests will find themselves when the cabins at the camp are filled, where presidential aides will bunk down for the night, where members of the press will register while chasing a story. Like many before them, they'll find themselves sitting down to a hearty country meal at the Mountain Gate, their thoughts straying up the mountain but their feet firmly planted in a real American town.

Chapter Eleven

CHANGING OF THE GUARD

Remember, change is our friend.
—CO Joe Camp to the Camp David crew

THE PRESIDENCY IS a transient job. As the saying goes, you're a tenant, not an owner. You come into office with years ahead of you to accomplish your goals. But in what seems like the blink of an eye, it's over, and you're passing the torch to the next leader.

The same is true, albeit on a much smaller scale, for those who serve at Camp David. Unlike the civilian support staff at the White House, a military crew runs Camp David, and members rotate in and out on a regular basis. Military personnel are accustomed to change. In fact, we welcome it because it's how we grow in our careers. But that doesn't mean that saying good-bye doesn't tug at our heartstrings.

And so, when I became CO at Camp David, I knew that in two years my term would be over and I'd be off to another assignment. The end came faster than I expected, and I've often thought about the lasting impact those two short years had on me and my family.

The speed of coming and going can be dizzying. CO Reuning marveled that one minute he was at Camp David, and two weeks later he was riding the Metro to the Navy Yard in Washington, DC. We all feel that shock of change, especially since Camp David is so special. Even when we're ready to go, a part of us wants to linger.

Leaving is like closing a book in the middle of the story. Since our terms don't coincide with the presidents', we don't get the clean break that administrations experience. We're left to look on from the outside to see how "our" presidents are doing—and when we're lucky, we get to see them again. Michele, the girls, and I saw the Bushes twice after we left camp, the first time in Hawaii, when we were invited to the reviewing line at Hickam Air Force Base as they were returning from an overseas trip. Similar to Bob Reuning's stark reality, we were at one moment on the flight line with the Bushes, catching up on things and posing for a family photo, and twenty minutes later we were in the food court on base ordering chicken nuggets for the kids. The second meeting was more memorable, and serious. On August 30, 2005, Bush came to Coronado to give a speech at Naval Air Station North Island commemorating the sixtieth anniversary of victory over Japan. Michele and I met the Bushes behind the stage for a brief chat and photo after his speech. The first thing they asked us, true to form, was "Where are the girls?" But after the pleasantries, the discussion turned more serious. The day before, Hurricane Katrina had hit the Gulf Coast, and Bush was extremely worried. He told me, "Mike, it was devastating, and the death and damage is significant."

In his remarks at the ceremony, Bush said, "This morning our hearts and prayers are with our fellow citizens along the Gulf Coast who have suffered so much from Hurricane Katrina." Later, looking at the photo we took with him, I was struck by how the presidency had aged him since our time at Camp David—before 9/11, the launch of the war in Iraq, and now Hurricane Katrina.

The Bushes were extremely thoughtful in remembering former commanders. After we left Camp David and while they were in office, we always received a Christmas card. The year they left the White House, Laura Bush sent us lithographed copies of all the new paintings and drawings she had placed in the cabins at Camp David. The cabin Red Oak had a picture of a red oak tree and birds. The lithographs came from the White House in a nice bound envelope.

After leaving camp, Mike Berry felt privileged to attend, along with other officers in his wardroom, the commissioning of the aircraft carrier USS *Ronald Reagan* in 2003 and the commissioning of the aircraft carrier USS *George H. W. Bush* in 2009. When Barbara Bush saw them at the latter event, she exclaimed, "Look, George, it's the guys from Camp David!" Their chaplain Jon Frusti, who was with them, told the president that they wanted to challenge him and his family to another wallyball game. President Bush was limping and using a cane after some surgery, but he looked at them and said, "We'd beat the socks off of you!" Still as competitive as always.

So, as much as Camp David is about the experience, it is an encounter with the bittersweet reality of endings. From the sidelines, the crews share the ups and downs of presidential comings and goings. When a president doesn't win reelection or chooses not to seek a second term, there's an especially poignant mood around the camp. CO Joe Camp remembered how downcast people were when President Bush 41 was defeated by Bill Clinton. The Bushes were much loved, and it was hard for some people to accept that they'd be leaving. However, the Bushes maintained a very positive attitude right to the end, although they couldn't help feeling sentimental. In her memoir, Barbara Bush described their last weekend at the camp as "very touching — and very hard." CO Camp organized a surprise farewell ceremony at the hangar that drew five hundred crew members and their families. He detoured the Bushes there on their way to the helicopter, and when they entered and saw the huge cheering crowd, they lost it. Camp gave a speech thanking the president and First Lady for all they'd done and how much they'd meant to the camp. When it was time for the president to say a few words, he was very emotional and choked up as he told the crew, "We Bushes have never considered you as troops. You are family... friends."

Aware of how sad the crew was, Camp told them, "We're going to have a new commander in chief. Remember, change is our friend. We embrace change."

A similar mood undoubtedly accompanied Lyndon Johnson's final days at the camp. According to Lady Bird Johnson, their last visit, on October 24, 1968, was "a gray and cheerless autumn day." But she added that the flight in had been beautiful, and "we looked down on the Catoctin Mountains — a magnificent show of gold and bronze and green, and every now and then the scarlet of maples." That was her final memory of the camp. Weeks later Richard Nixon would be elected president.

It would be a sad end for the Fords as well. Less than four years into his abbreviated administration, Ford was already out the door, having lost the election to Jimmy Carter. In *The President Is at Camp David*, W. Dale Nelson recounted Ford's final moments at Camp David: "The Fords made one more visit on January 15. The record for that final weekend closes with a telling vignette. As he waited for the last helicopter ride back to Washington, the thirty-eighth president of the United States stood in an empty field house near the helipad, practicing his golf swing."

Jimmy Carter's one term came to an end not only amid disappointment but also while he was immersed in the drama of the final days of the Iran hostage crisis. He never stopped pushing for their release, right up to the last second. Still working the phones, the president and Mrs. Carter nevertheless flew to Camp David on his last weekend in office. "I was torn about going," Rosalynn Carter wrote. "I had loved it so and anticipated great difficulty in going through the weekend, knowing that never again would we enjoy the solitude, the beauty, the relief, it had given us for four years. But this was not to be just like any other weekend." Carter was on the phone constantly, conferring with the State Department and the situation room. And by Sunday, the news was good—the hostages would be released. As they boarded the helicopter to return to Washington, the Carters were elated. "Instead of leaving for the last time with sadness, we left with happiness and the highest hopes," Mrs. Carter wrote. On the helicopter, the president leaned over and kissed her. Although it was disappointing that the hostages weren't officially released until moments after Reagan took the oath of office, nothing could take away from the Carters' satisfaction.

On rare occasions, through death (Roosevelt and Kennedy) or resignation (Nixon), presidencies end very suddenly, and this is as traumatic for the crews that serve them as it is for the rest of the nation. I've been told that the camp crews throughout the Nixon presidency were very fond of the First Family, and they must have felt rattled at the end, especially since Nixon's visits to the camp were more frequent during his final year. On the weekend before his resignation—before anyone, possibly even the president himself, knew he was resigning—Nixon came to the camp accompanied by Mrs. Nixon, Tricia and Ed Cox, Julie and David Eisenhower, and the president's close friend Bebe Rebozo. Four years later, in his memoir *RN,* Nixon described the mood as those gathered experienced "the history and tragedy that lay behind our weekend together in this setting." The Fords, when they arrived, went out of their way to establish good relationships, but it was a tough transition.

When a president leaves office after eight years, the ending can feel dramatic for the nation, yet even more so for Camp David. During that time the camp will have been through several commanders and turnovers of Navy crew. Even so, hitting the eight-year mark is a bittersweet time for the presidential family, especially those who have loved Camp David. The Reagans, with their record-setting attendance at the camp, had an emotional farewell the weekend before Bush's inauguration. A large gathering in the hangar included the Navy and Marine crew, as well as personnel from the communication agency, WHMO, and Catoctin Mountain Park. It was at this gathering that President Reagan dubbed the camp "the good ship Camp David," and said, "Of all the things about the presidency, we will miss Camp David the most." Fighting tears, Mrs. Reagan was unable to speak.

Bob Reuning remembered a similarly emotional farewell on George and Laura Bush's last day at camp. But not surprisingly, there was one twist completely unique to Bush. He insisted on doing a challenging bike ride the morning of departure. Surveying the terrain, Reuning was concerned. The weather had been very cold and the trails were icy to varying degrees. They'd had to cancel a ride the previous day. But Bush wouldn't be deterred. He wanted that ride. Slipping and sliding, they took off, Reuning holding the rear in case there was a problem with any of the riders. There were a number of spills, though not by the president. As the ground thawed it became muddy, so Reuning finished the ride covered in mud. Bush was happy although it was possibly his last ride ever at Camp David.

Reuning raced to Cedar to clean up and change into his dress uniform for the chapel service and farewell ceremony. These were very emotional; the president kept looking around, as if to capture the scene in his memory. What Reuning remembered most was the final walk to Marine One. Before Bush boarded, he gave Reuning a big bear hug and said, "You're a good man, Bob." Reuning replied, "God bless you, sir. We'll miss you." He was crying as he shook Mrs. Bush's hand and repeated that they'd miss her. "The boss went up the steps, turned to me, and saluted. I saluted him back, but he was already gone. I saluted again and held it until he sat, and then I began my walk. As the helicopter lifted, we started to wave. I could see them waving through the window. I gave the president a thumbs-up and I thought I saw one in return."

One of the great gifts of Camp David is the complete absence of politics. As citizens, we all have our political preferences, but as military in service of the president, we put those views aside. The party ceases to matter. It's the president of the United States who earns and deserves our respect—and he gets it. But nearing the end of a president's second term, when we know for sure there's going to be a change, we're eager to see who our new boss will be. This got a little bit complicated at camp in 2000.

At the time we were allowed to use Laurel for wardroom events when the president wasn't there, so Michele and I hosted an election-night party for the officers and their wives. We asked all the guests to bring a special dish from their home states. In addition to our dish, Michele made a red Jell-O mold in the shape of the United States with each state outlined. We had the TV on so we could watch the returns, and as each state was called for Bush or Gore, we'd slice that state off the "map," and someone would eat it. When Florida was called, it was cut off and eaten. And when it was *uncalled*, things got very messy. Most of the officers and spouses stayed well past midnight, but by around three in the morning, it was just Michele and me and the XO and his wife, John and Lisa Coronado. When it finally dawned on us that we weren't going to know who our new president would be for some time, we quickly cleaned up the remaining items, straightened out the pillows, turned the television and lights off, and departed Laurel. It would be weeks before the election was settled in George Bush's favor, and we went ahead with our usual planning without knowing that key detail. (In 2016, Michele sent her Jell-O mold to the camp commander for their election-night event.)

The final days of Clinton's administration were a busy time for the camp. The Clintons visited camp for New Year's and I had asked Mrs. Clinton if we could meet to discuss their final visit, and she suggested we spend a few minutes talking in Laurel after the service that Sunday. She was Senator-Elect Clinton now, having won her senate seat in New York, and I congratulated her. The president joined us, to my surprise, and we sat at the small table in the living room. We spent a few minutes talking about my next assignment, in Hawaii, and they said Hawaii was their favorite place—very relaxing and peaceful.

They told me that their last visit would be the weekend of January 12. They were very pleased with the idea of having a farewell ceremony in the hangar just before they flew away for the last time. And then, as we finished our meeting and stood up, they kept talking—one of those moments of not letting go. They expressed once again their pleasure with the Christmas decorations and how happy they were with the renovations we'd done at Aspen, and then some world events were discussed. Chelsea walked in and said that she and Buddy would be there for the last weekend as well.

Weeks before the final visit, President Clinton and WHMO held a farewell ceremony for the chief of staff John Podesta, and each WHMO commander was invited to offer a few words and present a gift symbolic of his unit. I headed to the gift shop in Shangri-La for mine. It was a favorite place for members of the government as well as outside guests. One of the most desired items is the Camp David bathrobe, available in white or blue terry cloth with the impressive presidential seal on the left breast pocket. I purchased a white bathrobe.

When it was my turn at the ceremony, I went onstage, said a few words, and presented Podesta with the bathrobe. People in the crowd shouted, "Try it on!" so I helped Podesta put on the bathrobe over his nice dark suit. When he took it off, his now not-so-dark suit was covered in white lint. Either he didn't really notice or he decided to be gracious. He smiled and said thank you, and back to my seat I went, cringing.

During a period of six days, many guests of the Clintons came to the camp—the cabins were always full. Large groups of White House staff members also came for a tour—their last chance. We were definitely the most popular destination that week.

The Clintons arrived in the evening on January 12. Observers at the landing zone included many of the cabinet secretaries and crew families, including mine, and the Clintons were greeted with cheers. Clinton walked the line to shake hands, and he reached out and gave Michele a big hug. That night Phoebe Snow performed in Evergreen.

The Clintons returned to Washington early the next day, Saturday, to do some packing, but we had a full plate at the camp. It was Capitol Hill Day, and we entertained many members of

Congress and their families. We had a heck of a time keeping people from taking photos. At one point, I had to stop a woman from photographing the president's office in Laurel. This occurred as I was giving a tour to the guests, something that our seasoned petty officers do on more typical weekends. We were so pushed that all hands on deck reported for duty. The CO was no exception. In my group were Senator Patrick Leahy, his wife, Marcelle, and Senator Jon Corzine.

That evening the Clintons returned, and they invited us to dinner at Laurel, where they would be entertaining some of the congressional guests. When we arrived, we were impressed by the way the crew had transformed the Laurel conference room into a dining room with twelve round tables. The room was packed. Before we ate, I had a nice conversation with Senator Max Cleland, a highly decorated Vietnam War veteran and a triple-amputee. He was as excited as a kid to be there. I heard him call someone on his cell phone and exclaim, "I'm at Camp David!" He was incredibly gracious and appreciative, and I thought to myself, *What a great attitude.* There's no way I could ever have a bad day in this assignment. Michele and I got in line at the buffet and then squeezed into our seats at the Leahys' table. It was good to recognize a few more familiar faces from the tour earlier that day. President Clinton spoke and told some jokes, his charisma on full display, and the mood in the room was very festive. After dinner we returned to the chapel, where Don Henley gave a six-song acoustic performance.

Sunday dawned, the final day of farewell for the Clintons. After a chapel service, we had a nice event in front of the altar where we made remarks and gave gifts to the First Family. We presented them with a reproduction of the chapel bell on a piece of flagstone. Michele and Ginger Williams, our chaplain's wife, gave Chelsea the photo of her dad talking to children that had hung in the chapel annex for almost eight years. Wayne Wold, the choir director, gave the president his choir folder and a copy of the last song he'd sung signed by all the choir members. I gave them a framed picture of the First Family in front of the USS *Endicott* bell. The president and First Lady each made warm remarks, and we all felt emotional.

That evening, over three hundred people gathered for the final ceremony in the hangar. It was an upbeat occasion, and the Clintons—including Buddy—mingled with the crowd and then stood for pictures with the crew. I opened with brief remarks, introduced Mel Poole, the Catoctin Mountain Park superintendent, and then President Clinton and Senator-Elect Clinton spoke. Chelsea and Buddy sat patiently on the stage to one side and took it all in. Later that evening, we assembled at the landing zone to see the Clintons off for the last time. (That's when Chelsea gave me the stuffed animals for our girls.)

"And so they were gone," I wrote in my journal. "I must admit, I felt an empty feeling of sorts, but I was also very anxious, excited and curious how our new 'neighbor' would be in *his* presidential retreat."

Seven months later, it was *my* turn to leave. Because the Bushes visited so often in that short period, we felt close to them and were anticipating our final good-bye. The Bushes were scheduled to visit camp one last time on my watch in late July, but, very untrue to form, they had to cancel the visit. I was disappointed that we wouldn't see them at the camp again. But one day I was in my office and received a call from Ashley Estes, the president's secretary, who said, "Please hold for the president."

President Bush greeted me very warmly, *apologized* for canceling the visit the previous weekend, and then invited my family to the Oval Office to say good-bye. It was a very gracious invitation. Michele, Briana, Ryanne, and I drove down to the White House and were ushered into the Oval Office. The president treated us like honored guests, spending thirty minutes showing us around the office and the Rose Garden, and he really focused on talking to the girls about his surroundings. He then wrote a few personal lines to each of my daughters, and we took a few family photos, which we later received with a handwritten note from the president. It was, needless to say, the high point of our farewell activities.

Mike O'Connor and his family were also invited to the White House for a farewell with Bush 43. The president said to eight-year-old Julia, "How'd you like to sit in my chair?" She came around and sat, dwarfed behind the large Resolute desk. He told her it was the first time he'd ever let anyone sit in his chair.

Mike Berry, who had served three years instead of the normal two, was ready when it was time to go. However, he'd be staying in town. Because his new post was in Washington, he and Dee decided to keep their daughter, Kristi, in high school in Thurmont; Ken had graduated the year before. They bought a house in Frederick and Berry planned to commute to work. "My commute took me three-plus hours a day," he said. "But that's what dads do."

When his replacement, Joe Camp, reported two weeks before the change-of-command, Berry was very busy showing him the ropes, remembering well his own take on things three years earlier, when he was a newbie — "like trying to take a drink out of a fire hose." There are so many people, agencies, staffs, and departments involved with Camp David and they're all interconnected in many ways, and all focus on the commander. It's no wonder a new commander can initially feel overwhelmed.

Meanwhile, he and Dee tried to have as many people over for

dinner as possible so they could thank them for all the support. They often said that what they'd miss most about Camp David was the great people they'd worked with — a sentiment shared by other commanders.

The day before Berry's change-of-command, President Bush 41 asked Berry and his wife to come down to the Oval Office, along with both sets of parents, and he surprised Berry with an award ceremony. It was overwhelming and humbling at the same time, but, Berry noted, it was so typical of President Bush to go the extra mile for someone on his staff. That night they were all invited back to the White House East Room as presidential guests for a performance of *Forever Plaid.*

It was perfect weather for the change-of-command ceremony the next day. When Joe Camp said, "I relieve you," and Berry responded, "I stand relieved," he said it felt as if a ten-ton load had been lifted off his shoulders.

But there's no question that leaving can be very emotional. "The last time Bush was at church before we left, we felt pride and sadness," Bob McLean said. "Change is constant, but you're sad about every place you leave. My wife, who is very strong, held it together, but when we drove out of camp she started crying. Leaving something so special was hard, especially knowing you may never come back. We had a feeling that life was never going to be the same."

Bob Reuning admitted that the end was not nearly as fun as the beginning change-of-command. "The most unique and memorable experience of my life was over," he said. "But I knew it was coming and did my best to savor every remaining moment in camp. I wiped a grain of sand out of my eye when we drove off for the last time."

"The end came up quickly," said Russ Rang, echoing other

commanders. One day, shortly before he left, he was walking to the game room with his daughter Anna, and she said—with little-girl logic—"Dad, the slower you walk, the faster you get there." He asked her what she meant, and she repeated it: "The slower you walk, the faster you get there." He knew one thing: the end came fast, no matter how much they tried to slow it down. On the last day, his older daughter, Lila, threw her arms around a tree and wouldn't let go. "I had to drag her off," he said. "We got in the car and drove out the gate for the last time, handing in our badges. I thought, *I don't work here anymore.*"

August 9, 2001, was my change-of-command date, time for me to depart and turn over the camp operation to CO Mike O'Connor. This is the reality of command in the military; one day you're the new kid on the block, and the next day you're packing your bags. We accept this, but sometimes it's not easy, and Camp David was no exception.

It was a beautiful fall day on the mountain and everything was set for the momentous occasion. Most of our family members were there. Naval Academy classmates, other Navy friends, and new friends were also there to share in our special day of turning over command after a successful time in charge.

There were several unique things about the ceremony. One was that I brought Briana and Ryanne and then Michele up on the stage, to recognize and thank them for their support during an incredible time. I gave them gifts—for Michele a diamond pendant necklace, and for the girls, Camp David teddy bears.

The second thing was my farewell speech, which was my last opportunity to recognize the crew and say thank you. I read a letter to the Sailors and Marines that I had served alongside for the past two years and thanked them for their incredible service, for their endless commitment, and for their kindness and friendship to me and my family. It was honest, heartfelt, and real. Michele later told me, "There wasn't a dry eye in the house."

After I concluded my remarks, Mike and I saluted, faced the WHMO director, and saluted again. Mike made his remarks, we were piped ashore, and the ceremony ended. Just like that, I was no longer the CO. It was time to cut a cake, toast the crew at the reception, and enjoy the company of family and friends. During the next few days we finished packing up for our move from Cedar, Camp David, Thurmont, Maryland.

At the end of it all, the one thing that I could assure Mike O'Connor of was that the president would not be visiting that night. And for me, my hat size hadn't changed.

LEAVING CAMP DAVID was much different from every other pack-out in my Navy career. The small truck with shipping boxes was parked in the Cedar driveway; it received its contents and went to the warehouse down the hill. We were moving to Hawaii, not a bad consolation prize for having to turn over command and relocate from the mountaintop after an extraordinary two years.

As I was shuttling in and out of the house, checking box numbers and watching everything, one of my favorite Tom Petty songs, "Learning to Fly," came on the radio. The poignant song captured my mood; once again I was adventuring out, feeling as if I had no wings, knowing I would learn to fly, yet still concerned about the landing.

I didn't know it then, but looking back on it from a sixteen-year vantage point, I saw how many leadership lessons and experiences came from this one tour. While I learn from every assignment, the assignment to Camp David was the most bountiful. How do you talk to a president and his family members? How do you deal with the handlers, those around the president who sometimes have separate agendas? How do you greet a head of state? How do you try to be perfect but not micromanage? How do you make the routinely mundane seem utterly exciting? How do you balance family with work, especially in this very unusual duty? How do you keep your humility? And, how do you let go when your time is over?

Finally, the last items were packed and the last crate nailed shut and banded. Security labels were fixed and I signed each one. We had already taken our car to the Port of Baltimore to be shipped, so we wouldn't be driving out of camp in the family car. A van with a driver arrived at Cedar to pick us up. We looked around one more time, feeling sentimental, and climbed in. Somehow, being driven out of camp added an even greater feeling of finality. We were no longer in control; we no longer had the freedom to go just anywhere. Our time was over. We were being escorted off the premises. We approached the gate and sentry, where we turned in our badges — the last time I would use badge no. 1.

There weren't tears, but there was quiet in the van and, for me, a feeling of deep thanks and appreciation for this incredible honor of serving at Camp David mixed with a deep void of *How can I possibly top this?* Riding down the mountain, the lush summer forest blooming around us, and the picnickers looking out from their ordinary summer pursuits, we found ourselves gradually returning to the world outside. By the time we reached Thurmont, we had been unavoidably swept away by the winds of our next adventure.

Chapter Twelve

THE TRUE MEANING OF CAMP DAVID

Camp David is a national treasure.
—CO Russ Rang

FROM THE MOMENT the president of the United States enters the Oval Office each morning, people are clamoring for his attention. Even the most serene and focused human being cannot escape the cacophony of need that is his daily fare, parceled out in meetings, briefings, ceremonies, phone conferences, debates, crises, papers to sign, problems to solve. The days fold into each other in a seamless drumbeat of cares and woes. As Lyndon Johnson once said, "The presidency has made every man who occupied it, no matter how small, bigger than he was, and no matter how big, not big enough for its demands."

Every president faces joys and burdens that are unique yet all too familiar to his predecessors—and each of them relishes the moments when the sense of history outweighs the burdens; they savor the victories when they come because they are so easily upended. In spite of the overwhelming effort of being president, you rarely hear any of them talk about being exhausted, yet it's observable in the heaviness of their shoulders, the pouches under their eyes, the graying at their temples.

But there are some days, perhaps on a Friday afternoon, when the president strides across the South Lawn, a little lighter in his step, boards Marine One, and lifts off, leaving the noise behind. Rising in a deliberate sweep above the city with its cluttered highways and dense neighborhoods, the helicopter heads north into a quieter landscape of small towns, two-lane roads, and mountain parks; half an hour later it comes down through the trees and gently lands in a different world.

Ronald Reagan expressed it well: "As president, the days I hated most were those of nonstop meetings, one after another, with no time in between to collect my thoughts.... The days I liked best were those Fridays when I could break away a little early, about three or three thirty, and take off for Camp David."

Throughout Camp David's seventy-five-year history, people have been trying to identify what it is about this White House in the woods that makes it so special and necessary to the presidency. It's not just a getaway, although it is that. It's not just a change of scenery, although it's that too. But other vacation spots have such advantages. It's not the luxury — although the president has the most professional crew anywhere at his service. It's not just the privacy, although it remains the only location a president can be assured that he will hear no protests. "There are resorts with more luxury," Mike Berry observed. "But none as *exclusive*."

Over the past seventy-five years, thirteen presidents have made Camp David their own. In this book, with the firsthand accounts of the commanders who served there, I've been able to offer an unprecedented inside view of the presidents at Camp

David. The question of why the retreat is necessary can best be answered by analyzing what it ultimately meant to those thirteen men. Each president has put his own stamp on Camp David — and it on them.

For Franklin Roosevelt, it was a landlocked ship necessitated by wartime that nevertheless brought him a rare opportunity for repose. On his screened patio, the documents of war stacked around him, he could ease back and contemplate the world he was making. He named it Shangri-La, but it was more grounded than mystical.

Harry Truman was known to dislike Camp David and used it rarely because his wife called it dull — a verdict that survived the decades and even made it into an episode of *The West Wing:* when President Bartlet was asked why he didn't want to go to Camp David, he replied, "Bess Truman found it dull." In fact, Truman was the only president of the thirteen who never took to Camp David, preferring Key West — a miscalculation, I think, as Camp David might have helped him during his embattled final years when the stress of working with a recalcitrant Congress embittered him.

For Dwight Eisenhower, it was a place he cared about enough to name it after his grandson and to which he brought his greatest adversary, Nikita Khrushchev. Some might wonder why he bothered going at all, since his Gettysburg farm was only twenty-one miles up the road. But the camp's namesake, David Eisenhower, a young boy then, remembered it as an idyllic site where he went on hikes in the woods and played by the pool while "Granddad, an excellent cook, would spend the afternoon in the Aspen kitchen, preparing the steaks for a cookout. After dinner, the grandchildren staged skits and sang songs on the porch behind the presidential cabin, then were packed off while the grown-ups watched movies." This homespun quality appealed to the Eisenhowers, especially the president, who found it restorative.

For John Kennedy, it was a bright place to enjoy time with his family. CO Howe's lasting memory of him was when he was laughing and kidding, released momentarily from the physical pains that plagued him, soothed by the heated pool. In particular, for the glamorous young family, there was the sweet privacy—as Pierre Salinger wrote, "You could be sure that no photographers were hiding in the trees." Everyone observed that Kennedy was lighter, more relaxed at Camp David, where he'd sleep late, take walks, and watch movies after dinner—a schedule not unlike an average American's weekend.

In the beginning for Lyndon Johnson, Camp David was just another place to work. People reported that he was like a bull in a china shop in the quaint, wooded setting. And yet as we've seen, the camp exposed a tender side—like his taking the CO's daughters for ice cream. As his aide Jack Valenti put it, "There's something about Camp David that makes you feel softer." This was an experience Johnson needed, and Lady Bird, for one, welcomed the effect it had on her often surly husband.

Richard Nixon shaped Camp David to his needs, and the camp reflected his moods. In the early years he luxuriated in the camp, modernizing it and building a spectacular pool (pictured on the cover of this book). But in his final years, beleaguered by Vietnam and Watergate, he sought solace and solitude there. He understood that the camp gave him something he could not get anywhere else. At a Thanksgiving Day meal in the crew galley in 1972, he told those gathered, "Of the places you could be stationed, Camp David, I am sure, must seem to be rather tiring and boring at times. I have been to most places in the world, and we have had many heads of state here—Churchill, de Gaulle, Adenauer, and the rest. They think this is a great place. I hope you do, too." He could have been speaking about Camp David when he said at the end, "Only when you have been in the deepest valley can you ever know how magnificent it is to be on the highest mountain."

Only two and a half years in office, Gerald Ford barely had time to get his sea legs, and soon after he became president, Betty Ford was diagnosed with breast cancer and underwent a mastectomy. A month after surgery, she came to Camp David with her husband and was met warmly by the staff at Aspen, who hugged and kissed her. She called Camp David the best thing about the White House. There the Fords, with their teenage children, could briefly be the family they were before the shock of Ford's becoming president, an office he wasn't expecting to assume.

For Jimmy Carter, it was the site of his greatest achievement, the Camp David Accords, but the agreement between Israel and Egypt might never have happened had Carter not recognized the spiritual and emotional impact of the setting. Camp David was the everyman's rest spot, as Stephen Hess of the Brookings Institution and a former aide to Eisenhower told Carter at the beginning of his presidency. "A president should be able to walk in the woods on a weekend if it helps him restore his spirit or rethink his concerns," Hess advised. Carter gambled that the camp would work its magic on Sadat and Begin.

For Ronald Reagan, Camp David was where he could be a husband and person on his own terms. From the moment the Reagans came off Marine One, he in jeans, Nancy in a velour tracksuit, it was their time. "If it weren't for Camp David, I would have gone stir crazy," Reagan said when he left office. It was, CO Berry said, "a place where the Reagans could be themselves"—a rare gift.

For George H. W. Bush, it was a family retreat—kids, dogs, and sports—but nevertheless a certain discipline prevailed. He and Barbara normally worked during mornings at the camp—she at Aspen and he at Laurel—before engaging in their favorite recreations. The many photos of Bush at play at Camp David mask the fact that he made some of the most serious decisions of his presidency there, including, as we have seen, the decision to go to war. Camp David provided an atmosphere that helped him make the tough choices. His reliance on Evergreen Chapel was evidence of that.

Restless by nature and craving company, Bill Clinton took some time appreciating Camp David, but he found ways to make it fit his personality. He invited lots of guests whom he could regale with his stories, but I also saw him gain an intimacy with the Marines and Sailors who were stationed there. Clinton was a man who enjoyed an audience, and Camp David provided him just that.

George W. Bush shared the family love of Camp David, and he used it vigorously, to say the least. But it was when he was at Camp David that the nation had an opportunity to see his thoughtful, spiritual side. It's no accident that he retreated to the camp after 9/11 to find the guidance and the words with which he could comfort and motivate the nation. Later, with the nation at war, Bush spent long hours during the holidays on the phone speaking to the troops overseas.

Barack Obama could sometimes seem inscrutable in the White House. At Camp David he let his hair down, and he invited many others to do the same. Obama came closest to making it "the people's camp." He felt it important to give his White House staff the Camp David experience. CO Autry recalled a cabinet retreat that included all of the cabinet and their staffs—more than

eighty-five people. Everyone met in the chapel and sat there looking around, wide-eyed. Autry saw how much it meant to them to
grab hold of a piece of history. As he neared the end of his second
term, Obama sent groups of White House staffers up so they
could have the experience.

Asked about the importance of Camp David, Ken Khachi-
gian, who served as an aide to Nixon and Reagan, told the author
Kenneth T. Walsh, "It's where a president can be a human being
again. It's a place where he can be normal."

Reflecting on the same issue, John Heckmann said, "In my
mind, the value to any future president should remain the same as
it has been in the past. Camp David is needed as a personal getaway location and a high-level meeting venue (state visit, cabinet,
et cetera) for representing the country." The value of Camp David
as a getaway spot is obviously a personal preference for each president, but there are few places that the president can conveniently
go that is as secure and connected as being at the White House.
During the Bush administration, a state visit to Camp David was
a status symbol second only to the president's personal residence
at Crawford. A visit to Camp David was key in the role it played
in diplomatic relations.

Camp David should not be viewed as a high-end resort to
be used by anyone. It is more significant and important than this.
Its legacy as a place to resolve and deal with national and international issues needs to be honored, respected, treasured, and
continued well into the future.

As John Dettbarn observed, "Any tour at Camp David is an
absolute honor, but the importance of the place seems to elevate
the importance of the role each crew member plays in its history.
I feel as though my family and I, along with all other crew members, own a piece of Camp David, and we would be greatly

insulted if it were ever misused, dishonored, or not sustained properly for the critical role it plays in our nation's leadership and influence to the world. At a simpler level, our time at Camp David was special because of all the patriots (military, civilians, and family members) we got to know. We were bonded by the special role that we had in serving our nation in this prestigious way, but the joy in the memories we have is because of the friends we made there."

In some respects the meaning of Camp David — the *spirit* — exists more in mood than in substance. It can be found in a stroll along the paths on a fragrant spring afternoon; in the energy and laughter of a hard-fought basketball game or the crash of a perfect strike in the bowling alley; in the high wind that kicks up when Marine One's blades are spinning; in the easy hop-in, hop-off transport of a golf cart; in the sharp salute of a Marine greeting the president; in the woodsy smell of a cabin on a summer day; in the sight of a deer peeking through the brush; in the camaraderie around the bar at Shangri-La, where a big, frothy mug of beer can be had for two dollars; in the pure chorus of voices lifting in song and prayer at Evergreen Chapel; in the giggles of children as they run through the woods; in a bike ride along the trails, the Secret Service in tow; in the whir of a chopper coming through the trees at arrival; in the unabashed delight of foreign leaders wearing their signature camp jackets; in the contemplative moment when a president sits in Aspen in front of a roaring fire; in the salutes and handshakes and hugs; in the tearful faces of young troops bidding good-bye to a president they've served; in the icy breath of a Marine on patrol on a winter night; in the bark of a dog chasing its thousandth squirrel.

The spirit of Camp David can be found in the deep quiet of the nights, everyone tucked into his or her cabin — even the president of the United States can drift off in a safe and cozy berth, the weight briefly lifted.

When my successor, Mike O'Connor, came on board, I told him, "You're going to love this job." I meant it. And after he'd served, O'Connor absolutely agreed. It wasn't all hikes and wallyball for him. Soon after he took command, 9/11 rocked the nation—and Camp David. But by the time he left, two years later, he had come to fully appreciate the way Camp David wrapped around a president and his family like a blanket of comfort. "The president comes from a different world," he said. "He circulates on a level we can't fully understand. At Camp David, he can set some of that aside." He recalled walking by Aspen one morning and seeing Laura Bush outside in her robe. "Hey, Commander, how're you doing?" she called to him, smiling and without a hint of self-consciousness. And he replied, "I'm doing great, ma'am. Have a good day."

Many of the commanders who have served at Camp David told me that their adult children, once Cedar kids roaming around the camp or chafing at the security or singing in the chapel choir, still talk about the significance of the Camp David experience.

When I began as CO at Camp David, my daughters gave me a journal with this inscription:

> *Dear Daddy,*
> *We want you to write stories about Camp David and the President in this Journal. Someday our children will be able to read them. We love you.*
>
> > *Love,*
> > *Briana and Ryanne*

They were little girls who could not possibly have grasped the significance of what they were saying. I'm sure their mother had a hand in it. Yet today, as young adults, they think of the experience as one of the most important and memorable of their lives. As do Michele and I. We were happy there, in our home in the woods on top of a mountain. And that was our mission for the presidents we served — simply, that they be happy.

ACKNOWLEDGMENTS

I am full of gratitude to all the people who have supported me, inspired me, and pushed me to be more than I could ever have been on my own.

Michele—you made every house we lived in a home due to your incredible attention to the special touches of home life, the holidays, and always welcoming family and friends. And you held the fort during those times when my career separated us and you had the house and girls alone. Thank you for making Cedar our special home at Camp David and for willingly sharing it with others. Like your favored sunflowers, you brighten the home, our lives, and the world around you with your love and support.

Briana and Ryanne—you are extraordinary women and you are the greatest joys in your mom's and my life. When asked how our girls are doing, I always respond positively in the present, but I am really thinking about the future and how you will grace this world with your unique talents, compassion, and leadership. Serving in the Navy was an incredible opportunity and fulfilling lifestyle for me, but my greatest responsibility and passion in life is to be your dad and admire how you flourish.

My parents, Tony and Mary Lou—thank you, Mom and Dad, for the stable and humble lessons of life and for raising me to appreciate family and the simple things. Thank you also for supporting my naval career and all of my pursuits after retirement, especially this book.

My brother and sister, Philip and Lu Anne—thank you for "letting" me be the big brother, but as you know, no one is the oldest without wonderful, younger siblings such as you. Clemson Drive will always be home to me because of you.

My parents-in-law, Coach and Patricia—Coach, I will always miss our quiet mornings on your porch, looking at the woods over coffee and the paper. Pat, we lost you much too early and I know that you would have loved being with us in Cedar. A special thanks to you for teaching Michele the values of family, the kitchen, and the holidays.

And thank you to my and Michele's grandparents, aunts, uncles, cousins, nieces, nephews, and extended family, who continue to give us years of special memories.

Outside of my family and closest friends, the U.S. Navy is what I am most grateful for. My life went on a very fulfilling and atypical path when I entered the U.S. Naval Academy and I have been extremely fortunate every step along the way. I have always been fearful of what would've been if I had not taken the oath that very first time on July 6, 1977. Thank you to the class of 1981 and to Nineteenth Company, the greatest collection of caring and extraordinary friends that Michele and I have.

Thank you to the U.S. Navy's Civil Engineer Corps for giving me a rewarding and fulfilling career and for the opportunity to report for duty to Camp David.

Another institution that has had a significant impact on my career is Penn State University. I went to graduate school in Happy Valley through the Navy in 1986 yet didn't reconnect until after I retired in 2010. Special thanks to Melissa Doberstein, Mike

Erdman, Nichola Gutgold, Meg Handley, Trish Long, Maureen Macaleer, Rick Schuhman, Greg Scott, and Roxanne Shiels.

Thank you to Joe Angell, Tom Carter, Bruce Gebhardt, Bob Morro, Rick Roth, and Mark Stangl for being among my closest friends.

Thank you, Joe Caruso, for your courageous and inspiring life story and for the many years of mentoring and friendship.

Thank you, Michelle Bergquist, for your support and friendship and for introducing me to Lindi Stoler.

Thank you to Mary Bennett, Don and Mary Crumbley, Kathleen Khoury, Ray and Debbie Mello, Amanda Montgomery, and Elena Salsitz for your professional support and advice.

To our friends in Coronado, California, thank you for your friendship and support for the many years we were in and out of this special community with the Navy; we could not have done it without you. A special thanks to Doug and Arlene Chase, Rich and Chris Keyes, Craig and Nancy Swanson, and Marc and Kelly Wing for their tremendous support and encouragement.

I am grateful to all the people who made my time at Camp David so extraordinary. Thank you, crew of Camp David! The camp's incredible seventy-five-year history of service is inspiring and highlights the caliber of the people in uniform who serve our nation.

To President George W. Bush and First Lady Laura Bush, thank you for the genuine kindness and warmth that you extended to me, my family, and the entire crew every time you visited your mountain-top retreat, and thank you for the Christmas cards and opportunities to visit with you over the years since we departed Camp David. Thank you also for your kind words of support for this book.

To President Bill Clinton, Secretary Hillary Clinton, and

Chelsea Clinton, thank you for welcoming me and my family on that first visit of June 25, 1999, and thank you for the privilege of supporting you during your final years at Camp David.

Thank you, White House Military Office, for selecting me and then letting me and the crew do our job. Your support and guidance were always there, as it should be, yet you recognized the talent of the crew and let us shine. A special thank you to Danny (Diana) Donnelly for support, advice, and friendship.

I am also thankful to White House head usher Gary Walters and grounds superintendent Dale Haney, who were always supportive and gracious during my time at Camp David.

At Camp David, John and Lisa Coronado, Kevin and Ruth Timmons, and George and LaVerne Havash were extraordinary colleagues and friends and were part of the very important military triad. Thank you for your support and guidance.

Serving with the exceptional crew at Camp David was a blessing, as I shared in this book, and I offer my gratitude for the support, extraordinary service, and continued friendship of its senior leadership and their families: Brad and Julia Abelson, Frank and Darlene Cervasio, Don and Melinda Clay, Chad and Jessica Drake, Pat and Kelsey Garin, Cameron and Jill Geertsema, Glenn and Jill Hubbard, Eddie and Cathy Hughes, Tim and Laura Jett, Chris and Kathleen Kurgan, Curtis and Valerie Mason, Burt and Liz Owens, Chris Perry, John and Jill Rasmussen, Fred and Chris Szabados, Bill and Krerica Whitmire, Bob and Ginger Williams, and Heather Wishart.

To my fellow Camp David commanders: You get it, you've been there, and you understand. Thank you for your support on this book and for the tremendous time you spent on the interviews, storytelling, and sharing your happy, sad, and poignant memories. I am especially grateful for the input of my fellow commanders Chuck Howe, John Dettbarn, Bill Waters, Jim Rispoli, Jim Broaddus, Mike Berry, Joe Camp, Mike O'Connor, Bob McLean, John Heckmann, Bob Reuning, Keith Autry, Wendy Halsey, Russ Rang, and Jeff Deviney.

Behind the scenes, helping to make this book a reality, was a remarkable, supportive, and enthusiastic group of professionals. What an extraordinary team! It all began with Lindi Stoler, my book strategist, whom I met two years ago in San Diego. Thank you, Lindi, for your guidance and for connecting me with Steve Troha and Folio Literary Management.

Thank you, Steve, for taking me on and for helping me to develop the scope and potential of this story. Your patience with me is greatly appreciated.

Thank you, John Parsley of Little, Brown and Company, for seeing and believing in the wide appeal of this book and realizing that it would offer the reader a rare look inside the presidential retreat in Thurmont, Maryland. Thanks, too, to Pamela Marshall for continuing to shepherd the book to publication with the assistance of Gabriella Mongelli.

Remove any one of these people and this book might never have happened, but without a doubt, Catherine Whitney, you were the key! You were the perfect writer and I am so blessed and fortunate that we found each other and have worked so well together since our first meeting in Thurmont in December 2016. Thank you for your prolific genius, for your exceptional craft of writing, for teaching me so much about this process, and for your friendship.

The Camp David Commanders

Lieutenant T. E. Wynkoop, SC, U.S. Navy
August 5, 1958–September 12, 1961

Lieutenant Commander M. H. Breen, CEC, U.S. Navy
September 12, 1961–April 15, 1963

Lieutenant Commander Chuck M. Howe, CEC, U.S. Navy
April 15, 1963–August 13, 1965

Commander John Paul Jones Jr., CEC, U.S. Navy
August 13, 1965–July 12, 1967

Commander Jerry R. Dunn, CEC, U.S. Navy
July 12, 1967–August 7, 1969

Commander John L. Dettbarn, CEC, U.S. Navy
August 7, 1969–January 30, 1973

Lieutenant Commander D. B. Miller, CEC, U.S. Navy
January 30, 1973–August 22, 1975

Lieutenant Commander G. A. Zimmerman, CEC, U.S. Navy
August 22, 1975–August 3, 1977

Commander Ralph M. Cugowski, CEC, U.S. Navy
August 3, 1977–May 19, 1981

Commander William A. Waters, CEC, U.S. Navy
May 19, 1981–June 15, 1983

Commander James A. Rispoli, CEC, U.S. Navy
June 15, 1983–July 15, 1985

Commander James Broaddus, CEC, U.S. Navy
July 15, 1985–July 26, 1988

Commander Michael G. Berry, CEC, U.S. Navy
July 26, 1988–August 6, 1991

Commander Joseph D. Camp, CEC, U.S. Navy
August 6, 1991–February 8, 1994

Commander Richard E. Cellon, CEC, U.S. Navy
February 8, 1994–May 8, 1996

Commander Robert A. Ramsay, CEC, U.S. Navy
May 8, 1996–June 25, 1999

Commander Michael A. Giorgione, CEC, U.S. Navy
June 25, 1999–August 9, 2001

Commander Michael J. O'Connor, CEC, U.S. Navy
August 9, 2001–July 23, 2003

Commander Robert A. McLean III, CEC, U.S. Navy
July 23, 2003–July 13, 2005

Commander John V. Heckmann, CEC, U.S. Navy
July 13, 2005–May 31, 2007

Commander Charles R. Reuning Jr., CEC, U.S. Navy
May 31, 2007–August 13, 2009

Commander Keith E. Autry, CEC, U.S. Navy
August 13, 2009–June 24, 2011

Commander Wendy M. Halsey, CEC, U.S. Navy
June 24, 2011–June 21, 2013

Commander Russell C. Rang, CEC, U.S. Navy
June 21, 2013–June 19, 2015

Commander Jeffrey C. Deviney, CEC, U.S. Navy
June 19, 2015–present

NOTES

Introduction: Into the Woods

4   *Even David Eisenhower:* W. Dale Nelson, *The President Is at Camp David* (Syracuse, NY: Syracuse University Press, 1995).

5   *"But it's so* spooky": Author interview with former CO Chuck Howe, December 29, 2016.

5   *After FDR's death:* William M. Rigdon and James Derieux, *White House Sailor* (New York: Doubleday, 1962).

5–6 *"It's a mystical":* Author interview with former CO Mike O'Connor, December 29, 2016.

6   *"Without Camp David":* Ronald Reagan, *An American Life* (New York: Simon and Schuster, 1990).

6   *"sense of liberation":* Ibid.

7   *"I'm free":* Author interview with former CO Mike O'Connor.

7   *"When the president":* Ibid.

8   *"Look," Reagan said:* Nancy Reagan, *My Turn: The Memoirs of Nancy Reagan* (New York: Random House, 1989).

8   *Apples loved cigarettes:* Author interview with former CO John Dettbarn, January 3, 2017.

9   *"Anything can happen":* Author interview with former CO Keith Autry, January 19, 2017.

9   *"If I'd dropped":* Author interview with former CO Chuck Howe.

9   *"What color green?":* Author interview with the current Camp David historian and Navy chaplain, December 14, 2016.

10   *"I look out"*: Rigdon, *White House Sailor*.

11   *one other change*: Author interview with former CO John Dettbarn.

12   *"For me, one of"*: Nancy Reagan, *My Turn*.

12   *"Its interior is simple"*: George W. Bush, *Decision Points* (New York: Crown, 2010).

12   *"Commander, you've got to"*: Author interview with former CO Bill Waters, January 19, 2017.

16   *"When the president attends"*: Author interview with the current Camp David historian and Navy chaplain.

17   *"there are no tourists"*: Scott Benjamin, "Q&A: Laura Bush on Camp David," CBS, December 24, 2005.

17   *"To me, Camp David"*: Claudia Alta "Lady Bird" Johnson, *Lady Bird Johnson: A White House Diary* (New York: Holt, Rinehart and Winston, 1970).

Chapter One: The Good Ship Shangri-La

23   *The origin of the Catoctin Mountains site*: Joel D. Treese, "Hoover's Retreat: Rapidan Camp," White House Historical Association.

24   *An article in the* New York Times: Warren Weaver Jr., "The Camp That Was Hoover's," *New York Times*, August 14, 1987.

26   *"This is my"*: Conrad L. Wirth, *Parks, Politics, and the People* (Norman: University of Oklahoma Press, 1980).

27   *There was no wheelchair*: Ibid.

27   *During the construction*: William M. Rigdon and James Derieux, *White House Sailor* (New York: Doubleday, 1962).

29   *"Well, Admiral"*: Ibid.

30   *The Navy likes to*: Ibid.

31   *He liked to take*: Ibid.

31   *When there were guests*: Grace Tully, *F.D.R. My Boss* (Chicago: Peoples Book Club, 1949).

32   *Recalling a typical*: William D. Hassett, *Off the Record with FDR, 1942–1945* (Crows Nest, Australia: George Allen and Unwin, 1960).

32   *"To give you"*: George Wireman, *Gateway to the Mountains* (Hagerstown, MD: Hagerstown Bookbinding and Print Company, 1969).

33   *Winston Churchill had*: Rigdon, *White House Sailor*.

33   *"You know, one works"*: Doris Kearns Goodwin, *No Ordinary Time: Franklin and Eleanor Roosevelt: The Home Front in World War II* (New York: Simon and Schuster, 1994).

34   *"It's fun to be"*: Letter from FDR to Churchill on the occasion of Churchill's sixtieth birthday.

34   *Mrs. Truman had invited*: Rigdon, *White House Sailor*.

35   *"Petitioner states"*: Dwight D. Eisenhower Presidential Library.

36   *"I am glad"*: Rigdon, *White House Sailor*.

36   *"I don't plan"*: John F. Kennedy, press conference in the State Department auditorium, February 8, 1961.

37   *A few weeks into his presidency*: Claudia Alta "Lady Bird" Johnson, *Lady Bird Johnson: A White House Diary* (New York: Holt, Rinehart and Winston, 1970).

39   *"I see you've kept"*: Author's journal.

39   *One consistent feature*: Author interview with former CO Jim Broaddus, February 7, 2017.

43   *"He's an urban"*: Juliet Eilperin, "For President Obama, Camp David Often Ranks as the Venue of Last Resort," *Washington Post*, March 20, 2015.

43   *"G8 tends to"*: Obama statement explaining change of venue from Chicago to Camp David.

Chapter Two: Reporting for Duty

47   *"I was a reluctant"*: Author interview with former CO Bob McLean, January 18, 2017.

50   *"Booster!"*: Author interview with former CO Bob Reuning, January 6, 2017.

56   *"There must have been"*: Author's journal.

57   *"If the president speaks"*: Author interview with former CO Wendy Halsey, December 30, 2016.

58   What the hell: Author's journal.

58   *it had been fifty-two:* Author interview with former CO Chuck Howe, December 29, 2016.

61   *Mike — the toilet:* Author interview with former CO Mike Berry, February 9, 2017.

61   *Berry wasn't overly:* Ibid.

62   *"Didn't your predecessor":* Author interview with former CO Joe Camp, December 30, 2016.

62   *Dettbarn lost his:* Author interview with former CO John Dettbarn, January 3, 2017.

63   *"My steps, my ice":* Ibid.

63   *Kennedy liked the pool:* Author interview with former CO Chuck Howe.

64   *Heather Wishart was:* Author diary and account of Wishart.

66   *"The television isn't":* Author interview with former CO Chuck Howe.

66   *Rispoli, who is color-blind:* Author interview with former CO Jim Rispoli, January 18, 2017.

67   *CO Mike Berry was delighted:* Author interview with former CO Mike Berry.

69   *There's an addendum:* Author interview with former CO Bill Waters, January 19, 2017.

Chapter Three: Living There

71   *By the time Mike Berry:* Author interview with former CO Mike Berry, February 9, 2017.

73   *Joe Camp's two sons:* Author interview with former CO Joe Camp, December 30, 2016.

78   *My successor, Mike O'Connor:* Author interview with former CO Mike O'Connor, December 29, 2016.

78   *"It was like being":* Author interview with former CO Russ Rang, February 10, 2017.

79   *"I was just wondering":* Author interview with former CO Chuck Howe, December 29, 2016.

79   *"She talked to us":* Author interview with Hank Howe.

79   *"Can I stay":* Author interview with former CO Bob Reuning, January 6, 2017.

79   *Wendy Halsey's daughter:* Author interview with former CO Wendy Halsey, December 30, 2016.

80   *Hank Howe's friends:* Author interview with Hank Howe.

80   *"Do you live":* Author interview with former CO Wendy Halsey.

80   *as CO John Heckmann observed:* Author interview with former CO John Heckmann, February 10, 2017.

81   *"Julia knew how":* Author interview with former CO Mike O'Connor.

81   *"These kids are not":* Author interview with former CO Jim Rispoli, January 18, 2017.

82   *"I thought my life":* Author interview with Hank Howe.

82   *"Freeze! Freeze!":* Author interview with former CO Mike Berry.

82   *"Do you know where":* Ibid.

83   *Wendy Halsey's thirteen-year-old son:* Author interview with former CO Wendy Halsey.

84   *Jackie Kennedy made:* Author interview with former CO Chuck Howe.

85   *"Where are my":* Author interview with former CO Mike O'Connor.

85   *During the first month:* Ibid.

85   *"Do you want":* Author interview with former CO Wendy Halsey.

86   *"What's wrong":* Author interview with former CO Mike O'Connor.

86   *Lyndon Johnson was:* Author interview with former CO Chuck Howe.

86   *Pat Nixon loved:* Author interview with former CO John Dettbarn, January 3, 2017.

87   *One day while the Reagans:* Author interview with former CO Mike Berry.

87   *The Heckmanns were:* Author interview with former CO John Heckmann.

87   *"That single two-minute"*: Author interview with Master Chief Joe Maioriello, December 14, 2016.

89   *"his congenial attitude"*: Author interview with former CO Bob Reuning.

89   *"If you want"*: Presidential Pet Museum, www.presidentialpet museum.com.

90   *Reagan's Cavalier:* Ibid.

90   *The Eisenhowers were forced:* Ibid.

91   *The dogs were in:* Ibid.

91   *CO Howe recalled:* Author interview with former CO Chuck Howe.

91   *Nikita Khrushchev gifted Kennedy:* Traphes Bryant with Frances Spatz Leighton, *Dog Days at the White House* (New York: Macmillan, 1975).

91   *President Johnson's beagles:* Presidential Pet Museum.

92   *At the time, the CO family:* Author interview with former CO John Dettbarn.

93   *Bush 41's English:* Barbara Bush, *Millie's Book* (New York: William Morrow, 1990).

93   *"My dog Millie"*: Presidential Pet Museum.

93   *"This is Sam's"*: Author interview with former CO Mike Berry.

94   *Russ Rang's family:* Author interview with former CO Russ Rang.

95   *Buddy achieved:* Hillary Rodham Clinton, *Dear Socks, Dear Buddy: Kids' Letters to the First Pets* (New York: Simon and Schuster, 1998).

97   *"Are you confident"*: Author interview with former CO Bob Reuning.

97   *Vice president Dick Cheney:* Dick Cheney, *In My Time: A Personal and Political Memoir* (New York: Simon and Schuster, 2011).

97   *"Barney was by"*: President Bush writing on the occasion of Barney's death in 2013.

Chapter Four: Happy Campers

99 *"How're you doing"*: Author interview with former CO Bob Reuning, January 6, 2017.

100 *"It was a bit"*: Ray L'Heureux, *Inside Marine One: Four U.S. Presidents, One Proud Marine, and the World's Most Amazing Helicopter* (New York: St. Martin's, 2014).

100 *"On the last hill"*: Author interview with former CO Mike O'Connor, December 29, 2016.

101 *"We love this"*: Author interview with former CO Mike Berry, February 9, 2017.

101 *"I don't want"*: Ibid.

102 *Jimmy Carter had*: Sarah Pileggi, "Jimmy Carter Runs into the Wall," *Sports Illustrated*, September 24, 1979.

102 *One day he picked*: Author interview with former CO Mike Berry.

103 *When the president got*: Author interview with former CO Keith Autry, January 19, 2017.

104 *"The master chief"*: Author interview with former CO Wendy Halsey, December 30, 2016.

104 *The highlight of*: Author interview with former CO Russ Rang, February 10, 2017.

104 *By nature, those*: George A. Baker III, *The Making of a Marine-Scholar: Leading and Learning in the Bear Pit* (Bloomington, IN: iUniverse, 2008).

106 *Relaxing was not*: Ibid.

106 *"The president wasn't"*: Author interview with former CO John Dettbarn, January 3, 2017.

107 *"I'm down here"*: Author interview with former CO Jim Rispoli, January 18, 2017.

107 *Weather permitting*: Author interview with former CO Mike Berry.

109 *"Oh, please forgive"*: Author interview with former CO John Dettbarn.

111 *"Whenever I could":* Author interview with former CO Keith Autry.

111 *"I have a rare":* Jimmy Carter, press conference, May 29, 1979.

113 *Dad gave his daughter:* Author interview with former CO Russ Rang.

113 *"Outside of golf carts":* Hillary Rodham Clinton, *Living History* (New York: Simon and Schuster, 2003).

115 *"You don't have to":* Author interview with former CO Bob Reuning.

115 *"How do you like":* Ibid.

115 *"Where is everybody":* Ibid.

116 *"'Heads up'":* Author interview with former CO Russ Rang.

116 *"Is it okay":* Author interview with former CO Jim Rispoli.

117 *"Terminator arriving":* Author interview with former CO Mike Berry.

117 *"Commander, do you":* Author interview with former CO John Dettbarn.

117 *"Did you hear":* Author interview with former CO Jim Rispoli.

119 *"How I love":* Barbara Bush, *Barbara Bush: A Memoir* (New York: Scribner, 1994).

119 *"My God":* Grace Tully, *F.D.R. My Boss* (Chicago: Peoples Book Club, 1949).

120 *"was one expression":* Blanche Wiesen Cook, *Eleanor Roosevelt,* vol. 3, *The War Years and After, 1939–1962* (New York: Viking, 2016).

121 *Lady Bird Johnson confessed:* Claudia Alta "Lady Bird" Johnson, *Lady Bird Johnson: A White House Diary* (New York: Holt, Rinehart and Winston, 1970).

121 *The Reagans relied:* Author interview with former CO Mike Berry.

122 *"The Camp David cooks":* Scott Benjamin, "Q&A: Laura Bush on Camp David," CBS, December 24, 2005.

123 *"We feel bad":* Author interview with former CO Jim Rispoli.

126 *"the twelve days":* Author interview with former CO Mike Berry.

126 *"Skipper, it's the president"*: Author interview with former CO Mike O'Connor.

126 *One year he picked:* Author interview with former CO John Heckmann.

127 *"I'll take over"*: Author interview with former CO Mike Berry.

Chapter Five: The Spirit of Camp David

129 *an invitation from President Eisenhower:* Dwight D. Eisenhower Presidential Library documents, September 25–27, 1959.

132 *"It's so beautiful"*: Rosalynn Carter, *First Lady from Plains* (Boston: Houghton Mifflin, 1984).

132 *Who should enter:* Ibid.

133 *"When the cooks"*: Ibid.

133 *National security adviser:* Zbigniew Brzezinski, *Power and Principle: Memoirs of the National Security Adviser, 1977–1981* (New York: Farrar, Straus and Giroux, 1993).

134 *"had not been designed"*: Jimmy Carter, *Keeping Faith: Memories of a President* (New York: Bantam, 1982).

134 *"The meeting was mean"*: Rosalynn Carter, *First Lady from Plains.*

135 *"Everybody at the dinner"*: Ibid.

135 *The children were active:* Brzezinski, *Power and Principle.*

137 *That night Carter had trouble:* Jimmy Carter, *Keeping Faith.*

137 *"What I remember"*: Brzezinski, *Power and Principle.*

137 *Earlier, photographs had:* Jimmy Carter, *Keeping Faith.*

139 *"I hope that"*: Clinton announcement, July 5, 2000.

143–44 *Bob obtained:* Author interview with former chaplain Bob Williams.

144 *"We worked day"*: Madeleine Albright, *Madam Secretary: A Memoir* (New York: Harper Perennial, 2003).

146 *"My two-year-old"*: Ibid.

146 *"I am not a great man"*: Bill Clinton, *My Life* (New York: Knopf, 2004).

146 *G8 "made my tour"*: Author interview with former CO Wendy Halsey, December 30, 2016.

147 *Thurmont hung:* "Hundreds of Protesters Gathered in Thurmont; Police Close Main Street," *Frederick News-Post,* May 19, 2012.

148 *"Each time I":* Author interview with former CO Wendy Halsey.

148 *"Actually, we made":* Ibid.

150 *"Do you know":* Ibid.

Chapter Six: The Lonely Sentry

153 *"Finally, a call":* Grace Tully, *F.D.R. My Boss* (Chicago: Peoples Book Club, 1949).

154 *As Nancy Gibbs:* Nancy Gibbs and Michael Duffy, *The Presidents Club: Inside the World's Most Exclusive Fraternity* (New York: Simon and Schuster, 2012).

155 *Lady Bird often woke:* Claudia Alta "Lady Bird" Johnson, *Lady Bird Johnson: A White House Diary* (New York: Holt, Rinehart and Winston, 1970).

156 *In an obituary:* Tom Wicker, "From Afar, an Indomitable Man, an Incurable Loneliness," *New York Times,* April 24, 1994.

156 *"When Nixon went":* Bill Gulley and Mary Ellen Reese, *Breaking Cover* (New York: Simon and Schuster, 1980).

156 *"he likes to be":* Ibid.

156 *Bob Haldeman and John Ehrlichman:* George A. Baker III, *The Making of a Marine-Scholar: Leading and Learning in the Bear Pit* (Bloomington, IN: iUniverse, 2008).

157 *"Haldeman was a tough guy":* Author interview with former CO John Dettbarn, January 3, 2017.

157 *"In the mountains":* Richard Reeves, *President Nixon: Alone in the White House* (New York: Simon and Schuster, 2007).

157 *"Reagan is not one":* Kenneth T. Walsh, *From Mount Vernon to Crawford: A History of Presidents and Their Retreats* (New York: Hyperion, 2005).

157 *The only person:* Alex Larzelere, *Witness to History: White House Diary of a Military Aide to President Richard Nixon* (Bloomington, IN: AuthorHouse, 2009).

158 *On August 8, 1974:* Gulley and Reese, *Breaking Cover.*

158 *In spite of Jimmy Carter's success:* William Leuchtenburg, *In the Shadow of FDR: From Harry Truman to Barack Obama,* 4th ed. (Ithaca, NY: Cornell University Press, 2009).

159 *George Bush 41 agonized:* George H. W. Bush Presidential Library.

160 *"I remember we":* Author interview with Hank Howe.

160 *As he watched:* Author interview with former CO Chuck Howe, December 29, 2016.

161 *"My parents were":* Author interview with Hank Howe.

161 *Jackie and the children:* Author interview with former CO Chuck Howe.

161 *"I feel strangely free":* Johnson, *Lady Bird Johnson.*

162 *The morning of September 11:* Author interview with former CO Mike O'Connor, December 29, 2016.

164 *"The comforting song":* Condoleezza Rice, *No Higher Honor: A Memoir of My Years in Washington* (New York: Crown, 2011).

164 *When it came time:* Author interview with former CO Mike O'Connor.

166 *Elizabeth O'Connor had gotten close:* Ibid.

167 *"Bad news":* Ibid.

167 *"In the skies":* George W. Bush, statement to the nation, February 1, 2003.

Chapter Seven: An Unusual Duty

171 *"Those also serve":* Julia Robb, "Service Took Seabee to Camp David," *Frederick News-Post,* November 11, 2002.

173 *"These were young kids":* Author interview with former CO Bob McLean, January 18, 2017.

174 *CO Berry recalled:* Author interview with former CO Mike Berry, February 9, 2017.

175 *Guard duty can be lonely:* The 8th & I Reunion Association is an organization of Marines who served at Marine Barracks Washington, DC.

176 *In May 1989:* Keith Snyder, "Secret Service Probe Crash at Camp David," *Morning Herald,* May 12, 1989; also author interview with former CO Mike Berry.

177 *To work at Camp David:* Author interview with former CO Mike Berry.

177 *I had a similar:* Author's journal and interview with Heather Wishart.

179 *After a visit to Idaho:* Author interview with former CO John Heckmann.

184 *CO Joe Camp shared:* Author interview with former CO Joe Camp, December 30, 2016.

184 *"The biggest difference":* Author interview with former CO Mike Berry.

184 *CO Autry acknowledged the stress:* Author interview with former CO Keith Autry, January 19, 2017.

185 *On occasion, though:* Author interview with former CO Mike Berry.

185 *In January 2007:* Author interview with former CO John Heckmann.

186 *Also in the context:* Grace Wyler, "How Barack Obama Prepared for Tonight's Foreign Policy Debate," *Business Insider,* October 22, 2012.

187 *When Chuck Howe was CO:* Author interview with former CO Chuck Howe, December 29, 2016.

188 *When Wendy Halsey:* Author interview with former CO Wendy Halsey, December 30, 2016.

188 *"When the leaves":* Author interview with former CO Joe Camp.

Chapter Eight: Pew One

191 *According to the late Thurmont historian:* George Wireman, *Gateway to the Mountains* (Hagerstown, MD: Hagerstown Bookbinding and Print Company, 1969).

192 *Kenneth Plummer:* Author interview with former CO Mike Berry, February 9, 2017.

193 *Berry was delighted:* Ibid.

193 *"I prayed that God":* Ronald Reagan, *An American Life* (New York: Simon and Schuster, 1990).

194 *"Well, I think":* Author interview with former CO Mike Berry.

196 *"The weather was dreary":* Diary of Dee Berry.

199 *"In many ways":* Author interview with former chaplain Bob Williams, January 16, 2017.

200 *Months after President Obama:* Amy Sullivan, "The Obamas Find a Church Home—Away from Home," *Time*, June 29, 2009.

200 *"Jackie Kennedy Onassis":* Hillary Rodham Clinton, *Living History* (New York: Simon and Schuster, 2003).

201 *"He had a marvelous":* Author interview with former chaplain Bob Williams.

201 *Once when Arnold Schwarzenegger:* Author interview with former CO Mike Berry.

202 *Again, everyone was expected:* Ibid.

203 *John Heckmann's daughters:* Author interview with former CO John Heckmann.

203 *"The question was when":* Author interview with former CO Bob McLean, January 18, 2017.

Chapter Nine: Guesthouse to the World

205 *"Camp David is a far more intimate":* Laura Bush, *Spoken from the Heart* (New York: Scribner, 2010).

206 *For example, while Khrushchev received:* Dwight D. Eisenhower Presidential Library.

206 *In his book* Silent Missions: Vernon Walters, *Silent Missions* (New York: Doubleday, 1978).

208 *"That's a way":* Nixon tapes, Richard Nixon Presidential Library.

208 *"Anything you suggest":* Ibid.

208 *"Diplomacy is not":* Richard Nixon, *RN: The Memoirs of Richard Nixon* (New York: Grosset and Dunlap, 1978).

209 *"Now, there are":* Nixon tapes, Richard Nixon Presidential Library.

209 *After Reagan won:* Charles Moore, *Margaret Thatcher: The Authorized Biography,* vol. 2 (London: Allen Lane, 2015).

210 *As they passed Cedar:* Author interview with former CO Jim Rispoli, January 18, 2017.

210 *"He was at his":* Margaret Thatcher, *The Downing Street Years, 1979–1990* (New York: HarperCollins, 1993).

210 *The visit of Mikhail and Raisa Gorbachev:* Author interview with former CO Mike Berry, February 9, 2017.

212 *The press was at camp:* Ibid.

212 *Barbara Bush and Naina Yeltsin:* Barbara Bush, *Barbara Bush: A Memoir* (New York: Scribner, 1994).

213 *In spite of Putin's opposition:* Author interview with former CO Bob McLean, January 18, 2017.

213 *President Putin had forgotten:* Ibid.

213 *"For decades, when":* President George W. Bush, statement to press, September 27, 2003.

214 *"I learned a lot":* Amy Chozick, "George Bush Recalls Putin's 'My Dog Is Stronger' Style of Diplomacy," *New York Times,* July 10, 2015.

214 *In February 1970:* Author interview with former CO John Dettbarn, January 3, 2017.

215 *The day before the barbecue:* Author interview with former CO Bill Waters, January 19, 2017.

216 *As she recalled in her memoir:* Laura Bush, *Spoken from the Heart.*

217 *When Blair came:* Author interview with former CO Mike O'Connor, December 29, 2016.

218 *"not to avoid":* President Bush's remarks to the press following discussions with Prime Minister Junichiro Koizumi of Japan, June 30, 2001.

219 *"My watch was appraised":* Author interview with former CO Bob Reuning, January 6, 2017.

219 *The supply officer lighting:* Author interview with former CO Russ Rang, February 10, 2017.

220 *Berry met Colin Powell's helicopter:* Author interview with former CO Mike Berry.

220 *"Here I go":* Ibid.

Chapter Ten: Down the Mountain

226 *Jacob Weller, a blacksmith:* George Wireman, *Gateway to the Mountains* (Hagerstown, MD: Hagerstown Bookbinding and Print Company, 1969).

226 *As Wireman explained:* Ibid.

227 *One, an elder: Almost Blue Mountain City: The History of Thurmont, Maryland,* produced by Christopher Haugh, 2014.

227 *Jackie Kennedy helped bring:* Wireman, *Gateway to the Mountains.*

228 *Until it closed:* Brian Shane, "The Cozy: Longtime Restaurant Near Camp David Closes," *USA Today,* August 8, 2014.

229 *At its peak:* Wireman, *Gateway to the Mountains.*

230 *"Wire service reporters":* Helen Thomas, *Front Row at the White House: My Life and Times* (New York: Scribner, 1999).

231 *Joe Reynolds:* Joe Reynolds, "Trout and Tradition," *Field and Stream* (May 1985).

231 *"Everyone made a mad dash":* Thea Rosenbaum, *No Place for a Lady* (Bloomington, IN: AuthorHouse, 2015).

Chapter Eleven: Changing of the Guard

234 *CO Reuning marveled:* Author interview with former CO Bob Reuning, January 6, 2017.

235 *"Look, George":* Author interview with former CO Mike Berry, February 9, 2017.

236 *In her memoir, Barbara Bush:* Barbara Bush, *Barbara Bush: A Memoir* (New York: Scribner, 1994).

236 *When it was time for the president:* Author interview with former CO Joe Camp, December 30, 2016.

236 *According to Lady Bird:* Claudia Alta "Lady Bird" Johnson, *Lady Bird Johnson: A White House Diary* (New York: Holt, Rinehart and Winston, 1970).

236 *"The Fords made one":* W. Dale Nelson, *The President Is at Camp David* (Syracuse, NY: Syracuse University Press, 1995).

237 *"I was torn":* Rosalynn Carter, *First Lady from Plains* (Boston: Houghton Mifflin, 1984).

237–38 *Four years later:* Richard Nixon, *RN: The Memoirs of Richard Nixon* (New York: Grosset and Dunlap, 1978).

244 *"How'd you like":* Author interview with former CO Mike O'Connor, December 29, 2016.

244 *"My commute took":* Author interview with former CO Mike Berry.

245 *"The last time Bush was at church":* Author interview with former CO Bob McLean, January 18, 2017.

245 *"The most unique":* Author interview with former CO Bob Reuning.

245 *"The end came up quickly":* Author interview with former CO Russ Rang, February 10, 2017.

Chapter Twelve: The True Meaning of Camp David

250 *Ronald Reagan expressed:* Ronald Reagan, *An American Life* (New York: Simon and Schuster, 1990).

250 *"There are resorts":* Author interview with former CO Mike Berry, February 9, 2017.

251 *"Granddad, an excellent cook":* W. Dale Nelson, *The President Is at Camp David* (Syracuse, NY: Syracuse University Press, 1995).

252 *CO Howe's lasting memory:* Author interview with former CO Chuck Howe, December 29, 2016.

252 *"You could be sure":* Pierre Salinger, *P.S., a Memoir* (New York: St. Martin's Press, 1995).

253 *"Only when you":* Nixon's farewell words to staff.

253 *everyman's rest spot:* Kenneth T. Walsh, *From Mount Vernon to Crawford* (New York: Hyperion, 2005).

253 *"If it weren't for"*: Ronald Reagan, *An American Life*.

254 *CO Autry recalled:* Author interview with former CO Keith Autry, January 19, 2017.

255 *"It's where a president"*: Walsh, *From Mount Vernon to Crawford*.

255 *"In my mind, the value"*: Author interview with former CO John Heckmann.

255 *"Any tour at Camp David"*: Author interview with former CO John Dettbarn, January 3, 2017.

257 *"Hey, Commander"*: Author interview with former CO Mike O'Connor, December 29, 2016.

INDEX

About the Author

MICHAEL GIORGIONE is a rear admiral who served for twenty-nine years on active duty in the U.S. Navy and retired in 2010. During his career, he had many prestigious assignments. He was called by the White House to be the commander of Camp David for Presidents Bill Clinton and George W. Bush.

The retired admiral is founder and president of LeadingLeaders, a leadership development and consulting firm. He is also chairman of the board for the Seabee Memorial Scholarship Association, an executive board member with the Civil Engineer Corps/Seabee Historical Foundation, and a fellow in the Society of American Military Engineers. He spent four years at the U.S. Naval Academy, where he received a bachelor of science degree in ocean engineering. He received a master of science degree in civil engineering from Penn State University and took advanced management and business courses at Duke University and the University of North Carolina. The magnitude of and experiences from his assignments have made him a much-sought-after speaker and teacher.

Michael Giorgione lives in Coronado, California, with his wife, Michele. They have two daughters, Briana and Ryanne.

More Great American History from
Back Bay Books

Ike's Bluff: President Eisenhower's
Secret Battle to Save the World
by Evan Thomas

"A brilliant and engaging book about the most important of subjects: how close we came to Armageddon in the seemingly placid 1950s."　　　　　—Jon Meacham, author of *Thomas Jefferson*

Miracle at Philadelphia: The Story of the
Constitutional Convention
by Catherine Drinker Bowen

"A remarkable account of the men and issues of that historic gathering."　　　　　—James Reston, *New York Times*

The Imperial Cruise:
A Secret History of Empire and War
by James Bradley

"Engrossing and revelatory . . . Revisionist history at its best."
　　　　　—Ronald Steel, *New York Times Book Review*

BACK BAY BOOKS
Available wherever books are sold